Acclaim for *Hon*

"A fast moving, gripping account of Jones' adventures as a combat soldier, dedicated cop and narc. The account of his training, indoctrination, sense of camaraderie, and disappointment in the bureaucratic leadership in both professions is mesmerizing and as good as it gets. Jones presents a moving and valuable saga representative of the millions of patriotic Americans who made the United States the most free and powerful nation in the world."
>   —Joseph D. McNamara, Police Chief, San Jose CA, Ret.

"Premier Army aviator with whom I entrusted my life without question."
>   —General Frederick J. Kroesen, US Army, Ret.

"Russell Jones' insights into the failed War on Drugs come directly from his first-hand experiences as a Vietnam helicopter pilot, police officer, narcotics detective, DEA task force officer and intelligence agent in Central America during Iran-Contra. No one can have a reasoned opinion on drug policy without considering his vast and hard-hitting experiences."
>   —Judge James P. Gray, Superior Court, Orange County, CA, Ret.

"Russell Jones' engrossing memoir, *Honorable Intentions*, is a story of adventure and heroism that becomes a personal journey of enlightenment as he breaks the bonds of supreme religious authority embedded at childhood and becomes immersed in public service as a police officer, soldier and spy, all with aspirations to contribute to the betterment of his fellow man. But along with the excitement and satisfaction of public service he comes to understand the dark corrupting influences imposed by those in leadership positions who depend upon men of his caliber to strip themselves of their individuality and become part of the collective though obedience, discipline, dedication, and pride, while they are exploited and used as the hunter/gatherers to feed the quota-based propaganda machines— traffic tickets, drug arrests and seizures, battlefield body counts— used to justify the tyrannical enforcement of failed public policy while the institutions they lead, once established to protect and serve, erode from the inside-out from the corruption of totalitarian ideology that always accompanies the perversions of coerced morality. This journey of enlightenment has served Russell Jones well as his voice today is an experienced, credible weapon used effectively in this book to expose and counter the failed 40-year ideology of totalitarian paternalism that we call the War on Drugs."

—Stephen Downing, Deputy Chief of Police, Los Angeles, Ret.

"Russell Jones exposes the truth that certainly angers and threatens the agenda of many."

—Micah Bowie, Pitcher, Major League Baseball, 1999-2008.

"If you desire an insider's view of how narcotics officers operate, this book is pure gold."

—Howard Wooldridge, Drug Policy Expert, Washington DC

"It's a fine piece of work and the author has been successful in causing this reader to think about the drug problem from an entirely different perspective."

—Major General Chuck Teeter, US Army, Ret.

"Wonderful book, the first in my life that I've read straight through in one sitting. It's full of information about wars of all kind that has never before been made public."

—Jack Cole, New Jersey State Police, Ret.

"The men who sacrificed for our country are rightfully honored, in spite of our nations failed policies."

—LTC Ralph Lemes, US Army, Ret.

To Carol & Chuck

Honorable Intentions

Russell Jones

Russell Jones

Copyright © 2012 by Russell Jones

HILL COUNTRY INK

www.honorable-intentions.com

ISBN: 978-0-578-09213-3

Printed in the United States of America

*Dedicated to the memory of these
brave men who served with honor:*

Roger Auld
Don Bartley
Hershall Bullock
Ernest Burns
David Crow
James Eisenhour
Gary George
Richard Huerta
Robert Jantz
Angus McAllister
Joseph Neske
Gerald Ortego
Gordon Silva
Gene Simpson
Douglas Stover

Contents

Preface

This book is my memoir spanning sixty years. Names and identifying circumstances are correct, except in a few cases where, having to navigate the tension between what was moral and what was good for this work, I deemed it prudent to protect identities. Conversations are true to their spirit and have been re-created to the best of my abilities. For the story to flow, some events aren't in chronological order and some have been condensed.

I caution the reader. Gritty language peppers military and law enforcement environments. I took care to avoid obscenities; however, I believed removing the profanity in some passages would have detracted significantly from the story's integrity.

Many, whose memories through the fog of time were able to fill in the gaps or validate mine, assisted me. For the sake of brevity, I'll limit my thanks to members of the Vietnam Helicopter Pilots Association, Americal Division Veterans Association, 196th Light Infantry Brigade Association, San Jose Police Benevolent Association, and the Intelligence Community Associations Network.

The opinions expressed in this book are mine and don't reflect the position of, nor the endorsement by any of the aforementioned associations, their members, officers, chapters, or boards.

To paraphrase Michael Verde, "Heaven or hell on earth might be, at the end of your life, having to sit and write your life story." For the times it was hell, I'd like to thank my bride, Sally, for her support and understanding. I wouldn't have completed this without her.

Prologue

You Are History

A part of me died long ago and was reincarnated as I visited the site of that earlier existence. It was 1994, and I was standing where I had taken my last steps in Vietnam twenty-five years earlier. A dirt road in front of me headed through the Que Son Valley toward Death Valley and the village of Hiep Duc. To my right was a knoll full of boulders we had named Baldy. Far to the south, across the mouth of the valley, I could see the top of a mountain that had been Firebase East.

As I took in the scene, Tran Bao leaned against the fender of his faded blue Toyota. He had used a thin belt to scrunch his oversized and well-worn slacks around his waist. His shirt was missing several buttons, and he wore rubber flip-flops. I offered him a Marlboro, which I carried knowing Vietnamese people appreciated American cigarettes as gifts.

Tran had been a soldier with the 7th Viet Cong Battalion. As I watched him enjoy his smoke, I considered the fact that we had once been soldiers pitted against each other. For whatever reasons, politics, perseverance, or stamina, his army prevailed. I thought of the incredible differences in our fortunes. *Is it chance, destiny, or grace? What fate now makes him the driver while I ride in comfort?*

I motioned it was time to leave, and we headed down the dusty road. While traveling along the north side of the Que Son Valley, we stopped at what had been Firebase Ross, where a monument now stood in tribute to the liberation by the People's Vietnamese Army. Continuing our journey, we drove past the rocky Nui Chom hills, where the blood of hundreds, if not thousands, was spilt.

At the west end of the Que Son Valley, the hills narrowed, and we entered Death Valley toward our final destination of Hiep Duc. Vibrant green rice paddies lined the dirt road. As we approached the village, I saw the familiar heavily forested mountains that rose to the clouds. Along the western edge of the town were the banks of the Song Thu Bon River, over which the road continued on a bridge that the US Army Corp of Engineers pontoons still supported. A few buildings had been added since I last saw the town, but they all seemed in poor repair. People scurried around in their conical hats, carrying farm products in large baskets. As they passed, they diverted their eyes as if I was someone to avoid.

"They don't like Americans?" I asked Tran as we walked the streets.

"You Russian, they think," he said in broken English. "Russians not friendly."

Since the fall of South Vietnam, a heavy Soviet presence had been there. But the politics in Vietnam had slowly changed, and the Russians had left. The government was allowing more tourists, including Americans, to travel throughout the country.

I was curious to see their reaction. "Well, tell them I'm American."

Within minutes of Tran letting out the word, a crowd surrounded me. Tattered clothes draped their frail bodies, and most wore sandals. I couldn't help but notice that many were missing an arm or a leg. They were laughing and talking, but I only heard the high-toned singsong of the Vietnamese language.

Upon learning I'd been a helicopter pilot during the war, one elderly gentleman took my hand and gave me thanks in his poor English. He then spoke in Vietnamese to a woman in the crowd.

"He wants you to know that we're thankful for what you tried to do," she said, translating in perfect English. "We don't blame you. We know it was the politicians."

I was amazed they would speak like that in front of Tran or others in the crowd who could have been government officials. She sensed my concern and waved off Tran, making it clear that she didn't care.

"I was a nurse in Da Nang during the war. Because of that, I was sent to a re-education camp for ten years. They don't scare me. See him over there?" She pointed to a young man who wore no uniform and was observing the crowd. "He's the policeman." Her look of disgust indicated he was insignificant.

Another gentleman came up and took me by the arm. Then he led me down the street to his home. It was built of rough concrete blocks with a tin roof, and the floor was hard-packed dirt. The dwelling had a kitchen, one bedroom, and a living room that also served as the dining area. There was no plumbing. A colorful poster taped to the wall displayed a male image appearing to be a composite of Rama, Krishna, and Jesus.

Sitting at the table was his wife and a man who seemed to be about thirty years of age. Beneath a piece of broken glass covering the tabletop were several photos showing a young Vietnamese couple standing beside a shiny red Camaro.

As the crowd outside peered into the doorway and window, the gentleman pointed to the young man in the photo.

"My son," he said while smiling. "He escape." His hand waved up and down as his arm slowly extended away from his body.

"By boat?" I asked.

"Yes, yes." He then pointed to the young woman in the photo standing alongside his son. "Wife, she Vietnamese. Live in Santa Ana."

"California," I said.

He stood back alongside his wife who was still seated. They both wore broad smiles.

Then a somber look crossed his face as he pointed to the man sitting at the table. "Number one son and I caught."

"You and this son also tried to escape by boat?"

"Yes, but no good. Sent to education camp ten years."

My mind went back to the couple I had met in San Antonio only months earlier. My wife and I were holding a garage sale for my mother-in-law, whose Alzheimer's required a move into assisted living. Near the end of the day, an elderly Vietnamese couple shuffled around looking at the few items left. The woman had her eye on a porcelain teapot. I started a conversation with the gentleman and mentioned my tour of duty in Vietnam. He told of how he'd been a captain with the South Vietnamese Army and spent fifteen years in a re-education camp. Upon his release, he and his family fled by boat. When he mentioned they had lost their son to starvation during their escape, my wife and I expressed our sorrow. After a few moments of uncomfortable silence, he quietly said, "That was the price of freedom."

I felt heavy as I stepped out of the house in Hiep Duc and went back into the cheerful and curious crowd. I thought of my friends who died here, those Vietnamese who died trying to escape communism, and those struggling in Hiep Duc today. I questioned the randomness of it all. But the villagers refused to play along with my mood and laughed and talked instead.

I noticed the policeman who had followed the gathering. He glared at the group as if he were aiming a gun. Our eyes suddenly met, and his hard stare seemed to say, "Don't worry about our lives. We are here because this is what's so. You are who you are, have been where you've been, and done what you've done because it's what's so." His eyes then softened. Before turning away, he appeared to add with an air of superiority, "I'm young and just beginning a life in a world far away from yours. You are history."

Upon leaving Hiep Duc, I directed Tran to take a dirt road that followed the southern edge of Death Valley. When we came to a familiar landscape, I could see, to my south, the top of a mountain that had been Firebase West. I asked Tran to stop and stay with the car. I walked out toward a small island of jungle in the midst of a sea of rice paddies. Twenty-five years ago, tension filled this air. Here, men had battled, some were taken prisoner, many died, and awards and decorations were earned.

A small stream ran along the edge of the heavy growth. In the shallow, slow-moving water, I caught my reflection. *Who am I? And why am I here? Am I just this abused carcass seeming to stare back? Or is there some meaning to all I've experienced? What do I believe? Is my life just what's so?*

I walked back to the middle of the rice paddies and squatted on my heels, much as the Vietnamese do. The scene was peaceful. Tran was dutifully waiting several hundred yards away and paced the road while finishing another Marlboro. He was in the same area where, in that previous life, armed Viet Cong had shot at me while I crouched in the muck behind the earthen dike of one of these ponds.

A soldier will leave the battlefield, but the battlefield never leaves him. So when Vietnam began allowing independent travel, I discovered an irresistible urge to return. On the surface, it was curiosity or nostalgia. But the visit was kindling unexpected emotions and questions. *Are we here by chance, Tran? Or was the crossing of our paths destined?*

I picked up a clod of dirt and threw it in the middle of the rice crop that had grown a few inches above the water. The resultant splash sent a series of large circular ripples and caused the thin leaves of the plants to toss back and forth. I noticed a large insect, disturbed by the motion, attempt to fly, but it hit the water at the edge of the dike. A bird immediately snatched it. The ripple I created took one life and yet nourished another.

Isn't it true that every act is the source of an infinite series of lasting effects? So wasn't my act of throwing that clod itself the result of a prior event?

I began to think of the far-reaching consequences from the ripples that had influenced my forty-seven years: my life as a military pilot, police officer, narcotics detective, DEA task force officer, intelligence operative, forensic consultant, college instructor, drug counselor, and ocean sailor.

I had plenty of reasons to be thankful. Three previous employers had paid me a comfortable sum, but I had earned twice that in self-employment and managed to keep most of that capital over the years. I never doubted if I were going to successfully put food on the table, and I never knew poverty or real hunger. I had owned eight residences, from humble dwellings to a spacious mountain home. At one time or another, I had possessed ten vehicles, three oceangoing sailboats, and two airplanes. I had been married three times and blessed with one son.

I looked up at Firebase West and noticed the top had grown back over with vegetation. The mountains now seemed close, and Death Valley looked narrow and small. I then wondered if I even dared consider some of the dreadful events that had caused me, at times, to abandon faith, not only in my country and her leaders, but that faith into which I had been baptized. I had roamed this world and mingled with people at their best, but also at their worst. Many had tried to kill me, and I carry the lead from AK-47s and shrapnel from rocket-propelled grenades in my body. A felon desperate to escape had purposely run me down with his car. Members of organized crime had placed contracts on my life. In the course of this, I had been directly responsible for the deaths of a dozen men and probably others whose bodies weren't found. I had wounded and maimed countless others.

From Vietnam to the jungles of Central America, from the streets of San Francisco to isolated islands in the Caribbean, I had associated, dined, conducted business, and fought with highly dangerous individuals. Yet in spite of those abnormal hazards, I had eluded destruction, both physically and financially, while participating for more than two decades in some of my country's turbulent history.

I got up and started walking back to Tran. *Am I history?* I certainly didn't think so. There were plenty of waves yet to make.

Chapter 1

Just Come Home Alive

From my earliest memory, I wanted out. I vividly remember the wooden fence around the kindergarten playground. The slats were four inches apart, and, by placing my face between the slats, I could see into the community with cars driving by, people coming and going, and customers entering and leaving businesses. Kindergarten wasn't fun and games. My rug, graham crackers and milk, recess, and story time didn't cut it. I wanted to escape to out there where I could experience life.

I snuck out the door, across the street, down the block, and into the five-and-dime store before anyone noticed. As a five year old, I was in wonder of all the toys, candy, tools, and household paraphernalia. Unfortunately, the kindly shopkeeper soon realized where I belonged and gently led me back to school where they were surprised to learn I'd been missing. What were later to become major personality traits—stealth, curiosity, lack of fear, and impatience—came into play at an early age.

It was that impatience that led me, in 1967, to enlist into the army. I wanted to get out into the world … or maybe just to get out.

I was also in the army to become a pilot. In the early 1950s, I stood at the observation platform on top of the San Francisco airport and watched with fascination as planes, such as the Douglas DC-4, arrived and departed while we waited for my grandmother's arrival. In 1958, I had my first trip in an airplane when I returned from Brazil with my family. I was thrilled to ride in one of the most graceful and beautiful airliners ever built, the Lockheed Constellation. It was always described with superlatives such as highest, fastest, and best.

The young truant and soon to be "fire starter," with my sister Cherie.

The crew welcomed me to the cockpit where they answered my many questions about the duties of the pilot, co-pilot, and navigator. They explained the controls, instruments, and radios. Later that night, when we were a couple of hours out of Miami at twenty thousand feet, the pilots summoned me back to the cockpit where, with twinkling lights of towns along the coast, I was able to see the outline of Florida and a brilliantly lit Miami. I decided then that I wanted to be a pilot.

I got my chance as a teenager in California. By the time I was driving, I was allowed to socialize on Sunday afternoons with members of our church. When Doug Harlow suggested one Sunday afternoon that a group of us go to the drag races, I was interested. Harlow was the typical 1960s teenage car enthusiast who was into the muscle cars of the day. I was more into antique vehicles, and I was rebuilding a 1929 Chevrolet sedan. But I had never been to the races, so I joined Harlow and others for a day at the Fremont drag strip.

I found it boringly repetitive as cars burned rubber, belched fire and smoke, and, with a deafening roar, tore down the quarter-mile track in a race that lasted all of five seconds. I was more interested in the sailplanes gliding softly overhead as they approached the little airport north of the drag strip.

The following Sunday, I drove to the glider field and found I was old enough to obtain a student pilot's license. To ensure it was within my capabilities, an instructor took me for a demo ride in a Schweitzer 2-22, a two-place trainer built of cloth-covered steel tubing. A powered airplane noisily towed us skyward, but, upon being released at an altitude of fifteen hundred feet, I could hear nothing but a gentle breeze as we soared over the eastern foothills.

The instructor had me take the controls and fly, and I turned left and right, slowed down, sped up, dove, and climbed. It was as if I had scrambled on a bicycle for the first time and rode off. I flew back to the airport and, following instructions, brought the sailplane down just short of landing, where the instructor took over. We touched down on the single wheel, and we had barely rolled down the runway when we came to a stop. I was ecstatic. *Piece of cake. I can do this.*

At the age of sixteen, against my parents' wishes and without their knowledge, I sold my prized possession, a six-inch reflecting telescope. I was able to pay for ten hours of lessons and received my Federal Aviation Administration (FAA) student rating for sailplanes.

After completing high school in 1964, I majored in administration of justice for two years at West Valley College in Campbell, California. Impatient to be out of my parents' home and on my own, I transferred for my third year to John Brown University, a reputable Christian university, in Siloam Springs, Arkansas. The university was the choice of several other members from our church, Calvary Baptist in Los Gatos, California. It wasn't, though, a well-thought-out choice for me. I wasn't ready for the rigors of a university, and a few of the courses in administration of justice from West Valley weren't transferable into any program at John Brown. So I was considered a sophomore while in my third year of college. Since the Selective Service System (SSS) didn't look kindly upon this, I promptly lost my college deferment and, at twenty years of age, found myself ready to be drafted into military service.

I knew being drafted most likely meant I'd be assigned to the infantry. That wasn't appealing, so I went to the local recruiter's office to see what they had to offer. The navy and air force both confirmed that I needed a four-year degree to get into flight school, and neither of their programs for military police seemed attractive. While in the army recruiter's office, I happened to notice a poster on the wall promoting their helicopter pilot program.

"Does the army require a four-year degree for flight school?" I asked the recruiter.

"No, sir. Only two years of college is required. Interested in flying?"

"I have a student pilot's license for sailplanes and some training toward my powered license." I did my best to impress him.

He was already writing an appointment slip for me. "We test tomorrow at 1330."

I slowly did the math in my head, coming to the conclusion that, on the twenty-four hour clock, 1330 hours meant 1:30 in the afternoon.

The next day, I took a written examination in a room at the back of the recruiting office. The following week, to determine my suitability in becoming an officer and gentleman, I was sitting before two men and a woman for an oral board. The questions were rather mundane, focusing on my family and educational background. Then the subject of the war came up.

One of the men asked, "How would you feel if President Johnson sends you to Vietnam?"

I had never given that much thought. I only wanted to learn how to fly. I was sure that, based on the news, the war would be over before I ever got through basic training and flight school, well over a year away.

The answer to the question, though, rolled off my tongue as if I had rehearsed it a hundred times. "Sir, I grew up in school having to practice hiding under my desk in case of a nuclear attack. I watched on television as the communists shot students trying to cross from East Berlin to the West. I was a classmate with two brothers whose family fled Poland after the communists took over at the end of the Second World War. I now have a friend who told me his stories of how, ten years ago, he left his family behind as he risked his life and escaped Hungary during the communist crackdown."

"I'm aware of the thousands who have fled the communist regime in Cuba, many dying in the process. I know the difference in the freedoms and quality of life for South Koreans as opposed to those who live in North Korea. I learned from my college history studies of the million or more who, before Ho Chi Minh militarily sealed the border, fled North Vietnam to the South."

The members of the board sat quietly, so I continued. "The leaders of South Vietnam have asked for our assistance in protecting their country from the communists. I have faith that my government is making the right decisions, and I will honorably serve if called."

I passed all tests. A couple days later, everyone in the recruiting office shook my hand in congratulations. The attitude in the office was as if I had already accepted the program, so, when they slid the papers in front of me, I signed up for Army Warrant Officer Rotary Wing Aviation School.

So in 1967, while long-haired hippies in tie-dyed clothing flashed the peace sign while stepping down from multicolored buses in San Francisco, I was getting off an olive drab bus for army basic training at Fort Polk, Louisiana. I found the training exciting. I especially enjoyed the times we were out in the field in our pup tents, washing out of helmets, eating from mess kits, crawling on our bellies under barbed wire, firing weapons, and learning how to camouflage ourselves. The highlight for me was the obstacle course. I excelled at it, as it required speed, agility, and dexterity. Basic training was offering me an outdoor experience in pushing my limits that I had been hungry for most of my life.

As a youth, I was never exposed to activities such as the Boy Scouts or Little League. My father was an associate minister at Calvary Baptist, and our family spent a year in Brazil as missionaries, so the church was always first in our family's life. On Monday evenings, there was Boys Brigade, a pitiful substitute for the Boy Scouts. Wednesday evenings were prayer meetings. On Friday evenings, the church organized youth activities, such as miniature golf or roller-skating, which were an alternative for whatever was occurring for the heathens at school. Saturdays were spent with house chores, ensuring I had no time for organized sports. My parents argued that Saturday evenings at the church gym provided basketball, foursquare, or badminton. With the limited attendance, I considered those activities nonsense. Sunday mornings, of course, were spent at church with a short respite at home for a nap before returning for the evening service.

So the military was an opportunity to excel, but it also had its mental and physical challenges. Assisting me over those mental hurdles was a mentor, Gerald Ortego. Much older at twenty-nine, he had been in the service before and reenlisted for flight school. We had kitchen duty together, and, while we peeled potatoes and scrubbed pots for twelve hours, he gave me advice.

As with other recruits, I tended to take it personally when the drill sergeant's face was inches from mine, spewing saliva as he instructed me on how to properly carry my rifle or execute an about-face. Ortego explained how to go with the flow and not take the sergeants too seriously when they were yelling and carrying on.

"It's a game. Important, but don't take it personal, and you'll do fine."

The physical challenges for me were the long marches. Stamina had never been my strong suit. I had bursts of speed and could beat many in short sprints, but no amount of training and exercise, including two years of soccer and one year of water polo in college, improved my endurance. So in boot camp, I began to dread the upcoming march of ten miles. On that day, up earlier than usual, wearing full backpacks, and carrying our rifles, the entire company of one hundred and ninety-eight men was marching off by 0800. One of the drill sergeants started calling a cadence to keep us marching in step.

In a loud voice, he yelled, "Your left, your left, your left right left," although it sounded more like he was saying, "Yurr leff, yurr leff, yurr leff rahh leff."

The sergeant then said, "Bring it on down." We responded, in step, "One, two, three, four, one, two, three, four!" stomping our feet with the last "three, four." I found the cadence, the sound of boots hitting the ground, and the feelings of camaraderie exhilarating.

The main purpose for cadences was psychological. It was to keep us in step and motivated and distract our minds from physical pain, which I was beginning to experience. Along with the cadences, I tried a suggestion Ortego had proposed, focusing on the weave of the material on the soldier's uniform in front of me. I got short of breath, though, sweated profusely, and wondered how much farther we had to go. It seemed like we'd been marching for hours, but the sun was still low on the eastern horizon. My uniform was feeling bulky.

As we continued, cadences changed to songs, and I found them fun as they took my mind off the march. "Around her hair she wore a yellow ribbon. She wore it in the springtime in the merry month of May. And if you ask her why the hell she wore it, she wore it for her soldier who was far, far away. Far away, far away, she wore it for her soldier who was far, far away."

What seemed like ten hours later, the sun was still not overhead. My feet hurt, the stitches on the uniform material of the soldier in front of me were twice the normal size, and my own uniform, drenched in sweat, was too large. My helmet bobbled around my head, and I struggled to keep everything I was carrying from falling off.

As the march progressed, so did the cadences. A sergeant sang out, "We tried it once or twice, and we found it rather nice."

The company sang back, "Lay me down, roll me over, do it again."

I wasn't sure what it meant, and the sergeant continued, "Jill was number one, and she was mighty fun."

The company sang in reply, "Lay me down, roll me over, do it again."

It only took a few men in the company who already knew the cadence to follow along with the sergeant, and the green recruits caught on quickly and energetically. I was following Ortego's advice and stared at thread holes on the uniform in front of me that looked a half-inch in diameter. And I decided the cadences we were now calling had a sexual slant to them.

The sergeant sang, "Beth was number two, and she screwed me 'til I'm blue."

The company sang back, "Lay me down, roll me over, do it again."

The sergeant continued the cadence with Liz as number three, Sue as number four, and so on, and the company continued singing and responding enthusiastically. I, on the other hand, was no longer hearing right. Everything was muffled. I gasped for what little air Louisiana had to offer in April. I couldn't help but notice guys falling out around me, exhausted, and I was sure I was also going to drop out at any moment.

"Company," a drill sergeant shouted. "Halt."

I crashed into the soldier in front of me while others plowed into me from behind, like a pileup on the freeway. After weeks of drilling, this wasn't our finest moment.

"Left face!"

We shuffled around, eventually finding the correct "left," and faced the drill sergeant. He instructed where the water was and where the line for lunch would be formed. After his order to fall out, I stumbled over to the nearest pine tree, dropped my gear, and collapsed. I finished my canteen of water, and I was resting my head on my arms, which were on my knees, when I noticed a shiny set of boots in front of me. I slowly raised my head, dreadfully expecting a drill sergeant. It was Walt Henderson, one of the recruits also headed for flight school. He was from Texas, was raised in a military family, and played high school and college football. His uniform was neat, clean, and sweat-free, and he was still wearing his pack.

"Grab your gear. Sarge says we're heading out." He looked sincere.

"You're kidding," I said with a hoarse gasp, not realizing he was joking. "I haven't had lunch yet."

My sweat-soaked uniform had collected mud from the dust. Holding my pants up with one hand, I stood and nearly passed out as the blood in my head stayed at ground level. Walt laughed along with other flight school recruits who had gathered around. We tended to hang out together on breaks. Based on their appearance, they handled the march somewhat better than I did.

Henderson had his hands on his hips. "Looks like you had a tough time, soldier."

I motioned to my gear dropped in the dirt. "It's a good thing I'm going to fly 'cause I can't see myself humping around all day with this." I wiped sweat from my brow. "And what's with this sexual stuff?"

"What do you mean?" Jim d'Arteney asked. He was from California, and spoke in a deep mellow voice.

"Why this singing about sex while we march? Is it necessary?" I was expecting a chorus of agreement from those soon-to-be officers and gentlemen.

Henderson, whose nickname soon became "Sugar Bear," gently placed his arm around me, cocked his head back, and looked at me in the eye. He then pursed his lips briefly. "Where have you been, son?"

Everyone cracked up. I hadn't yet learned that the attitude and military bearing of army warrant officers (WOs) was going to be different from my expectations.

Tom Andrews, also a Texan, came up behind me and put his hands over my ears. "Tell you what. I'll march behind you like this so you won't have to listen."

The laughter continued all around, and I began to sense that I should drop the subject. But the difference between the worlds I came from and the one I was entering continued to be a problem. My life had been centered on our church. During my high school years, Karen Snyder and I attended Billy Graham crusades whenever possible, and we went forward at the end of each service to rededicate our lives to the Lord. I never attended a school dance, and my evening dates with Susan Cadloni, my current girlfriend, usually consisted of bowling or roller-skating. If we went to the movies, there was nothing more than holding hands along with our popcorn and soda. I had been president of the church college youth group, and I had been trained to lead the church congregation in singing during the Sunday evening service. My dream of being out in the world was coming true, but in a way I hadn't imagined.

The friendship among those headed for flight school continued to grow as we shared stories about home, family, and friends. One day, we were sitting around during a break and showing off pictures in our wallet. I had a picture of Susan, and others had pictures of girlfriends or fiancées. A few, like Ortego, were married and had pictures of their wives. Don Isenberg, a farm boy from Indiana, pulled out his wallet and proudly showed a picture of his John Deere tractor, for which he took a lot of ribbing. We were beginning to bond, and I felt proud to be included.

We looked sharp with shiny brass, polished boots, and neat uniforms, and we graduated from basic training knowing that most of our company was soon heading to Vietnam. It seemed, though, that none of our drill sergeants were encouraging us to go "win the war." It was more like, "Just come home alive." That subtlety was lost on us at the time.

Eight of us were now warrant officer candidates (WOCs) and headed for flight school at the US Army Primary Helicopter Course, Fort Wolters, Texas. With a year to go before graduating from flight school, we believed the war would be over by then.

Chapter 2

Predestined

I arrived at Fort Wolters in July 1967, anxious to start flying, but found that the first month was in pre-flight—all classes and no flight training—with plenty of time spent with our TAC officer. We didn't have drill sergeants at flight school. We had TAC (pronounced "tack") officers, chief warrant officers who had spent a tour in Vietnam. Their job was to make proper army officers out of us, to prove they could triumph over such pedestrian stock.

Saturday morning inspections in pre-flight required everything to be perfect. Underwear had to be rolled neat and smooth to exact dimensions. Uniforms in the closet had to be hung with each hanger evenly spaced, down to the sixteenth of an inch, including the space from the sides of the closet to the first and last hanger. Boots and dress shoes had to be spit-shined to a high gloss. We even polished the soles. No matter what we had been through earlier in the week, absolutely no dirt could show anywhere on the footgear. Our bunks had to be made up to exact specifications and tight enough to bounce a quarter off the blanket.

During the inspection, the TAC looked for the slightest excuse to over-turn a mattress, dump underclothes out of a footlocker, and toss uniforms out of the closet, leaving the candidate no alternative but to start over. Failure to follow instructions and pay attention to the slightest detail, or not being "stract," meaning up to the highest military standards, resulted in the candidate not graduating from pre-flight.

On our third Friday evening, we were having a pre-inspection in preparation for the company commander's inspection the next morning. It was late, and the TAC had already been through twice before, unhappy with what he'd found. He had tossed everything before leaving and promised to be back.

Two hours later, at midnight, we were standing at attention by our bunks as he entered. The thud of his heels on the wooden floors of the World War II-era barracks broke the silence. As he walked, he slapped his swagger stick against his calf where his pants were bloused into his boots. His highly pressed uniform, with military creases in the shirt, hadn't a wrinkle. Below his aviator wings were several rows of ribbons, including awards and decorations from Vietnam. The leading edge of his shirt placket lined up with the leading edge of his belt buckle, which, in turn, lined up exactly with the edge of the fly of his trousers. His boots shone like patent leather. His brass gleamed like gold. This was topped off with a jet-black helmet, highly glossed and adorned with his chief warrant officer 2 (CW2) bar.

He stopped first in front of Candidate Johnson's bunk. "Candidate, who the hell taught you how to make a bunk?"

"Sir, Candidate Johnson, sir. I ... uh ..."

"I, uh, uh, what, candidate? Is that too tough a question for you? Sounds like a simple question to me, so let's try again." He was screaming in Johnson's face. "Who taught you how to make a bunk?"

"Sir, Candidate Johnson, sir. No one, sir."

That was the way candidates had to talk. Candidates said "sir" at the start of their sentence, their name, "sir" after their name, and "sir" at the end of the sentence.

"It looks like it." The TAC tossed the mattress off the bunk onto the floor.

Each of us had an individual trashcan, and, as the TAC continued down the row of bunks, he noticed Candidate Isenberg had thrown a piece of trash into his. The TAC went apoplectic. He started kicking trashcans, dumping lockers, turning mattresses, yelling, and screaming. He then stood nose to nose with Isenberg, who was standing at attention at the foot of his bunk. His lips curled as he spoke.

"What the hell is trash doing in your trashcan?"

"Sir, Candidate Isenberg, sir. It was trash, sir."

Sounds like a reasonable answer to me.

26

The officer started screaming. "What the hell is going on? I've never seen such a bunch of absolute misfits. Who the hell is the army sending me to try to turn into officers? Jesus Christ."

I cringed at his taking the Lord's name in vain.

The TAC then went back to Candidate Johnson. "Is there anyone here who can teach Candidate Johnson how to make a bunk?"

There was silence, as no one dared answer.

"I just asked a simple question. Am I addressing a bunch of morons here? Is there anyone who can teach Candidate Johnson how to make a bunk?"

"Sir, Candidate Ortego, sir. I will, sir."

The TAC walked over to Candidate Ortego and stared face-to-face with noses almost touching. Unfazed, Ortego stood as if molded in bronze, looking straight ahead and right through the TAC. For what seemed like minutes, the TAC continued, but Ortego held his own, unmoving.

The TAC finally wheeled and addressed us all. "You'd better start working as a team. You got that?"

"Sir, Candidate Jones, sir. Yes, sir," I shouted in unison with the rest of the platoon.

The TAC disappeared into the latrine area and shortly returned muttering to himself. He then shouted. "Who the hell's in charge of the latrine?"

"Sir, Candidate Henderson, sir."

"That isn't going to cut it, candidate." He passed Henderson and appeared to head out of the barracks. "It's dull and dirty in there."

You have to be kidding. That place is so clean that I'd eat off the floor.

He suddenly stopped at the door, turned, and faced us all. "It's your attention to details, candidates. The little details are going to kill you. You'll go over them again and again until they don't seem important anymore, like the pre-flight, the checklist, and radio frequencies." He stared. "Is your cargo properly stowed? Are all straps secured? Is your door gunner qualified? Are you over-loaded for where you'll land? You can pay all the attention to the big picture of the day, but, if you haven't paid attention to the details, it's going to get you or, worse, your crew killed." He paused again. "I'll be back at 0200." He wheeled to leave, but then spun back once more. He spoke softly this time in a serious tone, "I'll eliminate the whole flight, every one of you if I have to. I've done it before. I'll do it again."

Elimination was the term used when you were dropped from flight school. A classmate would disappear one day, along with all his belongings, leaving only an empty bunk. I had a mental picture of the candidate secretly being led out to a wall and shot.

> *Dear Mr. and Mrs. Jones, We regret to inform you that your son, Robert Russell Jones, was found to have lint on his sock. He was therefore not up to the standards required to become a warrant officer in the United States Army. He was eliminated on July 31, and his body disposed of per regulations.*
>
> *Sincerely,*
> *Iam Stract, CW2*

Our TAC finally left, and I heard a collective sigh. The barracks looked like a tornado had gone through it.

Isenberg spoke first. "I don't understand," he mumbled as he paced in circles and waved his arms around. "It was trash. Isn't that what a trashcan is for?"

I silently agreed. I was as confused and angry as Isenberg was, although for additional reasons. "I don't understand the swearing and cursing."

Andrews glanced at me with a look that said, "You're kidding. You're worried about the cursing?"

"Are we in this together?" Henderson appeared from a small group huddled at his end of the barracks.

"Yes," we answered, sounding weak and tired.

"Okay, then. Everyone get your own gear together and then start checking everyone else. Help wherever you can to get this place back in shape."

An hour and a half later, we had the place looking sharp, at least as sharp as it had been at midnight. I noticed plenty of cheerful commotion down at the latrine end of the barracks and headed off to see what I was missing. Apparently, Henderson, d'Arteney, and others had obtained paint from the maintenance shed, and, in response to the TAC's statement that the latrine was "dull and dirty," they had completely repainted the latrine from a pale white to a baby blue and pink. They then painted little colored fishes on the walls. I was learning that, when pushed to the limit, a cohesive group found a way to respond. I couldn't help but smile, but, at the same time, dreaded the TAC's reaction.

At 0155, we were all standing quietly near our bunks, ready to hit the position of attention if someone sighted the TAC.

"What does TAC stand for?" I asked.

No one immediately seemed to know, but Ortego finally said, "I think it stands for training, advising, and counseling officer."

"They must have had a good laugh when they came up with that one," I said. Everyone chuckled.

"I could use some counseling right about now," d'Arteney added in his baritone voice.

There was more laughter as we were all in a punch-drunk mood due to lack of sleep, the past pressure from the TAC, and the anticipation of his next appearance.

"Flight, attention," a candidate at the door cried out.

We snapped to attention at the foot of our bunks. The TAC entered and slowly walked down the barracks, his boots clunking and his swagger stick slapping the bunks as he passed. He said nothing. At every other bunk, he stopped, looked the candidate in the eye, walked around the bunk, and then checked out the footlocker. He continued to say nothing, and we all stood perfectly still, staring straight ahead.

It seemed like an agonizing hour for him to get to the far end of the barracks, but he finally disappeared around the corner and into the latrine. We held our breath, and he seemed to stay there forever. When he emerged, he did so at a quicker pace. He stomped to the other end of the barracks. As he passed, I could see he was livid, beet red with anger, and ready to explode.

He finally spoke, but in a forced attempt at a normal tone, "You've worked so hard to get here, and, just like that, you've thrown it away. Your education, your dreams of becoming a pilot, you've tossed it, every one of you." He hesitated, as if to let it sink in. "You want to be a grunt, I guess. You want to hump through the jungles of Vietnam? Okay." He turned and, as he walked out the door, simply said, "Lights out."

We scrambled into our bunks. *Would they really eliminate the entire flight?*

In less than two hours, we were back up for a quick breakfast and then final preparations for the morning inspection by the "Old Man," the company commander with the rank of captain. He arrived right on time, along with a couple of his staff and, of course, our TAC. The captain certainly appeared to be much older, at least thirty years of age. In his dress greens loaded with ribbons indicating numerous awards and decorations from Vietnam, he stopped at each candidate, had a short quiet talk as he inspected everything, and then moved on to the next. He asked us not to shout.

"Good morning, Candidate Jones. How are you?" He was almost whispering.

"Sir, Candidate Jones, sir. Fine, sir."

"Where are you from, candidate?"

"Sir, Candidate Jones, sir. California, sir."

After checking my gear, he stopped in front of me and continued with his questions. "What was your major in college?"

"Sir, Candidate Jones, sir. Administration of justice, sir."

"Do you plan on using your flying skills in law enforcement if you choose not to make a career out of the army?" he asked, as if it were something he might consider himself.

"Sir, Candidate Jones, sir. Yes, sir."

"Interesting. Thank you, candidate."

The quiet questioning and personal inspections continued with each and every candidate in the platoon and, well over an hour later, concluded with the latrine. The captain and his covey of followers then quietly emerged and came to the center of the barracks. The captain stood tall and exuded a military bearing.

"Candidates, thank you for your time. I've heard some wonderful things about you and want you to know how proud I am of you." His voice was soft and reassuring. "I know you're anxious to start your flight training. In the meantime, my office is always open so, if you need anything, please stop by."

As they left, our TAC turned and said, "You'll have to stay on base, but you have the rest of the weekend off. Be back by 1700 on Sunday."

We were stunned and stood there looking at each other for a moment. I made eye contact with Ortego.

He smiled and seemed to say, "See, it's only a game."

Cheers and laughter then erupted, and everyone was amazed that they didn't say anything about the latrine. I felt good, but couldn't help but remark to Ortego, "It's not a game for those who've already been eliminated."

"For them, it wasn't meant to be," Ortego said.

"Not meant to be? You make it sound like it's predestined."

Ortego appeared to be in thought. "You couldn't have put it better."

A chill ran through my body.

I looked forward to spending the day away from the barracks. I caught a movie with Henderson and Andrews at the base theater and hit the sack early. Then we attended church Sunday morning. After church, we had a chance to talk to a candidate wearing a blue disk on his cap that indicated he was a blue hat with the 3rd Warrant Officer Candidate Company.

After pre-flight, candidates went "up on the hill" to one of the ten WOC companies. WOC was pronounced as "wok," the stir-fry skillet, or, as TAC officers might say in taunting, as "wock, something you throw at a wabbit." Each WOC Company was assigned a color. The colored hat worn with your flight suit was your company color. When wearing the dress uniform, the cap had your company's colored disk in front, held on by WOC brass.

The pecking order was alive and operational within the program, with those in pre-flight being at the absolute bottom of the rung. On the top rung were senior candidates with only a month remaining before graduating from Fort Wolters. Their orange epaulet, a small shoulder strap, which had a black stripe, identified them. Among candidates, seniors had the same status as an officer, meaning junior candidates had to respect them with salutes and "sirs." Candidates who were not yet seniors, but who had soloed, wore a solid orange epaulet.

This candidate at church, wearing the blue disk on his cap, along with the epaulets without a stripe, was willing to lower his standards and spend a few moments with lowly pre-flighters, Henderson, Andrews, and me. Our primary interest at this point was flying, so we had plenty of questions about the training. The conversation, though, eventually got around to the WOC companies.

"When do you graduate?" Andrews asked.

"Two months to go. When are you guys headed up the hill?"

"Next week. We're senior pre-flighters," Andrews said.

We all laughed.

"So who's graduating next week?" Henderson asked.

"I think 4th WOC, yellow hats. Maybe 1st WOC, red hats. They're graduating soon, too."

"I like the sound of red hats," I said.

"Oh, no, you won't. You don't want 1st WOC. The TACs think they have to be the best, hard-core, number one." He raised his finger along with his voice, getting roused up. "We all stay clear of 1st WOC and their TACs." He left with a parting warning. "Don't go to 1st WOC."

"As if we have a choice," Andrews said.

Henderson laughed. "Just get me on the hill. Heck, I'll wear a pink hat."

"I just want to start flying," I said.

We headed back to the barracks. Our pass was coming to a close.

The following Saturday, filled with apprehension about the unknown, we marched up the hill. Sure enough, our new assignment was the dreaded 1st WOC, the "Big. Red. One." No sooner had we arrived into the company area than the TAC officers went on the offensive.

CW2 Barryhill stood in front of our company, and he wasted no time in assuring us that the rumors we'd heard about 1st WOC were true. "You'll be first in everything you do. Is that understood?" he shouted.

"Sir, Candidate Jones, sir. Yes sir," I yelled in unison with everyone else.

CW2 Horning, standing off to the side, then added, "If you think you can't cut it, you'd better get out now. Understand?

"Sir, Candidate Jones, sir. Yes sir."

"I can't hear you," Barryhill shouted.

We yelled back even louder.

"So who wants to drop out now?" Horning bellowed.

No one answered, and suddenly the TACs were in our faces, demanding that we resign now.

"Half of this group will not be here in sixty days, so quit wasting my time candidates," Horning screamed as he passed by me.

We were in a formation in back of the building, and they had us dump our duffle bags, which contained our entire possessions, on the ground. Several other TACs joined in, and they went through everything we were bringing in, as if we had a chance to obtain contraband while marching in formation from pre-flight. There was so much yelling that it was hard to decipher it all.

"Candidate Auld, what are you doing with a comb?"

"Candidate Lambie, do you think you're going to bring those boots into my building?"

"Nose clippers, Candidate Kinkusich? What's a matter, candidate, you can't pull your nose hairs like everyone else?"

And, of course, during all the yelling of questions, the candidates tried to answer. It was a cacophony of shouting, hooting, wailing, and crying.

I suddenly felt hot air on the back of my neck.

"Who the hell are you looking at?"

I dared not turn since I was at attention.

"I'm talking to you, candy-date," he bellowed.

A round face, an inch away from mine, started to appear as a TAC began to circle to my left. He was on the overweight side, heavy jowls with flopping lips, looking like a caricature of a human bulldog.

I shouted as loudly and as confident as I could, "Sir, Candidate Jones, sir."

He whistled loudly to get everyone's attention. Silence fell across the company with a heavy thud. "I got a live one here," he yelled for all to hear. "So Candy-date Jones, who were you looking at?"

I hadn't seen this TAC before and certainly hadn't been looking at him because he came up from behind.

"Sir, Candidate Jones, sir. No one, sir," I said.

"Are you calling me a liar, candy-date?" he asked, as if an accusation had stunned him.

His bad breath mixed with his body odor from the Texas summer sun. "Because, if you're calling me a liar, then we've got some real problems here. Now

I think you were giving me the eye, candy-date. So let's try this again. Who were you looking at?"

The entire company was listening. I had no idea where this conversation was going, but decided this might be the time to go along to get along. "Sir, Candidate Jones, sir. You, sir."

"See, you were looking at me. Thank you, candy-date, for your honesty." Every word spewed across my face. "So do you like me or something?"

Clearly, this question had no correct answer. I was in trouble no matter how I answered. I decided to take the most direct route and tried to get it over with. "Sir, Candidate Jones, sir. No, sir," I said loudly.

He screamed, "No what?"

"Sir, Candidate Jones, sir. No, I do not like you, sir."

"I think you do, candy-date," he said with an air of appreciation. "I think you like me." He couldn't have gotten any closer without his lips flapping against my cheeks. Then, looking as if he'd just come to a realization, he stood back and shouted, "Well, goddamn, I think you'd like to bed me, wouldn't you, candy-date?"

I flinched at the swearing. The TAC continued circling and brought his face back within an inch of my neck. His salty breath overcame the mounting temperatures as he pivoted around me.

"Do you hear that, company? Candy-date Jones wants to snuggle up and bed me." He then stepped back and started dancing on his toes, holding his arms like a ballerina as he sang, "Mother, mother, Candy-date Jones wants to bed mother."

He spied my Bible among my personal possessions strewn on the ground before me, picked it up, and pushed it tight against my nose. "You think this is going to help you, Candy-date Jones?"

"Sir, Candidate Jones, sir. Yes, it is going to help me, sir."

He stared eyeball to eyeball a few more moments and then finally went on to someone else. The other TACs started up where they left off, and the loud vocal dissonance continued.

The TAC was from 2nd WOC, and his nickname was "Mother," which explained a little more about his tirade. He loved to work the mess hall where any

TAC could create havoc, screaming in a candidate's face about his lack of table etiquette and therefore his inadequacy to become an officer and a gentleman.

Once the training began, we were up at 0445, not a minute earlier and not a minute later. With our rooms ready for inspection, we were to be fully dressed and in formation at 0500. The first couple of mornings found several of the candidates, including myself, half-dressed with shaving cream still around our ears. It was soon easy, though, and those who hadn't been eliminated in the first week or so were looking fairly sharp in starched fatigues and shiny brass. We spent half of the day in classroom training, covering everything from helicopter power plants and transmissions to navigation. We spent the other half of the day at the airfield taking flight lessons.

The Mattel Messerschmitt

My first flight instructor, a civilian, appeared old enough to have flown with the Wright brothers. We climbed into the army's TH-55, a small, lightweight helicopter that the Hughes Tool Company built. It was known in the civilian world as the Hughes 269A. Candidates referred it to as the "Mattel Messerschmitt."

The doors were off, and I noticed that, as I sat in the helicopter, my right shoulder and hip were actually hanging out over the edge of the seat into thin air. I secured my helmet on my head and plugged in my intercom system as the instructor started the engine. He took off and leveled out at an altitude of fifteen hundred feet. By the way the aircraft responded to my instructor, I could tell that he hadn't climbed into the helicopter. He had strapped it on his back. He flew as if the aircraft were an extension of his body.

"Now, let's talk about the cyclic first," he said. The cyclic, known in fixed-wing aircraft as a "joystick," came up from the floor between the pilot's legs and was held by the right hand. "Go ahead and get on the cyclic with me and follow along. As you can see, when I move the cyclic slightly to the left, we turn left. Move it to the right, and we turn right. See how little we have to move it to get the helicopter to respond?"

I was amazed at how little he had moved the cyclic. I gently squeezed the intercom switch on the cyclic with my forefinger. "Yes, sir."

"Cut the 'sir' when in the aircraft. Now, if we move the cyclic forward, we drop the nose, gain speed, and lose altitude. If I pull back on the cyclic, the helicopter will want to climb and slow down. All right, go ahead and play with the cyclic a bit. You have it."

"I have it." I lowered the nose, raised it, and then made a few turns. I was surprised to find that the helicopter, unlike the airplane, turned with only the cyclic and didn't need input from the pedals.

Piece of cake.

"Great. Okay, I have it," said the instructor.

"You have it." I let go of the cyclic.

"Now follow along on the pedals. Notice if I push the left pedal, the nose turns left. The right pedal turns the nose right. Now you try it."

I gently pushed the left and right pedals, and the nose of the helicopter swung left or right, but continued flying, although awkwardly, along its intended path. I was beginning to get the feel, as taught in class, that the body of the helicopter swung like a pendulum below the rotating disk of the blades above.

"Great. Now the collective. Just follow along."

The collective is a lever on the left side of each seat that pivots in the back. The end of the collective was similar to a bicycle handlebar grip. I knew from classroom training that rotating the grip controlled the throttle. As I placed my left hand on the end of the collective, I could feel the instructor lift it ever so slightly. As he did, the helicopter gained altitude.

"Now you try it, but be careful not to turn the throttle."

I pulled on the collective, known as "pulling pitch," and felt us quickly rise as if in an elevator. I pushed it back a bit and could feel the bottom fall out from under me.

"Great. Now, notice the engine RPM[1] gauge. You'll notice the RPMs are in the green arch. Place your hand back on the collective, and, without raising or lowering the collective, notice how the RPMs change when I turn the throttle."

I heard the engine RPMs increase and saw the needle slightly rise to the top of the green arch, but I never felt him turn the throttle. The RPM needle then returned to the center of the green arch.

"It takes little pressure. So you try it now."

At first, I had the tendency to overcorrect with the RPMs, sending the needle on the gauge close to the red line. With a little practice, though, I had it down.

"Great. Now get on all the controls, and keep us flying straight and level."

Piece of cake. We wobbled through the sky with my overcorrections. *I'll be soloing in no time.*

"Great. Okay, I've got it." He dropped us like a rock out of the sky and into a large cow field. We came to a perfect hover three feet off the ground.

"Now take the pedals and keep us pointed at that tree straight ahead."

I had no problem with that.

"Turn us ninety degrees to the right."

I went farther than ninety, but eventually settled us into the new heading.

"You overcorrected a bit. That's natural at first. Now forget the pedals, take the cyclic, and keep us over this spot."

---

1. revolutions per minute

We moved around a little, but I was fairly successful. I was proud of myself and positive I was making a great impression.

"Great," he said again. He loved that word, and I enjoyed hearing it. "Now, hands off the cyclic, and take the collective. I'll worry about the throttle. You keep us at three feet."

After a few moments of ups and downs, I finally settled at a fairly decent hover.

"Great. Now forget about the collective and handle the throttle."

That was difficult as the throttle was touchy, and it seemed that only thinking about rotating counterclockwise raised the RPMs, but I had it down after a few minutes.

"Great," the instructor said again.

I was beaming at my accomplishments, imagining I might set a record for soloing in the shortest amount of time.

"Now, get on all the controls, and you've got it."

"I've got it," I replied with confidence.

We remained in a steady, constant hover for a half-second. We started to drift back, and I applied forward cyclic. At the same time, the nose started turning left, and, when I applied right pedal, the RPMs fell. As we began to turn, drift, and fall, I increased RPMs, and we shot skyward. We were climbing, spinning, drifting, falling, and then spinning the other way. We were just short of crashing, burning, and dying at the far end of the field when the instructor calmly said, "I've got it."

We were immediately back in the middle of the field at a constant, steady, smooth three-foot hover.

"Remember what you learned in class. When you increase or decrease throttle, it'll result in gaining or losing altitude. And the nose will swing left when you decrease power and right when you increase power. If you move the cyclic forward, you'll lose altitude, so you'll have to increase throttle, which means applying left pedal. Everything you do, every movement by one control, will result in having to make a correction with another control."

We spent another fifteen minutes in that field, and I made absolutely no progress. I was all over the field, sliding right and left, back and forth, up to twenty-five feet, spinning, and then nearly crashing. The instructor recovered and placed us in the center of the field at a perfect hover before turning the controls back over to me. In a second, the instructor would have to take over again. He never yelled nor raised his voice, but rather assured me that it would take practice.

Upon arriving back at the main airfield, I was thoroughly soaked with sweat, devastated and embarrassed. *I can fly airplanes, so why can't I hover this little toy of an aircraft?* I looked at the faces of my classmates, and I could see they were as dejected at their progress as I was with mine.

On the bus ride back to our barracks, Candidate Irby said, "It's kind of like balancing a broom on its end with one hand while sitting. It's pretty easy. Then the instructor says balance another at the same time with the other hand. It's a little harder. Then he wants you to continue while adding two more brooms to balance with each foot."

We laughed in agreement.

Candidate Lambie added, "And all the while licking an ice cream cone."

The hooting and banter continued all the way back to the base as we realized we all had the same difficult day.

Harassment and inspections continued back at the barracks, but, for most of us, they were getting easier as we adapted. For a few others, whether it was the inability to pay attention to detail, follow instructions, or maintain strict military discipline and decorum, they couldn't make the grade and were eliminated at the TAC's discretion. Other classmates were recycled a class back due to their lack of performance in flight school or academics.

Classes continued on the flight characteristics of helicopters and the potentially disastrous consequences when anything went wrong. Flying continued, which was the easy part. I had no problem with flying in the pattern around the airfield. The hovering was giving me and everyone else the fits until it happened one day. I hovered. A ninety-degree turn left, one hundred eighty–

degree turn right, land, and pick it up to a three-foot hover. It seemed to all come together at once.

I knew I was getting close to soloing when, at five hundred feet, the instructor suddenly closed the throttle, simulating an engine failure. Now, a helicopter doesn't glide like a fixed-wing airplane. When power is cut, it immediately drops like a rock out of the sky. At five hundred feet, I had less than fifteen seconds before contact with the ground. I needed to make a decision on where to land in the first couple of seconds, and then turn in that direction. In the final twenty feet, after flaring to stop forward flight, I needed to pull the collective, or "pull pitch," gently setting the aircraft on the ground using the remaining RPMs left in the rotors.

I had only one chance to get it right since all rotor blade momentum would be used on the first attempt. If I pulled pitch too high, I would run out of rotor blade momentum and slam into the ground. If I pulled too low, I would crash before the remaining momentum in the blades sufficiently slowed the helicopter's descent.

When the instructor cut the throttle, I immediately dropped the collective to maintain rotor RPMs. With seconds to make a decision on where to land, I immediately chose a field to my left. I made a tight, one hundred and eighty-degree left turn. As I turned, my fixed-wing experience kicked in, and I applied full left pedal, exactly the wrong thing to do in a helicopter in that situation.

When power is reduced or shut down to idle, as in this case, regardless of which way the pilot is going to turn, he wants to apply right pedal to counteract the reduction in force applied to the rotor blades. I applied full left pedal, and we immediately went into a nosedive. This isn't a normal operating position for any training helicopter at any altitude, especially one at less than five hundred feet.

The instructor yelled as he grabbed the controls, "I got it!"

The engine screamed to life as he rolled in power and yanked in collective to gain control. He pulled out of the dive and recovered only feet above the ground. He set the helicopter down, rolled off the throttle, sat for a moment with a few deep breaths, and then simply said, "Do that again, and I will give you a pink slip."

I knew he was serious, and I knew it only took two pink slips to be, at best, recycled to the class behind you or, worse, eliminated. And I knew exactly what I had done wrong.

The next day, we again flew the pattern. He gave me several more simulated engine failures, which I handled successfully. Then he had me land next to the tower where those not flying waited.

He unstrapped, got out, secured his seat belt, and then, before disconnecting his intercom, said, "Continue to fly the pattern, and set down after each approach. I'll be in the tower monitoring your progress and will let you know when to shut down."

With that, I found myself alone. Although I had soloed numerous times in fixed-wing aircraft, I was nervous. I flew the pattern, came to a hover, and tried to set down the helicopter. But as I wobbled around at three feet, I couldn't seem to set the skids on the ground.

Come on. Land. Darn it, what's the problem?

I was sure everyone was watching as I was stuck at a couple feet. I finally cheated by rolling the throttle off slowly within the last foot.

Whew! I landed.

After receiving clearance, I took off and flew the pattern again, landing properly. Upon shutting down for the day, I found I had beat Candidate Hudson by barely ten minutes, becoming the first in the flight to solo. On the ride back to Fort Wolters, Hudson and I were the happiest two guys alive. The bus made the obligatory stop at the Holiday Inn in Mineral Wells, where our classmates tossed the two of us into the motel swimming pool. The next day, we proudly wore our wings on our red caps, indicating to all that we had moved up one more step in the candidate hierarchy.

Graduation in January from Primary Helicopter Flight School came more with relief than excitement. It was on to Fort Rucker, Alabama, for the continuation of our training, where pressure from TAC officers was light, but classroom training became more difficult as we dealt with turbine power plants and instrument flying. Again, we spent half a day on the flight line.

We started at Fort Rucker learning to fly solely on instruments in the army's OH-13, an antiquated observation helicopter, which, along with the army's OH-23, saw plenty of service in the Korean War. To create the experience of instrument flight and to prevent the pilot from seeing outside, the right side of the helicopter had the bottom of the bubble painted over. The student also wore a shield that prevented any side or forward viewing around or above the instrument panel.

Instruction in instrument flying is important because, in bad weather, when the ground or horizon is no longer visible, the pilot has no way to tell if he's climbing, descending, turning, or flying in any given direction unless he's able to read and believe his instruments. Believing is crucial because the pilot who's in instrument flight will experience sensations known as vertigo that tell him he's either turning left or right or climbing or descending when, in fact, he's not or is actually doing the opposite. A disoriented helicopter pilot flying in instrument conditions will result in tragedy within moments. The necessity of keeping the aircraft straight and level is then coupled with the need to get to where the pilot needs to be and not into a mountainside.

We then moved on to the UH-1 Huey, the helicopter made famous by the Vietnam War. Flying the Huey was like driving a Cadillac in comparison to the training helicopters we previously flew. The controls were hydraulic-assisted and felt smooth as silk. The throttle was regulated, which meant that, once set, the RPMs were constant while in normal flight conditions. We learned how to fly the Huey into restricted landing zones, narrow hilltops, and sloping hillsides. We practiced formation flying, daytime low level, and nighttime cross-country.

I had found marching in large formations, with the cadence, stomp of the boots, and feelings of camaraderie, exhilarating. Formation flying with the Huey was spine tingling. The large blades of the Hueys created their own special beat, and, when six or nine Hueys sat on the ground in close formation and then lifted off together, the feeling was astounding. The thumping of my aircraft's blades and whine of the turbine engine usually overcame all other sounds, but, in close formation, I could feel the rhythm of the surrounding helicopters in my bones. This was particularly true in flight when the formation reduced power during approach and the Hueys' blades slapped the air with the unmistakable sound that still echoes in the mind of all who served in Vietnam.

Graduation day with Mom and Dad

With a week to go before graduation, the anticipation regarding our upcoming orders began to take precedence, and rumors spread like prairie fires.

"Don't go to the 1st CAV. They have the worst living conditions. They sleep in their choppers."

"The 173rd Airborne has it all together."

"My cousin says to get assigned to the Saigon area. It's the most secure."

"You don't want to go to I Corps. That's where the heavy fighting is."

Vietnam was divided into four different Corps, with I Corps (pronounced "eye corps") being the farthest north along the border with North Vietnam. IV Corps was the farthest south. Saigon was in III Corps. Whatever the rumors were, staying out of I Corps seemed to be a common theme.

Class 68-503 graduated in May 1968. One of the first ceremonies was for the entire company to fly in several formations over Fort Rucker, and, as a result of graduating second in class, I led the second flight. For me, though, leading the flight wasn't the same experience as being in back where the helicopters were majestically spread out in front, undulating in the formation like ocean swells.

Our last contacts with flight instructors, TAC officers, and classroom instructors came with the same advice we had received in basic training, "Come home safe." No one said, "Go win the war" or "Defeat communism." With a faraway look of knowing in their eyes, the attitude of those who had been there seemed to be that "You can't win this war, so just survive it."

As a new warrant officer (WO) with flight wings, I received my orders. Report within a month to the American Division in the Republic of South Vietnam.

"Who's the American Division?" I asked.

The usual reply was a blank stare.

"Never heard of it," someone said.

Wonderful. Everyone is going somewhere with at least a reputation. I'm going to a division no one has heard of.

The best information I was finally able to get was, "Yeah, that's the 23rd Infantry, an old World War II division reactivated last year. They're up in I Corps."

I Corps, great. I succumbed to the rumor mill in believing that I Corps was the last place I wanted to be assigned.

I felt better, though, when I learned Gerald Ortego had also been assigned to the American Division.

We left Fort Rucker still in that age of innocence. We were proud army aviators, flyboys, wearing aviator sunglasses and large watches. We strutted as if we were wearing white scarves around our necks.

The realization that, in a few weeks, I'd be heading off to a war that our government had yet to resolve tempered my enthusiasm. A war that had been distant and abstract was about to become tangible and dangerous.

Chapter 3

Welcome to Vietnam

"Bull. He shouldn't have been flying," a WO said. The pilot sitting across the table from him threw his arms in the air. "Wait a minute. Don't blame him. Who asked him to fly?"

It was June 1968, and I had been in Vietnam less than a week when Captain Krause and I grabbed a table for dinner at a small officer's club located at the south end of Chu Lai. Storm shutters were pulled up, allowing the gentle breeze off the South China Sea to clear the smoke from the dimly lit building. From a makeshift stage, a civilian hailing from Australia was singing his rendition of a country-and-western song.

Krause was finishing his second tour in Vietnam, and he was assigned to an administrative position where we had met while I was processing into the Americal Division. He was considering flight school. He enjoyed the company of helicopter pilots, had access to a jeep, and liked visiting the officer clubs of the various aviation units in Chu Lai. War might be hell, but I quickly learned that, for pilots in Chu Lai, there were plenty of great clubs serving drinks, steaks, cheeseburgers, and fries and regularly showing full-length movies.

While enjoying our meal, we couldn't help but overhear an increasingly loud and boisterous group of four rough and tenured WO pilots wearing faded uniforms sitting at the other end of our long table. They wore their hair long with sideburns and bushy mustaches. Empty beer bottles and full ashtrays littered the table in front of them. Profanities laced their conversation.

"You're right," one said. "Cotton had less than a month, right? Shouldn't have been flying."

A third man chimed in, "Cotton wasn't asked. He was ordered."

I was beginning to get the picture. Someone named Cotton had been hurt or killed. The conversation disturbed me. Krause and I just sat and listened.

One of the guys finished a bottle of beer and then slammed it down. "Do you believe that story about one shot from the tree line?" He swore as he wiped beer from his chin with his sleeve. "It's a cover-up, I tell you. Something stinks to high heaven here."

One changed the subject. "I got his boots. He kept his stuff nice."

I couldn't believe what I was hearing as they continued to talk about his personal gear, such as a guitar.

"They're not going to send that home. His wife isn't going to want that, so why not?"

I dropped my head and stared at the table. Cotton had apparently been killed. Krause slapped me on the shoulder and motioned to go. Heading out the door, I turned to watch as they stood on the benches and, with beers raised high, sang a toast.

When I entered the military, I had an image of military pilots with crisp, clean uniforms, shiny boots, broad smiles, bright teeth, close haircuts, white scarves blowing in the breeze, big aviator watches, and a gleam in the eye. The pinpoint of reality had just pricked that bubble of a dream.

We were quiet on the drive back through the base. I was disgusted with what I thought was complete disrespect and irreverence for a fallen soldier, but didn't bring the subject up as we talked outside my quarters.

"So, Krause, one year of combat on your first tour wasn't enough? Why the second tour so soon?"

Krause leaned forward against the steering wheel. "Some of us begin to feed on the adrenalin of combat. Kind of becomes a rush you can't live without, you know?"

No, I don't know. But I listened.

"This war is some kind of addiction, and I couldn't stop cold turkey."

"So back to Nam and right back into the field?"

"Yeah, six months of some good action with the 11th Brigade and then I took this job to kind of wind down. Hope it works." He laughed.

His demeanor changed as he suddenly became sullen and stared out into the black sky. He spoke softly, more to himself than me. "I'm afraid I've been changed forever." Krause then turned to me. "I'm out of here in a few days, so take care, okay?" He hesitated. "About those guys back at the club. I know you can't grasp it right now, but it's their way of dealing with a bad situation. Until you've been in their shoes, you won't. I hope you never are." Krause stammered a bit. "But you probably will be. Maybe then you'll understand."

I didn't sleep well that night as thoughts raced through my mind. *Who was this aviator, Cotton, who served with honor? Did he have faith when he said good-bye to his bride and boarded that plane to Vietnam? Did he have faith in his commanders, who might have ordered him on a mission when he was just days away from returning home? Was this all destined when he entered flight school?*

The war was real now, even though I had yet to fly a mission. Someone had died. I hadn't given it much thought before, but it was beginning to sink in that a passenger, crew, or fellow pilot could be hurt or killed while aboard my helicopter. The weight of that responsibility was clearer. No longer was it a TAC officer barking how my lack of attention might get someone killed. As I tossed and turned in my bunk, I was having trouble coming to grips with how I would handle that if it happened on a helicopter under my command.

I began to think back to my wedding reception and the last talk I had with Pastor Bishop. Barely a week after graduation from flight school, Susan Cadloni and I were married in Los Gatos at Calvary Baptist. She was my best friend, and I knew she'd make a wonderful wife and mother. We had discussed whether we should get married before or after Vietnam, and we decided to get married before. After the wedding ceremony, we held a reception in the church gymnasium. Knowing I was off to Vietnam, everyone had a word of support for me.

"We'll be praying for you."

"We have faith that you're doing the right thing. God bless you, and, remember, to God be the glory."

"We're so proud of you. You'll be in God's hands, so don't you worry now."

Pastor Bishop managed to get a few words in with me before he left the reception. He was short and balding and wore glasses, and he could give a sermon ending with an altar call equal to any gospel crusade.

"Now, don't forget your Lord, Russ. Keep up with your Bible studies and attend church. We expect you to be a witness for him while you're serving our country. We'll be praying for you and asking God to bless you with a safe return."

"Doesn't God already know what's in store for me?"

Pastor Bishop gently placed his left hand on my shoulder, and, with a soft smile and a twinkle in his eye, simply said, "Yes."

It's predestined, already written in the book.

As if he could read my mind, Pastor Bishop concluded, "Have faith in our Lord Jesus Christ."

When I was thirteen, Pastor Bishop had given a sermon on the topic of predestination, and it stuck with me through the years. "It is written. It has been decided. God knows who is among his flock. And it is by grace you are saved. It is by grace that your name is written in the book." He then opened his Bible. "Follow along with me, Ephesians chapter two, verse eight. 'For by grace are ye saved through faith—not of yourselves, it is the gift of God.'" Pastor Bishop then looked across the congregation, seemingly right at me, and repeated, "Through faith."

As I lay there that night in Vietnam, I couldn't help but think about that word, faith. I had to have faith that my government was doing the right thing in Vietnam and my commanders, making life-and-death decisions, would be making the correct ones. I had to have faith that my Lord would return me safe and sound back to Susan, my bride. *Yet hasn't it all been predestined?*

Typical of the army, it took over a week of "hurry up and wait" around the Chu Lai processing center before Major Allison picked me up and took me to my new home, the living quarters, or hooch, for the pilots assigned to the 196th Light Infantry Brigade's (LIB) Aviation Unit. It was a single-story, wood-framed barracks with wood floors. The exterior had wood siding up to four feet and then four feet of screen that allowed for plenty of airflow when necessary. Storm shutters dropped to cover the screens during inclement weather. Galvanized metal was on the roof. Our hooch was upgraded to include a plumbed shower. The sun heated the water, stored in a black barrel on the roof. I was quite pleased and, after later seeing the housing for other aviation units, realized how good the pilots of the 196th LIB had it.

Several long rows of hooches lined the side of a hill, and we were about four rows up, two from the top. We had a great view to the east overlooking the Ky Ha helicopter airfield, with the South China Sea in the background. The Vietnamese hamlet of Ky Ha, for which the heliport was named, lay just beyond the heavily wired and guarded perimeter over the hill to our west.

It was explained that, because our hooch sat on the side of a hill, facing the ocean with the mainland behind it, we were safe from a rocket attack. If a rocket cleared the hill, it would pass safely overhead as its flat trajectory would make it unable to hit where the hooch was. Apparently, that didn't apply to mortar rounds.

One morning, just as a blistering sun was rising over the South China Sea, I sauntered down the hill and past the control tower, and I was crossing the dirt road to enter the Ky Ha heliport. A sergeant was approaching on foot from my right. Few others were stirring except for civilian Vietnamese arriving for work. On my left, I suddenly heard a muffled explosion and saw dust, about a hundred yards away, billowing out of the ditch along the side of the road. I stopped just as the sergeant walked up beside me with his hands in the pockets of his well-faded fatigues. He was watching the same dissipating cloud.

"What the heck was that?" I asked.

"Mortar round," he said knowingly.

It didn't seem very loud for a mortar round, but what would I know about that yet?

"Are we under attack?"

He stood there for a few seconds, as if to see for himself. "No, but, if another one drops, I'm hitting the ditch."

"That one landed in the ditch," I said.

He rocked back on his heels and laughed. "Okay, you got me on that one. I think that was probably a bracket round."

"Bracket?"

The sergeant understood he was talking to a clueless WO who had recently arrived in country. "Some time later today, a hooch maid[2], maybe yours," he said with a smirk, "will casually walk by where the mortar round landed and estimate how far off that round was from your helicopters. She'll report that to the VC so they can adjust their fire. When they think they have it right, they'll send a bunch of rounds in."

Wonderful! Nothing like having the support of the locals.

No other rounds landed, so I crossed the ditch and entered the helipad. A bubbling wave of ninety-degree heat off the perforated steel panels greeted me along with the smell of aviation fuel. On the southeast corner of the helipad was the 54th Medical Detachment, a helicopter medical evacuation unit complete with a hospital. The 123rd Aviation Battalion (AvBn) occupied the northern end. My unit occupied the southwest corner.

Major Allison, who left the unit shortly afterward, was the 196th Aviation Unit's commanding officer. Next in line was Captain Benny Walton, then we had Warrant Officers Bob Moore, Ronald Redeker, Bert Hampton, John Hambrick, and now myself.

Redeker, who had recently taken a bullet through a calf muscle, was healing fine and gave me my initial tour of the unit, including our four helicopters. The 196th had two Hueys, used primarily for command and control (C&C) by the brigade commander. Outfitted with comfortable thick seat cushions for the passengers, they were set up with extra radios in the back that allowed the colonel or other high-ranking officers communications with various ground units.

Then Redeker showed me two OH-23s. I could hardly believe the army was still using Korean War-era aircraft. I was also quite disappointed to learn that, having recently graduated from flight school and qualified to fly the turbine-powered Huey, I was going to be flying this antiquated helicopter in combat situations. The 196th not only used the OH-23 for ferrying personnel around the area of operations, but also for armed scout missions while assisting the 1st Marine Division (MarDiv) in the Da Nang area.

What lifted my spirits was the discovery that, after a short walk down the

2. Hooch maids were Vietnamese women who were bussed in each day, and they cleaned, washed uniforms and linens, shined boots, and drank the soda pops out of our refrigerator. Every hooch had one maid, a rule that gave employment to the local community.

hill to the flight line, across the helipad, and then down a bluff, I could sink my toes into the beautiful white beach along the blue waters of the South China Sea. I was to spend many off days snorkeling, playing football, or simply sunbathing in a prime and coveted location in I Corps.

Back early from flying one afternoon, I walked into our quarters to get a soda out of the refrigerator. Redeker was sitting at our bar having a drink with a pilot from the 123rd AvBn whom I hadn't met, WO Hugh Thompson.

Our young maid interrupted the conversation. "Hey, GI, get me Coke?"

"You pay for these, Hai?" I asked her jokingly.

"You numba one, GI. I love you too much." She laughed as she took the soda from me and headed out the door, probably to step off how far the last mortar round landed from our hooch.

Thompson continued his conversation with Redeker. "They were indiscriminately killing hundreds of civilians, women, and children. I had to do something."

Hundreds? I knew civilians died as a result of war. What he implied, though, that civilians were targeted, sounded incredulous. I could only pick up bits and pieces of the continued conversation, but one of his comments about the army infantry unit involved, along with his aero scout unit commander, stuck with me. They had claimed the civilian deaths as body count. I couldn't comprehend the concept of collateral civilian deaths being claimed in such a manner.

Being the new guy in the unit, I didn't feel comfortable joining the conversation and asking questions, so I went on with my business, yet wondered what it was all about. If Thompson hadn't appeared so credible, I would have assumed he was exaggerating a recent unsettling event. Redeker later commented that it sounded like things got out of hand and a massacre occurred south of Chu Lai, at a place called My Lai.

The flying I did in the first week was mostly orientation of the Chu Lai area and, specifically, Ky Ha. Take-off was usually east, right over the beach and ocean. Landing from the west, I couldn't help but notice the barbed wire, bunkers, and guard towers, which reminded me that the front line in that war was the perimeter of any base. Outside of that, it was hostile territory.

After Redeker returned to flight status, I had a flight with him that turned out to be a valuable noncombat lesson. He and Moore were flying up to Da Nang on what they called an administration mission and asked if I wanted to come along. Several enlisted men from the maintenance section loaded up in the back with me. No one had said much about the trip to the new guy, so I was pretty much along for the ride without a clue.

We landed at a navy supply depot close to the ship docks, and I was instructed to wait in the helicopter, running at idle. Redeker and one of the enlisted men met with a sailor. He looked in a shoebox Redeker was carrying, and then took the box and left. In a few minutes, someone drove a forklift over carrying a crate approximately three feet by four feet. They loaded it in the back of the Huey.

Arriving back at Ky Ha, I found out that the crate we brought back contained a new mini refrigerator for the enlisted men. Everyone remained tight-lipped, and, although I never found out what, I knew something had been traded. More important, I remembered where we had been.

I now understood why our hooch was better furnished than others I had seen. We had beds with full, thick, six-inch mattresses instead of the army bunks with a sagging, thin, two-inch mattress. We had two full-sized refrigerators, a couch, table and chairs, and a full bar with stools and counter.

By July, I was flying regularly and learning the area of operations for the brigade. The 196th held the most northern portion of the Americal Division's territory. The coastline in this area ran approximately north and south. Highway 1 followed the coast and lay anywhere from five to ten miles inland. The land between the coast and the highway was sandy, generally not farmable, and covered lightly with skimpy brush. On the western side of the highway, the land was a broad expanse of valuable farmland sectioned into rice paddies that extended inland as far as twenty miles before rising to steep mountains covered in thick vegetation.

Thirty miles north of Chu Lai, a fertile valley called the Que Son ran westward. The importance of the farmland in the Que Son, both economically as well as strategically, made it hotly contested between the 2nd Division of the North Vietnamese Army (NVA) and the 196th.

Bordering the northern side of this valley were the Que Son Mountains, which held fire support bases (FSB) Ross, Ryder, and Buck. FSBs, also referred to as landing zones (LZ), had artillery units that provided support to the infantry units on patrol. At the eastern end of this range of mountains, alongside Highway 1, was a small hill of large boulders called LZ Baldy, the headquarters for the 196th LIB.

Twenty miles south of Baldy along Highway 1, at the foot of the southern range of mountains along the Que Son Valley, lay Tam Ky, the provincial capital. This range of mountains held FSBs East, Center, and West.

Forming a V between these mountain ranges, the Que Son Valley ran west and came to a point about twenty miles inland at the small farming community of Hiep Duc. This most western part of the Que Son, the scene of heavy fighting only six months earlier, was called Death Valley.

In the steep, thick mountains across the Song Thu Bon River at Hiep Duc were nearly sixty-five hundred soldiers of the 2nd NVA. They emerged occasionally in various unit sizes to strike throughout the valley.

I began flying the C&C missions as the "peter pilot." The army didn't use the designation of copilot, but rather aircraft commander (AC) and pilot, and ACs referred to their pilots as "peter pilots," a minor humiliation to be suffered until promotion. A crew chief and a door gunner made up our crew. The crew chief, whose responsibility was to maintain the helicopter, flew as a door gunner on the right side, with the other gunner on the left. On a typical day, we lifted off Ky Ha in time to be at LZ Baldy by 0700 for Colonel Kroesen, commanding officer of the 196th.

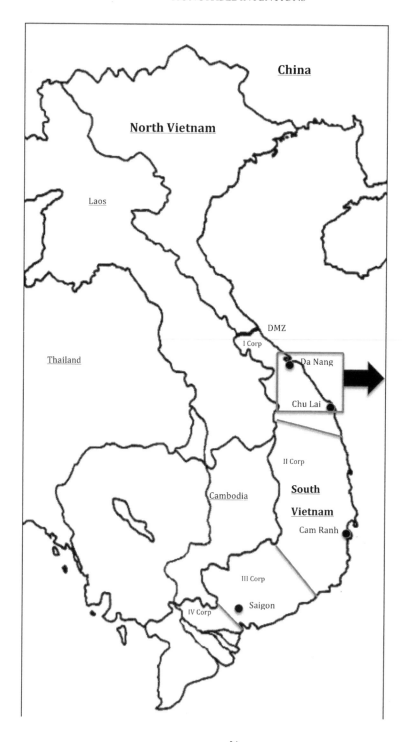

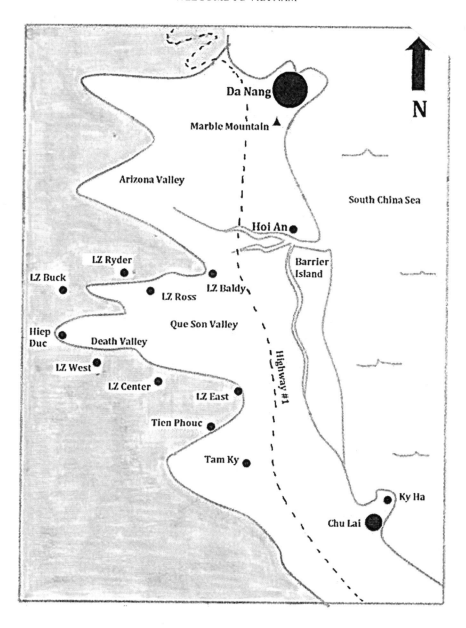

Colonel Kroesen served as a lieutenant in Europe during World War II and as a major in the Korean conflict, earning Purple Hearts in both. He was tall, lean, and fit, and I always thought that, in appearance, he could be a John Wayne stand-in. He carried himself with just the right display of personal pride and dignity. He listened more than he talked, made his point in few words when he had something to say, and instilled confidence in those around him. More than once, when talking to the troops out in the bush who were ready to step off into the blistering heat of the day for another patrol, I heard him say that he wished he were going with them. Everyone knew he meant it. Colonel Kroesen's management style was to tell his men what needed to be done and see they had the necessary resources. He then allowed his subordinates to make decisions and accomplish their missions without interference and micromanagement.

When we arrived at LZ Baldy, Colonel Kroesen could be ready to go right away, or we could end up waiting for hours. When he was ready, it was usually to fly out to one of the FSBs, such as Ross, Center, or West. It only took fifteen or twenty minutes to arrive, and, once there, we'd shut down and wait until he was ready to go elsewhere.

Flying C&C for brigade commanders and higher-ranking officers was what most pilots in other units considered them to be, picnic missions. The pilots and crewmembers spent hours reading books or playing card games while waiting between missions. We usually had lunch at a regular mess hall and were home by nightfall with only three hours of flight time logged. After a dinner of steak and potatoes and a movie at a club, my day ended with a hot shower and then to bed in clean sheets on a real mattress.

Moore had only weeks left in his tour. I was his peter pilot. After dropping off Colonel Kroesen at division headquarters in Chu Lai one afternoon, we were instructed to pick up a Vietnamese woman and her sick child and transport them to a hospital in Da Nang. With Moore monitoring my abilities as a pilot, I landed at a small village on the outskirts of Tam Ky where the mother and child boarded. As I was lifting off and climbing to altitude, a single shot was fired. Moore stayed off the controls and remained silent as if nothing had happened.

I keyed the intercom. "Did we just get shot at?"

"Yep, just got your cherry busted," Moore said.

That wasn't what was on my mind. I remained quiet for a moment as I thought about it, getting mad. *Someone down there is willing to kill a mother and a child while we're on a goodwill mission to help them.*

I keyed the intercom again. "With that small of a village, don't you think everyone knew why we were there and who we were flying out?"

"Welcome to Vietnam," Moore simply said.

Damn. I was ashamed that I almost swore over the intercom.

By the end of July, I had finished my transition training in the OH-23. In spite of initially detesting the antiquated aircraft, I found that the missions assigned were more interesting than flying C&C. They didn't necessarily sound exciting, such as flying the brigade S-2, the intelligence liaison, here or there. But the liaison sergeant was as willing to look for some combat activity as I was.

The sergeant and I were headed back to Chu Lai one evening to catch dinner at a decent mess hall. I was cutting across the valley, low level, at a good sixty knots and rounding the base of the hills east of LZ East.

Low level meant I was flying the helicopter with the skids only a few feet off the ground while banking and weaving between the trees and hedges. When a helicopter is at altitude, someone on the ground can hear it approaching from far away. When it is coming at a high rate of speed and at ground level, the helicopter suddenly appears out of nowhere and passes by before those on the ground have time to react.

The sergeant was sitting to my left, his M-16 in his lap at the ready. I was hugging a line of brush to my right, then I zipped tightly between two trees into the next rice paddy. *Hey, was that a soldier with a weapon?*

I had passed by him before I had time to get a good look. I pulled back cyclic, dropped collective, and rolled off the throttle to prevent gaining altitude. I then kicked in right pedal and spun one hundred and eighty degrees, and we actually flew backward a bit. The helicopter shuddered as I rolled throttle back in and tried to gain forward momentum.

My OH-23

"Yes," I said to myself, "and it's an NVA."

He was running across to the far tree line, and I had him on the sergeant's side now. Everything seemed so crisp, clear, and vivid. We started to gain on the soldier just as he dove into some brush.

"Damn," I cursed to myself, "these twenty-threes are slow."

The soldier rolled over and brought his weapon up at us.

Don't you see him, Sarge? Fire now! I cringed as I kept trying to gain speed so we would be a moving target. I suddenly heard the sound of the sergeant's M-16. It happened so fast that we never said a word between us.

I exhaled with a long, drawn-out, "Whew!" My heart pounded, and my hands quivered with excitement as I circled over the area to ensure it was clear. I then landed close to the body. I continued to take deep breaths as the sergeant retrieved an AK-47, rucksack, and ammo belt. While taking off, automatic weapons from far-off positions fired upon us, but we were gone before taking any hits. My voice betrayed my enthusiasm as I reported the location to brigade headquarters.

We both had big grins of excitement for the rest of the ride back to Chu Lai. The short period of combat had rammed so much adrenaline through my system that fear had never been a factor, just exhilaration.

Back at Ky Ha, we checked out the contents of the rucksack. The sergeant was pleased because he had plenty of papers to turn over to intelligence. I was happy because I had an AK-47 to hang on my wall pending a trip to Da Nang to do some trading.

I went to the officer's club that evening with continued feelings of exhilaration from the deadly encounter. I had experienced a rush of adrenalin that day like never before, and I liked it. The enemy had targeted me, and they had missed. We had returned fire, killing one. I had no ambivalence over the taking of that life, as he was just some "communist gook."

A crowd gathered around me, and, while telling my story, someone bought me a rum and Coke. I had tried liquor several times before. A friend from church, Ralph Turrentine, was on the soccer team with me at West Valley College, and we had managed to obtain a bottle of rum one weekend. Not knowing what we were doing, we decided to go light and only fill a glass halfway full with rum and then the rest with Coca-Cola. It tasted terrible since, of course, it was too strong. We decided booze tasted bad, dumped it out, went into town, and bought a pizza.

In flight school, while on pass, Henderson, Andrews, and d'Arteney had taken me out to gently introduce me to the wilder side of life, but that didn't turn out too well either as it all tasted bad and made me sick. Now, under these circumstances, the rum and Coke tasted good so I had another. I enjoyed the camaraderie, and it was a great day to be a pilot in the army.

The following day, while heading out to Baldy on a C&C mission, I noticed F Troop, 17 Cav heavily engaged in the vicinity where we had killed the NVA. Colonel Kroesen commented on the accomplishment the Cav unit was having as a result of the intelligence from my action the previous day. That was clear evidence to me of our success in Vietnam and victory was at hand.

I was still a new guy when I started getting cocky. Flying the OH-23, I delivered a payroll officer atop LZ West and was then asked to take a captain out to a unit in the field near Hiep Duc. After my passenger was strapped in, I pulled pitch, executing a normal takeoff, but then dropped off the north precipice, leaving the captain's stomach back on the mountaintop. I skimmed the trees all the way to the valley floor, hugging the ground, weaving between the trees, or hopping up over them at the last minute. The captain loved it and looked cheerfully exhausted when I dropped him off at the base of a dark green jungle-covered mountain shrouded in mist.

I wasn't due back at LZ West for the payroll officer for several hours, so I headed back out of the valley toward Baldy for lunch. Again, I was flying low level, called "nap of the earth," clipping vegetation with my rotor blades as I went. With LZ West high off my right to the south, I was following a dirt road through Death Valley when someone started shooting at me, emptying a clip of AK-47 rounds. I flinched and ducked in my seat, but felt confident that nothing had been hit and continued for several miles.

Before the narrow valley floor began to widen into the vast Que Son, I began to feel a shudder in the helicopter through the seat of my pants, like driving a car with a flat rear tire. *Well, hell.* I switched my radio over to the frequency called "guard," which is used for emergencies. "Any station, Charger 630 is going down in Death Valley directly north of LZ West." I then changed channels to contact LZ West. "Polar Bear base, this is Charger 630, being forced down in the valley just north of your location." Someone responded, but I was unable to catch the full transmission since I was busy trying to find a suitable landing place for a helicopter I thought was ready to come apart.

I set the helicopter on top of a wide berm along a rice paddy that had only inches of water. I shut off the engine and climbed out. Except for the gentle whoosh of the rotor blades as they wound down, it was amazingly quiet. It was the first time I had set foot outside of a secure, dusty, treeless, sand-bagged perimeter, and the vibrant green, lush, and clean-smelling farmland took me in. I could hear birds and the rustle of the breeze through the surrounding trees. After walking around the aircraft, finding no signs of damage from enemy fire, I wondered if I should stay by the helicopter, sitting alongside an artfully landscaped rice paddy, or move over to an island of trees and bushes along the banks of a nearby stream. On many occasions, I had looked down at the meandering creeks and rivers and thought how great it would be to sit on the banks with a fishing pole, drop in a line, and enjoy the peaceful countryside.

Suddenly, it sounded like someone had snapped a whip three times along the left side of my head. Then the sound of three cracks from a rifle caught up and came from along the dirt road several hundred yards away.

Damn! I dropped off the dike. The sweet smell of the countryside suddenly turned putrid as I disrupted the water and knelt in the muck. The mire sucked at my boots as I crouched low and headed back toward the chopper. Getting on the radio to put out another call suddenly became urgent. I heard several more snaps over my head, followed by reports from a rifle, and I dropped again and hugged the mud. My heart was racing.

The sounds of the bullets reminded me of the furious bees zipping overhead as I, only a few years earlier, lay on the ground in an orchard. To hasten the prunes to the ground so I could pick them up and into a bucket, Dad had shaken a tree without realizing a hive was there. *It's curious the things people think about at the most inopportune times.* Raising my head slightly and looking over the dike in the direction of the gunfire, I saw three figures running full tilt toward me as they followed the dirt road along the edge of a tree line. They wore nothing but what appeared to be black pants, and one was carrying a rifle. My gut felt hollow as I reached for my only weapon, a thirty-eight-caliber revolver on my hip. I desperately wanted a rifle and swore to myself that, if I survived this, I'd carry my own M-16.

Relief came quickly, though, when I heard that familiar slap of rotor blades approaching from behind. I rolled over to see a Huey on a long final approach. The paintwork on the nose of the helicopter indicated it was with the 71st Assault Helicopter Company, based out of Chu Lai. As the pilot flared and pulled pitch to land, I got up and started a dash toward him. I could hear several more reports from the distant rifle, and the Huey, still three feet off the ground, immediately turned slightly right and, instead of landing, made an awkward, sideways departure.

"Come on, damn it!" I dropped back into the rice paddy and put another earthen dike between the shooter and me.

The Huey climbed out to about fifty feet, flared hard, spun, dropped back, and landed close by. This time, the crew chief and door gunner were blazing away with their M-60 machine guns. I ran and dove in as the helicopter lifted off. As I sat up on the cargo floor, I could see the AC, wearing a beat-up flight helmet, grinning back at me. The helicopter climbed out to altitude as the door gunner gave me his helmet so I could communicate with the pilots. While putting it on, I noticed another Huey full of troops headed for my aircraft on the ground. I was surprised at how fast the response had been.

The AC had a beaming smile. "Sorry 'bout that. My peter pilot's a FNG.[3] He had the controls the first time and got a little shook up over the incoming."

I gave a thumbs-up along with my smile to indicate no problem. "All's well that ends well" was how I certainly felt at the moment.

"You know, we lost a gunship crew in that same area a couple months ago," the AC said. "Buddy of mine, good guy. The peter pilot E&E'd[4] for two days and made it out. The others, we don't know. They never recovered any bodies." His voice trailed off as he peered down through his side window as if he might spot a clue.

I later learned he was referring to the vicious battle months earlier over the control of Hiep Duc, giving this area the name Death Valley. The 196th lost sixty-four soldiers, two hundred and four were wounded, and the NVA took ten as prisoner of war. Delta Company, 3rd of the 21st Infantry (D/3/21), suffered nearly half of the killed in action (KIAs) with twenty-eight. Early in the battle, WO Frank Anton, flying as AC in a Huey gunship, was shot down in the middle of the night. Intense enemy anti-aircraft fire prevented any successful rescue, and, although unknown at the time, he was taken prisoner. Major Patrick Brady, the commanding officer of the 54th Medical Detachment, flew evacuations that

---

3. FNG was a derogatory way of referring to a "new guy."

4. escaped and evaded

night. In darkness coupled with thick fog, under intense enemy fire while using three different helicopters due to enemy damage, he and his crew made four evacuations totaling fifty-one seriously wounded soldiers.

"I got word you have someone from maintenance headed this way," the AC said as we circled and watched a squad of soldiers unload from their Huey and take up defense positions around my helicopter.

"In that case, drop me back off. I'll wait with the little bird."

What was, when I first landed, a serene setting was now thick with tension. The look in the soldiers' eyes, their walk, stance, crouch, and physical bearing indicated everything was a deadly threat. The cry of a bird and the rustle of wind through the trees meant something completely different to these men. As a result of their sloshing through the adjacent rice paddies, the aroma of rotting vegetation and manure hung heavy in the air.

As it turned out, my chopper was unscathed from enemy fire, and the problem had been a failing joint at the drive to the tail rotor gearbox. The problem was fixed before dusk. I was airborne and safely home by dark.

Being shot at without taking hits or being forced down by maintenance problems ranked low on the scale of war stories, and, even though I was anxious to tell the story of my adventures that day, no one back at Ky Ha was interested. I was learning I sometimes had to suppress emotions.

------- * -------

Although other aviation units usually handled resupply missions for the 196th, there was a need for my unit to fly resupply on August 18. Using the second Huey in our unit, Captain Walton and I had the longest day of my tour, logging twelve hours flying supplies to units in the field throughout the Que Son Valley. We didn't have a proper breakfast and didn't stop for lunch, and we were too late for dinner at a mess hall by the time we arrived back at Ky Ha. I was tired and starving. I had a migraine, and I was generally feeling sorry for myself.

But a flight school classmate, James Eisenhour, also had a long day on August 18. Flying for the 240th Assault Helicopter Company in III Corps,

Eisenhour was attempting an emergency extraction of a long-range reconnaissance patrol that was in serious contact with enemy forces. Three other helicopters had already tried the extraction, resulting in two deaths and six wounded. One soldier was still on the ground, and Eisenhour went to get him. His aircraft took numerous hits from enemy fire, and Eisenhour, who had hopes and dreams for his wife and daughter back home, lost his life.

My next three days were spent on a volunteer-only mission that I relished, which was flying out of Da Nang on a temporary duty (TDY) assignment with the 1st MarDiv. Since the marines didn't have scout helicopters, the Americal Division supplied pilots and scout helicopters from the 11th, 196th, and 198th Infantry Brigades, on a rotating basis. Our mission was to patrol an area referred to as the "rocket belt."

Miles of flat farmland bordered the city of Da Nang, a large coastal city sixty miles north of Chu Lai. From this farmland, the NVA would fire 122-millimeter rockets, bombarding the city and inflicting devastating damage. Over six feet long and nearly five inches in diameter, inaccurate yet deadly, these rockets usually claimed civilian lives. Carried down the Ho Chi Minh trail from the north, down one of the valleys such as the Arizona that led into Da Nang, the rockets were easy and quick to set up and launch, allowing the NVA soldier to then hastily exit the area. The rockets had a low trajectory and had to be fired within a certain distance from Da Nang, not too close, not too far away.

Scout missions in Vietnam were typically conducted from the small observation helicopter that flew at treetop levels over the terrain looking for signs of the enemy. By mid-1968, most aviation units in Vietnam with scout helicopters were supplied with the turbine-powered Hughes OH-6A, which carried an observer who handled an M-60 machine gun. The pilot controlled a mounted 5.56-millimeter "mini-gun," which could deliver a devastating six thousand rounds a minute.

During a mission, the scout helicopter received cover from two heavily armed helicopter gunships, which flew above what the gunship pilots affectionately called the "little bird." When the scout aircraft discovered the enemy, the door gunner dropped a smoke grenade to mark the spot, and then the pilot flew out of the way, allowing the gunships to work over the area.

LIBs were low on the list of priorities for receiving the new OH-6A helicopter, so the 196th still flew the obsolete OH-23. Unlike other aviation units, we also didn't have gunships to provide cover. On a few occasions, I flew the rocket belt with another OH-23 following, but usually the mission was single ship, unescorted. The only firepower we carried was the M-60 machine gun that the door gunner handled.

I never felt the pressure on scout missions that I felt when flying the Huey because I didn't feel the heavy responsibility of ensuring I returned at the end of the day without having lost the life of crew or passengers. On these scout missions, my door gunner, Johnny Hanson, also a volunteer, knew the dangers, and the two of us had a special bond as teammates in a game of life and death. With his gun, Hanson was an excellent shot from a fast-flying, low-level helicopter, and I always insisted he accompany me when I took the 1st MarDiv assignment. For Hanson and me, the only concern was "catch 'em alive, leave 'em dead, and return with war booty." Then, with a couple of beers at the end of the day, we'd joke about "body count, medals, and a fast promotion."

We varied the time of our flights to keep the NVA off guard and took off late morning on August 21. I was clipping along at sixty knots (seventy miles per hour), hopping trees and skimming several feet above the rice fields south of Marble Mountain, the largest of five massive marble rocks that rose spectacularly from the flat farmland just off the coast and south of Da Nang. Hanson knew to be alert, as, on our first mission together, we had surprised three NVA soldiers setting up a 122-millimeter rocket site with assistance from, what appeared to be, local farmers. We killed the soldiers and allowed the civilians to leave the area.

On this day, Hanson sat sideways on my right, back to me, with both feet on the skids. His M-60, attached to the OH-23 by a bungee cord, hung at the ready in his hands. Swooping down over a thin tree line and into the next rice paddy, we surprised four NVA soldiers who started running along a strip of waist-high vegetation.

"Your side! Your side!" I yelled over the intercom as I rolled off the throttle, dropped the collective, and banked hard right, putting Hanson facing straight down from barely ten feet off the ground.

He saw them, but couldn't get a shot off as we flew by. I then jammed left pedal, and we spun completely around. I could see they were heading toward the remains of a battered, roofless, concrete French-style home.

Hanson remained calm. "Come around the south side of that house."

I circled tight to the right and slowed as we came up on the south side of the ruins. Just as I saw an old, blue, banged-up, fifty-five-gallon barrel lying on its side a short distance from the building, I saw one of the soldiers aim his AK-47 over it at us.

Oh, shit. Nail him Hanson!

I cranked in power, pulled pitch, and banked even tighter, forcing the NVA to rise up to aim.

"The barrel!" I shouted, probably loud enough to be heard without the intercom.

The NVA fired first. Within twenty yards, all was clear, colorful, and in slow motion. I could see the whites of his eyes, the smoke from his rifle, and the empty shells eject.

As the enemy shot, Hanson cut loose with a string of fire. The fury resumed full speed, and dust, rocks, and debris kicked up all around the barrel as we passed. I kicked in hard right pedal to keep the action on Hanson's side. I expected to see a body, but there wasn't one.

Damn it.

"The building!" Hanson cried out.

I straightened out to keep the structure on our right and then banked hard as we flew over it. The little bird responded as if it was an extension of my body. I heard shots again from the AK-47 right before Hanson let go with another burst. One body with an AK-47 now lay in the rubble.

"Is that the guy who was behind the barrel?"

"Yes!" Hanson yelled.

"Where are the others?" I wondered aloud over the intercom as we circled the area.

Hanson sounded out of breath as he stood on the skids and visually scoured the area. "Don't know."

Where the hell are they? I expected gunfire from them at any moment. It wasn't wooded enough for someone to be hiding in the trees, and we could see nothing around the ruins of the old house. The moments of frenzy began to fade as I scoured the area.

A marine patrol happened to be three hundred yards away, so I got on the radio and asked them to head our way. Once the marine captain and his men had the area secured, we landed. We had killed the enemy before, but this was different. This soldier went toe to toe in a deadly exchange of gunfire, and I wanted to meet him.

He lay face up in the debris. I was fascinated that none of the wounds to his chest or abdomen bled. I gathered his effects while his eyes, open and looking through me, began to dry and cloud over from the sticky heat of the day. His papers identified him as 1st Lieutenant Phung with the 90th Regiment, 2nd NVA Division. I looked at photographs of his wife and children, and for a moment realized that this was a man with a family. *What were your hopes, lieutenant? Were you serving your government honorably?*

I had no reason to believe he hadn't. The thoughts were quickly pushed from my mind as a call from Hanson brought me back to the realities of war. Hanson had walked over to look at the barrel. Just inside was the badly mangled body of a soldier. Hanson pulled him aside, then reached in, and dragged out another body that his sixty-caliber bullets had ripped apart. Finally, a wounded third NVA crawled out, dragging his intestines with him. The scene was brutal. Other paperwork, gear, and ammunition were found, but no further weapons. I called another chopper in to take the prisoner to the hospital in Da Nang, and Hanson and I took off and headed back to the 1st MarDiv Headquarters with Phung's rifle and gear.

During a period of disconnection with the real world, we had routed the enemy. I found it all intensely pleasurable. I was pumped with an intoxicating rush of adrenalin, and I was anxious to refuel and return for an evening mission.

Phungs AK-47. Notice the door gunner's M-60
hanging outside the chopper on the cord.

Body count was the infamous measurement of our success in that war, which the high command constantly stressed. Pressure was put on all units to obtain it. Hanson and I were headed back with a body count of three KIAs and one POW, and, as expected, the news was well received. The staff at 1st MarDiv was convinced that Hanson and I had thwarted a sniper attack on the marine patrol, and there was talk of awards, medals, and commendations. That night at the Marine Officers Club, I had plenty of free drinks and slaps on the back as I told the story over and over.

"They were in the barrel?" someone asked, sounding skeptical.

I smiled. "Now, this ain't no shit, but apparently these three little farts crawled into the barrel that the lieutenant gets behind and shoots at us from."

Everyone laughed, commenting on what it must have been like to be stuck in a barrel with M-60 rounds coming through. The booze flowed while girls on the rickety stage sang.

At one point in the evening, an older, gruff-looking marine colonel walked into the bar, stood at the door, and bellowed, "Anyone who can't tap dance is a—"

The noise drowned out the rest of his statement as forty men immediately jumped up and did a little dance. We all laughed, sat back down, and continued with our war stories while enjoying the camaraderie. War didn't get any better than this.

A classmate friend, Hershall Bullock, also flew that day. In III Corps with the 135th Assault Helicopter Company, a multinational outfit sometimes referred to as an Experimental Military Unit, Bullock was flying a Huey gunship with an Australian pilot when they took a direct hit from a rocket-propelled grenade. The entire crew was lost.

The following morning, back on scout duty, we spotted two military-age men with backpacks trying to hide by ducking into a large bunker. As I hovered up sideways to the opening so Hanson could roll in a grenade, we noticed what appeared to be a female face peering out. I was concerned that civilians might be inside the bunker, so I instructed Hanson to motion for them to exit.

We were unnecessarily exposed to enemy fire, but we continued to hover around and finally convinced a frightened group of four adult women and several children to emerge. After it was clear that no one else was willing to exit, Hanson rolled in two grenades. There was no way to tell what the results were.

After lunch and while preparing to head back home to Ky Ha since my TDY for that period was ending, the marine lieutenant who supervised our assignment approached me.

"Mister Jones, we got a problem. You're not getting credit for those KIAs yesterday."

"They were Hanson's, but what's the problem?" I loaded my gear and the captured AK-47 into the chopper.

The lieutenant looked embarrassed. "The captain in the field took the credit."

It took a moment for what he said to sink in, and then I considered recent events. One of the other 196th pilots, Hambrick, had reported in one day with several KIAs. The marines had refused to give him credit because he had failed to have the body count verified. That wasn't usually possible because we flew single-ship missions and the chance of a patrol being in the area to verify was remote.

"So the troops on the ground, who we called to verify our body count, took the credit?"

"I know. But what am I supposed to do when the major accepts the captain's daily report?"

"You stand up for your men. When we're up here, we're under your command."

Hanson and I then climbed in and took off. We kept quiet on the flight back, but the more I thought about it, the more I began to stew. Body count verification had been an issue with all the pilots since Hambrick's incident, so I decided to fly south of Chu Lai to Duc Pho and discuss this with Ortego and the other pilots of the 198th LIB. As I flew, I couldn't help but wonder if the pressure for body count was so important that the units in the field would lie about it. *How else are they lying to boost their figures? How accurate is body count in determining success in this war?*

"This is bull," one of the 198th pilots remarked right off the bat.

One of the other pilots opened a beer. "Why bother? Don't tell them anything anymore."

"Why are we risking our necks? To give some jarhead an attaboy?" another asked.

Profanity loaded their conversation.

Ortego tried to bring some common sense back into the discussion. "I don't know what the big deal is. Just do your job and come home. Who cares who takes the credit?" It was more of a statement than a question.

"Damn it, it's the principle of the matter," one guy argued as he polished off a beer and started another. "It's not right, and nothing will destroy cooperation and morale in the men quicker than not following the principle of doing what's right." He sounded like he was giving a speech.

"Well, there's a way to handle these situations," Ortego said as he motioned toward the group, "and this isn't it."

"Yeah, right. File a complaint with the rear echelon," someone said sarcastically, adding vulgarity.

They were getting riled up. Ortego got up to walk away and gave me a look that said, "Nice to see you, but we don't need this."

I didn't have the opportunity to visit with Ortego often, so I left the group and went over to change the subject with him. Because of the controversy I had brought with me, though, my attempt at small talk was awkward.

Ortego came back to the subject at hand. "Yes, it was a betrayal, but, by making it known in this manner, you've created an us-against-them mentality."

Ortego was right, and I left feeling uncomfortable. I made a mental note to get together with him at a later date when we could return to those friendlier big brother talks I had always enjoyed.

I rounded up Hanson, who was having his own grievance session with the enlisted men and headed back to Ky Ha. I informed Hambrick of the matter, but, otherwise, kept the issue low key. I knew, though, that the problem wasn't going away.

Except for Hambrick and Captain Walton, all the old-timers had finished their tours. I made aircraft commander in September and began flying more of the C&C missions in the Huey. I had become an old-timer in the unit with only three months in country. We, as a unit, were experiencing the same problem as the troops in the field. Experienced soldiers ended their tours and rotated home, replaced by "green" soldiers who joined other slightly experienced troops.

Hambrick, tall and lanky, slow and laid back, had laughing eyes that always seemed to suggest he had something to share but dared not. He was the only WO now senior to me, and he loved flying the little bird missions.

Newer than I in the unit were WOs Terry Reid, Rob Nebel, Gene Chalecki, and Lieutenant Mike McMahon, all fresh out of flight school with neither combat nor prior military service experience. McMahon was a good-natured officer who, junior in flight experience to the rest of the unit, left his rank outside of the helicopter and allowed his WOs to do their jobs. Chalecki was a skinny kid who always had a big smile regardless of the situation. Nebel, good-looking, friendly, and single, wasted no time in becoming a friend and confidante with the nurses and Red Cross volunteers who were living in the Chu Lai area. Reid, married with a child on the way, was low-key, easygoing, and confident. He was the best pilot I ever flew with. Those pilots would have described me as impatient and impolitic.

In Hambrick, I met my match in terms of someone who loved to play with explosives and blow up things. For me, it started as a boy in Brazil where I could buy a handful of fireworks for pennies at small street corner shops. I'd take them apart, consolidate the powder, then package my own mini-bomb. Later, taking lessons from my Campbell High chemistry teacher, Mr. Lithacum, I learned how to make hydrogen at home and fill large balloons. I set them aloft at night with a fuse, which ignited the balloon several hundred feet in the air, resulting in a wonderful, billowing ball of orange flame followed by a deep rumbling explosion. Calls from concerned neighbors over the exploding UFOs brought a police officer into the neighborhood, but, of course, they found nothing. I moved on to experimenting with carbide, which I used to make other explosives and firearms. Then, using chemicals I purchased from the local pharmacy, I graduated to making my own gunpowder, which I mixed in a wet solution and then dried in the kitchen oven when no one was home.

Without constant supervision, I always seemed to gravitate to dangerous activities. I remained unscathed during those experimental years, but not all went well for some of my friends. One was nearly electrocuted while we were experimenting with some high-voltage apparatus that could launch a bolt of electricity several feet. Another lost two fingers while loading explosives into a small CO_2 cartridge, and a third friend was forever scarred on both legs due to one of our failed experiments with carbide.

In Vietnam, Hambrick could always be found in possession of C4, a highly explosive soft plastic that he carried around in his pocket like one might carry a package of chewing gum. He and his door gunner made their own bombs and, when flying scout missions, dropped them on bunkers or huts where the enemy was suspected of hiding. The list of things that could go disastrously wrong using those homemade devices in or around a helicopter was long, but Hambrick, sporting a thick handlebar mustache and wearing a bush hat, simply grinned at any suggestions of caution.

As AC, I was usually paired up with Reid, which was unfortunate for him because he was quickly qualified as an AC in his own right. I had been qualified as an AC before him, though, so when assigned to fly with me, he had to log the time as the pilot. The days flying C&C were slow and low-key with only a few hours of flight time. Like the old saying, it was "hours of boredom interrupted by a few moments of terror." The moments of terror, though, were few and far between. If we weren't flying Colonel Kroesen, we had missions called "ash and trash," that is, providing resupply to units in the field. We sometimes carried Mary Laraine Young, known to us as Larry, and other Red Cross workers, referred to as Donut Dollies, out to the FSBs for a quick visit before returning to Chu Lai. One day, comic actress and singer Martha Rae was my passenger.

Flying the OH-23 continued to be more exciting. I was on a courier mission one afternoon, therefore without my door gunner. I was shut down on the helicopter pad at LZ Baldy, bored and half-asleep when Captain Walton walked off the hill and over to me. He was unfolding a map.

"We think there might be some activity over here. Scout it out and see what you can find."

I rubbed the sleep out of my eyes and saw he was pointing to an area east of Baldy. The Song Cua Dai River, fed by numerous other rivers and streams, emptied into the sea there. The main river feeding the Song Cua Dai from the north was the Song Hoi. The historic town of Hoi An sat at the intersection of those rivers. The main river entering Song Cua Dai from the south was the Truong Giang, which entered about six miles inland, and then ran south, angling back toward the coast all the way to Chu Lai, creating an island along the coast. Walton wanted me to check out this barrier island of white sand and small, scraggly, bare bushes.

"You can't hide a rabbit out in that. What do you expect me to see?"

Walt folded his map back up. "Probably nothing. I've got someone coming down to fly door gunner for you."

As Walton walked back up the hill, I stretched and yawned as a soldier approached carrying an M-60. In combat, a soldier can do everything right and still catch that bullet with his name on it. After-action studies and accident investigations show, though, that usually a combination of errors costs lives. The first error might seem insignificant, but it compounds with the second, and, like the snowball effect, the situation becomes unmanageable and disastrous. At that point, who lives and who dies is simply random luck.

On this day, the first error was that I had reached that euphoric time in my flying career that I doubted my mortality. I didn't expect much from the mission and paid little attention to the gunner as he climbed in the chopper. He knew how to operate the intercom, so that was good enough for me. After all, I was only a few miles from Baldy. *How much trouble can I find?*

I entered the barrier island directly east of Baldy and started working north, crisscrossing from the Truong Giang River to the coast and then back to the river. I knew this area well. A couple of weeks earlier, I had caught and dispatched the poor soul of a Viet Cong (VC) wearing what looked like black underwear and carrying an SKS rifle. Trying to hide out there was like trying to hide on the beach, but that also meant that, no matter how low I flew, I was visible from a long way off.

Midway through the mission, five miles from the end of the island at the Song Cua Dai, as I was making my turn at the Troung Giang, many small arms weapons opened up. *Shit, here we go again!* I tightened my turn and headed one hundred and eighty degrees back across the bare sand toward the sea as I started to put out a call to Baldy.

"Well, hell," I said to myself as I realized I was still on the frequency from my earlier mission for a unit out of range and now worthless.

I flinched as a string of firearms opened up in front of me. I banked hard right ninety degrees and headed back south, the direction I'd been working up from. I noticed two holes had appeared in the Plexiglas bubble. I then realized I hadn't heard anything from my door gunner. I glanced over at him, and I could see he had the M-60 in his lap, and he was frantically fooling with it.

"Get some damn heads down out there," I yelled over the intercom.

I hadn't seen anyone and was wondering just where the hell they were when another round of small arms fire opened up from the south.

"Start firing that gun!" I yelled over the intercom as I banked hard left one hundred and eighty degrees and headed north. The door gunner never said a word.

They were behind me, on my left and right. I thought that maybe I could get out of there by flying north, but that thought only lasted seconds. Another round of fire came from the front. Again, I banked hard, this time in a circle to the right.

I was flying only a few feet off the ground, and I continued a broad right-hand circle. As long as I stayed in that area, I wasn't shot at. Instincts told me I couldn't climb. It would take too long at too slow of an airspeed to reach a safe altitude of fifteen hundred feet. I knew I needed to stay low and fast.

I had a worthless door gunner, and I was on the wrong frequencies to advise anyone of my situation. I was flying low, fast, and in a constant turn that required I keep both hands on the controls. I wasn't in a position to change the radio frequency, so I couldn't contact Baldy or artillery support.

I had called in artillery on numerous occasions before. Sometimes in the Que Son, we missed NVA as they ducked into heavy vegetation, an old building, or small hole in the ground. I'd then call one of the FSBs, which had nothing better to do but spend tens of thousands of tax dollars blowing things up in and around where the enemy was hiding. It was an incredible amount of power available to a twenty-one-year-old kid. I was now in a situation that begged for artillery assistance, and I felt impotent.

In the few frantic seconds that this was occurring, I began to imagine the shooting coming from bunkers in the rolling sand dunes, camouflaged by scraggly brush. Narrow openings probably restricted their field of fire, so I was apparently fairly safe until I began to fly closer to the bunkers. That also meant their field of fire, as I approached and passed by at high speed, would be short-lived.

I gotta get out of here. I circled to a west heading, straightened out, pulled in full pitch and power, and went for it, inches off the ground. Again, a hail of gunfire and bullets and a few more struck home. Within seconds, though,

I was across the Truong Giang, and all firing had ceased. Luck had been with me, and, minutes later, I was shutting down at LZ Baldy, noticing the blades were making a different sound as they coasted down.

"God damn it! Get out of my helicopter!" I yelled to the door gunner, adding a few other expletives.

His voice was weak, and his hands were shaking. "The gun jammed."

"How the hell can the gun jam before you even fire? Get out of here." I was frustrated at my own failings, and I was taking it out on him.

Lugging the M-60 with both arms and dragging a belt of ammo behind him, my passenger shuffled away. As I sat there watching him, I realized I had crossed a personal barrier. *Come on, I'm not just swearing, I'm committing blasphemy. But we about got our asses killed out there! All right, damn it, but I don't need to take the Lord's name in vain.* I was arguing with myself and swearing in the process.

I started to walk around the helicopter, but about fell down as my legs were like rubber. I sat back down on the edge of the seat and started to shake all over, like I had the chills that came with a fever. My throat constricted, and, for a moment, I was sure I was going to throw up. The seriousness of the situation began to sink in as I realized that, had we been shot down, it would have been hours before anyone would've started looking for us. And this hadn't been my regular volunteer door gunner. I had unnecessarily risked this boy's life.

I began to hear the voices of a dozen TAC officers, "Candidate, your failure to pay attention to details is going to get you and your crew killed."

I had failed to pay attention and ask more details of my mission from Captain Walton. I had failed to pay any attention to whether the door gunner knew what he was doing. I had failed to pay attention to my radios. Any one of those details could have cost us our lives.

After a few minutes, my heart rate came down. I stopped shaking, and I was able to walk around. The aircraft had four holes in the bubble, two in the tail boom, and three in the rotor blades. One of the rounds through a rotor blade was at an angle, creating a large gash.

I briefed Walton, and, within hours, the area was surrounded. A Korean army unit, who had the responsibility of the area around Hoi An, set up a blocking force to prevent the enemy from evading north. The 196th put block-ing forces on the western and southern positions. They then moved in from the south and swept the island to the north. They met scattered resistance and had a few firefights, but, when it was all over there, no bodies, few weapons, and little intelligence was gathered. Whoever had been out there had vanished. I was fascinated with this enemy.

That wasn't the only time the 196th had such an encounter during my tour. A large contingent of NVA from the 2nd Division was discovered in the Que Son Mountains. The 1st MarDiv, which had responsibility for the northern side of that mountain range, set up their forces while the 196th set up on the southern side. A joint sweep of the mountain range from the west was then conducted in an effort to trap and engage the enemy. This went on for days.

At the briefings, the maps showed the daily locations where the NVA were. The 196th unit commanders showed where their troops were, where they were receiving resistance, and how the area was being squeezed. The enemy, though, was avoiding major conflict. It was that vexing problem of war pre-sented by the refusal of the enemy to behave as expected. Near the end of the operation, flying for Colonel Kroesen, I looked down on a heavily forested mountain range hiding thousands of NVA. It was exciting, as the trap was ready to be shut.

I showed up at Baldy the next day, ready for the climactic finish, only to find out it was over. No big battle, no large body count, and no large numbers of prisoners. It was like out on the barrier island. The enemy had just slipped away. I felt that, in what I was beginning to realize was a stagnated war of attri-tion, we were shoveling sand against the tide.

Another TDY assignment with the marines came up, and I arrived in the afternoon of September 28, ready for a short briefing with the marine lieu-tenant before heading out. Upon entering division operations, I could sense tension in the air. No one wanted to make eye contact or talk, and the lieuten-ant I usually reported to wasn't around.

"He's in a meeting," was the curt answer I received.

Hanson and I took off and flew an uneventful recon of the rocket belt. Sometimes looking for trouble, we extended our mission westward up the

Arizona Valley, searching the routes used for smuggling the rockets. We were on the west side of Highway 1 at the mouth of the valley when we spotted two young boys leading an ox pulling a cart full of straw. They looked like they were only about eight years old, but I had already learned that Vietnamese tended to appear to Americans as much younger than they actually were, so I figured they were teenagers.

When flying scouts, I was hyper vigilant, ready to see the smallest abnormality in the environment or people I flew over. I circled the ox cart at no more than twenty feet above.

"Something isn't right," I said. "Look at the way they keep walking and don't look up at us."

I made a wider path at least two hundred yards out and found no one anywhere close. It was all dry rice paddies with neither trees nor bushes to hide anyone for a least a quarter mile in any direction, so I came back over to the ox cart. The kids kept moving and talking among themselves as if we weren't circling overhead.

I knew the answer, but asked anyway. "You want to check out the cart?"

Hanson started removing his safety strap. Clouds of dust kicked up as I set the little bird down in the road. Hanson grabbed my CAR-15, a carbine model of the M-16, and exited. The two kids took off in different directions without looking back. The ox hadn't seemed to mind the helicopter, but didn't like the idea of Hanson approaching. It tried to make a U-turn, but the cart became stuck in the slight ditch on the side of the road. Hanson fired a few rounds off into the hay without results. He then jumped into the cart and kicked out some of the hay, coming up with three AK-47s, ammo, and a box of what Hanson later said was "stuff." Hanson ran over, placed the AKs in the chopper, and then, over the engine noise, shouted, "It's too much to carry."

"Burn it!" I yelled.

Hanson smiled and ran off. He piled some of the hay he had kicked out back into the cart, lit it, and scrambled back into the chopper. As we were taking off, I noticed the ox, with his cart fully involved in flames, was a little more motivated. He hurried off down the road in the direction he came from, trying to get away from a fire that followed.

After ensuring the cart and contents were well enough consumed, we went back to the 1st MarDiv. Hanson started tidying up the chopper as I walked over to a waiting lieutenant whom I hadn't met before. He looked distressed.

"What's the matter?"

He took on a look of disbelieving. "You don't know? Yesterday, someone flew in here with two KIAs that he wanted credit for."

I pictured bodies being ceremoniously dumped on the 1st MarDiv Headquarters helipad. *It's Hambrick. No one else has the mettle to pull that off.* I couldn't stop myself from laughing aloud, which, of course, incensed the lieutenant.

"You don't understand, mister. Heads are going to roll around here."

"What, pray tell me, lieutenant, did you expect? This whole war is based on an insidious plan of accounting for bodies. My gunners are taught that numbers count. We start reporting body count ..." I motioned over to the 1st MarDiv. "And some REMF'er[5] comes up with a policy that our KIAs must be independently verified. So Hanson nails three a couple weeks ago, plus a prisoner. Abiding by your new rules, I have it verified. Your captain in the field, though, claimed them as his body count. So you don't take our word for it. You steal the credit when we have it verified, and then you get your shorts in a knot when we bring a body into your precious compound." My voice was steadily rising. "What continuing cooperation are you going to expect from our guys?"

A major had overheard the argument and walked up to put in his unwanted opinion. He was aware of the problem with the bodies being flown into headquarters, but apparently not what led up to it. He held the stub of a cigar in the corner of his mouth as he talked.

"What's the problem, mister?" He got right in my face like a TAC or drill sergeant. "You have a problem with our way of doing things?"

"No, not at all. It's just a misunderstanding of how the army operates versus the marines. An army officer would never consider taking credit for body count that should be credited to the aircrews supporting him. He'd be ashamed and know it was dishonest."

---

5. REMF, rear echelon mother fucker, referred to officers on administrative staff who, working in secure rear bases, wrote policy making life miserable for those who risked their lives in the field.

The major backed up a bit and stared. He then shifted his gaze to the lieutenant. "What the hell is he talking about?"

I jumped right back in. *What are they going to do? Send me to Vietnam?* "I'll tell you."

"No," said the lieutenant. "I'll explain it." He waved me off to go back to the chopper.

After their short talk, the major stomped away, and the lieutenant came over.

"He agrees that what they did wasn't cricket, whatever that means."

"Yeah, well, we'll see, I guess the proof will be if they reverse the previous denied claims of body count." I paused a bit. "Oh, yeah, cricket. Cricket's a game played in England, similar to baseball. It's a gentleman's game with strict adherence to the rules, behavior beyond reproach, and honor."

The lieutenant's face failed to hide the sting of the rebuke. He broke eye contact and walked over to Hanson who was securing the AKs in the chopper. "You get the weapons from this morning?"

Hanson said nothing, but just looked at me.

"No, nothing to report." I lied. "Brought them with us from Chu Lai. We promised these to some navy guys." I smiled at the lieutenant.

"All right, I get the picture." He spoke more to himself as he turned and walked back to headquarters.

I took off with Hanson and headed to the military compound in Hoi An. A South Korean unit, soldiers of high caliber, controlled the territory around this village, and the area was secure. They also ran the best mess hall around. I was getting to know the chef, and, on this occasion, I took him a souvenir, one of the AK-47s that Hanson had retrieved from the ox cart. He was jubilant, jabbered away in Korean, and motioned for us to take a seat at a table. Before long, a waiter came out carrying a tray, fancy restaurant style, with plates loaded with steak and lobster, vegetables, wild rice, a fresh salad, and hot bread.

At the other end of our table, wearing their pressed fatigues and shined boots, sat several majors and captains. *REMF'ers.*

Although they had a fine dinner of roast beef, the officers couldn't help but notice what had been prepared for the two grubby helicopter crewmembers who obviously had been flying around in the hot countryside. The aroma of the shellfish, mixed with the smell of medium rare steaks, drifted through the mess hall, and, as we dug into our steamed lobster, we couldn't help but smile. The officers stopped their conversation, and we knew it was killing them. Finally, one of them got up and sauntered over, working a toothpick in his mouth.

"So how do you rate steak and lobster around here?" he asked, like he was a long-lost friend.

"Rank has its privileges," I said with a big grin.

Hanson suppressed a laugh. The captain tried to get an honest answer out of me, but I continued to smile and dance around with my replies. I could see the Korean chef watching us from the doorway to the kitchen. He sensed what was occurring and had a big, laughing smile. It had been a great day.

It hadn't been a great day for Trent Fair, my friend from Calvary Baptist Church. In a letter from home, I read that Trent had been running and splashing along the Santa Cruz beach with his girlfriend. He had dove into a wave and, in a freak accident, broke his neck. *He'll be fine. It's not like he was taking bullets while flying helicopters or while pounding the ground as a grunt in the Que Son.* With death and destruction around me, it was difficult to relate to a random event on a California beach.

I didn't fly on November 21. I spent the day playing football on the beach and swimming in the surf. Near the end of the day, a pilot with the 198th LIB met with us in our hooch. He explained how Gerald Ortego, on the mission with the 1st MarDiv, was killed that morning when, preparing his OH-23 for the morning mission, a 122-millimeter rocket slammed into the helipad.

I was stunned. This couldn't be. I had faith in a just and loving God who oversaw an ethical universe in which someone like Ortego wasn't supposed to die. A sense of spiritual abandonment and meaninglessness came over me.

In shock and feeling socially severed, I left the group and walked down to Ky Ha, climbed in an OH-23, and set off for Da Nang. I felt the need to be there and see for myself. I quickly thought better of it and circled over the South China Sea, crying. I had lost more than a classmate. Ortego was a personal friend. He had hopes for himself, his wife, and a future family. He had faith. Now he was dead. Dead, dead, dead. I hadn't gotten back together with him, and I still had things to say.

Later that evening, several of us flew a Huey down to Duc Pho to meet with a few of the pilots from the 198th. We had an opportunity, not available to troops in the field, to take the time to mourn the dead. We gathered at the club, drank, told stories about Ortego, and bitched about the war, military policy, body count, and the marines. We were ill mannered and vulgar. Sitting in the back of the Huey on the ride back to Ky Ha, I couldn't help but wonder what others in the club, who knew little of the circumstances other than someone died, thought of our behavior.

Letters to my wife were getting fewer. I could only write about the small stuff so many times and couldn't imagine writing a letter like this:

> *Dear Susan, I'm beginning to feel like a short-timer with six months to go. Today, we were near the site where an armored personnel carrier hit a mine. I landed and got out. Some poor guy had been sitting on top, and, when the vehicle flipped over, it squashed him underneath like a bug. Only his legs stuck out. I'm finally flying the OH-6A. What a hot machine. It is so much quicker, quieter, and easier to sneak up on the gooks and waste them. Tonight, I'm the hero as the guys are barbequing steaks I got in trade for an enemy rifle. A couple days ago, we caught this commie sitting on a rice paddy dike. He reached for the rifle, and my door gunner blew his head off. He was carrying pictures of his mother. One of my buddies from flight school was killed a few days ago. He left a wife back home. I had a hard time with it for a while, but things are better now. I'm fine, and don't you worry. None of this is going to change me at all. Love, Russ*

On December 11, Walt "Sugar Bear" Henderson was shot down. Assigned to the 173rd Airborne in II Corps, he was flying C&C when anti-aircraft fire hit them. Trapped in the wreckage while a battle raged around him and at one point given up for dead, he was finally extracted after an eight-hour rescue mission.

———

Back in Da Nang with the marines, I was refueling my new OH-6A when I ran into flight school classmate Peter Krutschewski.

"Did you hear about Jantz?" he asked.

Aw, crap. With that question, I already knew. Robert "Bobby" Jantz from Kansas was a year younger than most of us and was one of our more wild and crazy classmates. He had a heart of gold and would give me his last five dollars if I asked for a loan. On many occasions, when I needed a ride, he threw me the keys to his car with no questions asked. Krutschewski from Michigan, a year older than most of us, was a little more mature, tough, and streetwise. He would also loan five dollars, but with interest.

Krutschewski informed me that, on January 2, Jantz was killed while flying with the 116th Assault Helicopter Company out of Cu Chi. In the course of a war that I was beginning to believe was senseless, I was becoming numb to such news.

I thought of Karl von Clausewitz, whose works in military strategy were accepted as the Bible. *Didn't he condemn a war of attrition as the pit of hell?* I shook my head and looked out across the airfield to the military administration buildings along the hillside. Somewhere among the drab buildings was a dreary office where men were doing the cold math of counting the dead.

While bad news about the injuries and death of unknown helicopter pilots and crew arrived weekly, the news of classmates seemed to arrive on a regular monthly basis. Next was Angus McAllister. Tall and handsome, he had a personality larger than life. He was from Biloxi, Mississippi, and I always imagined him standing in the doorway of a grand antebellum home and, in his boisterous voice, declaring, "Frankly, my dear, I don't give a damn," although he wouldn't have been able to say that without a broad smile. McAllister was assigned to the 176th Assault Helicopter Company in Chu Lai. On February 24, he was flying what should have been a simple resupply mission for an American Division artillery unit. He received unexpected anti-aircraft fire, and the entire crew was lost. That day, I was lounging on the beach.

Despite the controversy with the marines, I enjoyed flying the rocket belt. It was aerial swashbuckling, flying with utter disregard for the rulebooks, and unsafe. It was the perfect job for taking out frustrations and anxieties over lost friends. I'd have been satisfied flying our new OH-6A around the rocket belt for the rest of my tour, but it was not to be. A reorganization within the Americal Division was shifting the duty of flying C&C missions for the 196th to A Company, 123rd AvBn. Colonel Kroesen made it clear that he wanted his pilots to be Reid and me, so we were transferred.

Terry Reid and I pointing to bullet holes he took in our OH-6A.

Although the pilots assigned to A Company were a great group of guys, the command staff was, in military terms, "chickenshit." They decided the C&C missions would be a great way to safely build flying hours and rub shoulders with colonels, so they delayed giving me my unit check ride, which kept me grounded for several weeks while several of the staff flew Colonel Kroesen.

My UH-1 Huey.

At the end of the mission one evening, Colonel Kroesen instructed the staff officer who was flying as AC to return to Chu Lai. Following a riverbed for reference in the Que Son Valley, the pilot headed off into the fog. After a brief time, the colonel pointed out that they were flying west toward Laos. Chu Lai lay southeast. Not having a clue as to where they were, the AC flew due east until he crossed Highway 1 and then headed south. Upon arriving safely back at Chu Lai, Colonel Kroesen put his foot down. The next day, I had my check ride, and Reid and I were ready to resume the 196th C&C missions.

Chapter 4

Be Merry, for Our Time of Stay Is Short

It was spring of 1969, and, for several months, the area of operations for the 196th had been quiet. The village of Hiep Duc was secure. Refugees had returned home, fields were replanted, the harvest was successful, and the district was reborn into a thriving, healthy, happy place. It was a model for the army's pacification program.

The next valley south of Que Son, though, over the ridgeline from LZ East, was beginning to heat up. The 3rd NVA Regiment was found to be fully ensconced in the foothills around the village of Tien Phouc, and the 1st Battalion of the 52nd Infantry, with the 198th LIB, was ground down and unable to proceed after eight days of fighting the NVA from bunker to bunker. The American Division therefore extended the area of operations for Colonel Kroesen and attached the 1st/52nd to the 196th. One of the colonel's first moves was to commit the 3rd/21st, which was fresh from a three-day stand down at Chu Lai, where the soldiers had been able to play on the beach, clean uniforms, and hang out in bars.

On March 6, Delta Company, 3rd/21st, approximately one hundred and forty men strong, moved off LZ East toward Tien Phouc. Each man carried more than a full load because he didn't expect resupply for days. Despite the insufferable heat, they wore their steel helmets and flak vests and had their sleeves rolled down to protect their arms from the thorny "wait-a-minute" vines. They didn't know if they would face an enemy soldier, but they knew that, for the next week, they'd have to deal with fatigue, hunger, dehydration, jungle rot, and dysentery.

Troy "Muleshoe" Anders

The next day, they continued their hot walk in the sun. Sergeant Taft's squad took the lead. Private Conover walked point, which meant he assumed the first and most exposed position in the formation as they advanced through the hostile territory. In addition to his fifty-pound backpack, he carried another fifty pounds, which included extra rounds for his weapon, two claymore mines, six hand grenades, two smoke grenades, an entrenching tool, six canteens of water, and six days worth of C rations. As he moved forward, Conover was hyper-alert, looking at everything three or four times to make sure it was as it appeared to be.

Behind Conover walked twenty-year-old Specialist Troy "Muleshoe" Anders. Troy was from Muleshoe, Texas, where his mom and dad made a living running a team of mules. Working sun up to sun down to provide for their family, the Anders used their mules to clear trees and haul hay, and any other work that would be accomplished by tractor today. Troy's mom died when he was only six, and his dad carried on alone in raising Troy, his two brothers, and two sisters. Upon graduating from Muleshoe High in 1966, Troy immediately went to work for the rural electric company to help provide for the family.

Drafted in 1967, Troy found himself with Delta Company in May 1968. He quickly earned the nickname of Muleshoe, and, by March, he was one of the more experienced and trusted soldiers in the unit. His primary weapon was the M-79 grenade launcher, which many considered to be the finest infantry weapon in the field. When the enemy was discovered pouring rounds in on the squad from fifty yards, too far away to throw a grenade, too close for artillery, and nearly impossible to approach and knock out without excessive casualties, Muleshoe silenced the enemy with one of his well-placed high explosive grenade rounds. The M-79 was his life, and it fulfilled his purpose with the platoon that depended on him during combat.

Fifteen yards behind Muleshoe walked Private Gary Schneider. Barely eighteen, Schneider was new to the unit and considered "green meat" as he had yet to experience combat. He'd already learned, though, that, when out on patrol, he left behind the safety of the LZ.

Following close behind Schneider, teaching and assisting as they moved out, was Sergeant Taft. He was tough on his men, but displayed confidence and they respected him.

Farther back was nineteen-year-old Private Joseph Neske from East Islip, New York. Neske came from a close-knit family that included a brother and sister. A handsome, good-natured, and well-liked kid, Neske aggressively approached every activity with enthusiasm. If he thought he or someone close to him was being wronged, he wouldn't hesitate to go to blows if necessary. Neske was an all-around athlete, and tennis was his second love. His first love was his girlfriend, Judy. Below his senior class picture, Neske had written, "Be merry, for our time of stay is short." When Neske came home on leave before heading to Vietnam, his friends cut school and hung out for the day. They noticed how passionate and proud he was to be in the army. On March 7,

Neske had been with the Delta Company less than two weeks, having arrived in country a month prior. This was likely the second day of his first mission.

Also in this mix were Specialist Gary George and Private Kenneth Vehige. George, from Renfrew, Pennsylvania, had graduated from Knoch High School, where he had been a member of the track team. He had been in country since June 1968, and he was experienced. Vehige was from Wentzville, Missouri. Realizing he was more interested in partying than college, Vehige had volunteered for the army.

Around 1400, their fatigues drenched with sweat, Conover, Muleshoe, and Sergeant Taft broke through heavy vegetation into a small hamlet. The experienced soldiers had been here before. Not the exact same area, but similar villages, rice paddies, and jungle-covered hills had been patrolled and cleared again and again. They were looking for and fighting an enemy who spoke and dressed as the villagers. It was those villagers, simple peasants wanting only to farm, tend a few animals, and mind their own business, who were caught in the middle. They knew nothing of communism or capitalism. However, older members of the villages had experienced imperialism, and, to them, the American soldiers seemed like the imperialist French, dressing in the same type of clothes, patrolling and harassing as the French had. They also knew that, while the United States Army might pass through occasionally, the VC were there day and night and were merciless when they dealt with villagers who cooperated with the South Vietnamese (ARVN) and American soldiers.

It frustrated Muleshoe because, while clearing a hamlet, the few women present would promise there were no VC or NVA in the vicinity. Yet within minutes of leaving, a sniper often wounded or killed a member of the squad. And although the women of the village would claim there were no booby traps in the surrounding areas, someone in the unit often tripped a wire or stepped on a mine with devastating results. Sergeant Taft knew that the VC, working the rice fields by day and planting booby traps by night, were always tracking their every move. He also knew the NVA soldiers were watching, never entering a fight unless it was on their terms.

March 7 was turning into a long and boring day as Reid and I flew Colonel Kroesen to various LZs in the Que Son Valley. We finally landed at LZ West and shut down. My crew sat around, played cribbage, and waited while the colonel conducted his business in the battalion tactical operations center (B-TOC).[6]

LZ West

I opened some C rations, ate peaches and pound cake, and then walked around among the soldiers who had just returned or were getting ready to move out on patrol. Their body language showed bravado, but their haunting eyes and faces displayed a common denominator of loneliness, bewilderment, and fear. I returned to the chopper and tried to lie on the floor for a nap, but it was too hot. I looked at my watch and saw it was only 1420. The day was dragging.

Colonel Kroesen soon exited the B-TOC and motioned he was ready to leave. I looked at Reid and swirled my forefinger in the air, indicating to "kick the tires and light the fire." I put on my "chicken plate," a heavy ceramic vest that protected me from shrapnel and, hopefully, small arms fire. Its canvas

---

6. B-TOCs were sandbagged bunkers with low ceilings and dim lights containing radios and battlefield maps of unit and enemy positions.

cover smelled of my previous missions and anxieties. With it secure across my torso, I climbed into the left seat as Reid was throwing switches.

"Clear?" Reid asked over the intercom.

"Clear right."

"Clear left," came the replies from the crew.

Reid pulled the switch on the end of the collective. A ticking could be heard in the engine compartment, followed by a slight muffled combustion as the turbine ignited. The chopper rocked as the blades began to turn, the whine of the turbine increased, and, in a few minutes, the rotor RPMs were up to speed. Colonel Kroesen was seated and strapped in.

"All right, let's pull pitch," I said.

Reid lifted off, and we headed north over Death Valley, then turned east toward LZ Baldy.

About the time we lifted off LZ West, Conover began the move out of the hamlet and toward a large clearing of tall, sharp-sided grass that extended up the side of a hill. He slowly and quietly led them through the banana plants and scrub bush along the western edge of the clearing. Then he started to descend around the western side of the hill toward the south. A sudden roar of gunfire blasted from the foliage. Conover immediately went down from AK-47 rounds through his right arm and chest. Everyone else dove to the ground. As in any clash with the enemy at close range, there was immediate shock and confusion coupled with disbelief.

Muleshoe was quick to locate the enemy and began firing rounds from his M-79. Sergeant Taft ran forward to assess the situation and hit the ground in a slight depression next to Schneider, who had rolled out of his backpack. While hugging the ground as close as he could, Schneider was trying to get a bearing on where the shots were coming from so he could return fire. Suddenly, a hand grenade landed and exploded next to Sergeant Taft and Schneider. Taft received the brunt of the explosion with over seventeen wounds along his torso. His left leg, arm, and hand were useless, and his rifle was blown apart. He could only lie there and shout directions to his men.

Having tried frantically to avoid the grenade, confused from the sudden blast that left his ears ringing, Schneider rolled around and looked unsuccessfully for his rifle. Conover began crying for help, and Schneider, feeling helpless without his weapon, began crawling toward him. Gary George rushed up from behind with others and, under Sergeant Taft's direction, began laying down gunfire. Schneider had snaked several yards through the thick, green underbrush before someone dropped beside him.

Schneider could taste the soil collected in his nose as he dragged his face through the dirt in order to see who lay next to him. It was a medic. The side of the newcomer's face was pressed tight to the damp earth as bullets flew overhead, scattering leaves, branches, and debris.

The medic was out of breath and hard to hear over the gunfire. "How far ahead is he?"

Schneider tried to look forward through the grass without lifting his head, but a translucent leaf on its edge blocked his serpent's view. For a moment, Schneider had the strange memory of a science class assignment.

"Ten yards!" he yelled back.

Schneider started edging forward, but the medic grabbed him. "Stay here. You've been hit."

"Where?"

"Your back. Stay tight. I'll be back." The medic then started toward Conover, scurrying like a beetle through the soil and gunfire.

Schneider thought it strange that he didn't feel any pain until the medic confirmed he'd been hit. Then he began to feel a deep throbbing in his lower back.

Several lieutenants, along with the sergeants, struggled to regain control of the situation and deployed the men as they learned the extent of the enemy's positions. Under their direction, the return gunfire from the troops on the scene was heavy and on target. Neske, anxious to prove himself, positioned himself as instructed.

Farther back, where the unit had first begun to move along the western edge of the clearing, the company commander, with a call sign of Black Death, set up his command position. The medic, with Schneider's assistance, managed to get Conover and Sergeant Taft back to that point. Once Black Death had a grasp of the situation and felt his lieutenants and sergeants had the upper hand, he got on the radio while crouching low in the tall grass.

"Gimlet Three Oscar, Black Death."

Someone in the B-TOC at FSB Center answered promptly, "Three Oscar here, go ahead."

"We're in contact." Black Death's voice carried a tone of urgency. "About one click south of last RP,[7] size unknown. Need dust-off[8] for at least one, over."

"Three Oscar copies. Stand by."

The firefight continued, and, based on the info he was receiving from his men, Black Death maneuvered his men to protect both flanks. After what seemed like hours, yet was only minutes, his RTO[9] handed him the receiver.

"Black Death, go ahead," he said as he lay in the tall grass.

"Oscar Three here. Do you have a sit rep?"[10]

"They're dug into the hillside to our east. Maybe company strength. We're holding and preparing to move on them." His voice labored as if he had been running for miles. "I need that dust-off, one urgent with sucking chest wound, three other serious."

"Oscar Three copies." After a short pause, he continued, "We cannot, I repeat, cannot locate a dust-off. Will advise."

Black Death rolled over and faced the medic behind him. With all the gunfire, he had to yell. "How's he doing?"

While trying to stay low, the medic was frantically working to seal the wound in Conover's chest. Failure would mean the lung would collapse, bringing death. The look on the medic's face told Black Death that Conover's situation wasn't good.

Conover fought desperately to roll on his side and double up, the only way he could ease the pain and breathe. He knew his lung was sucking air through his wound, but he didn't consider death. He just knew he was going home.

---

7. reported position

8. Dust-off was the term for a medical evacuation by helicopter.

9. radio operator

10. situation report

The medic yelled back over the roar of gunfire, "What's the ETA for that dust-off?"

Black Death didn't answer. He didn't want Conover to hear the bad news. He was about to hand the radio receiver back to his RTO when he heard another call.

"Black Death, Charger 6," Colonel Kroesen called from his bank of radios.

"Black Death here."

"Black Death, this is Charger 6. I've been monitoring. I'm going to have my pilot come up this push.[11] Stand by one."

Colonel Kroesen then came up on my intercom. "Mister Jones, I'm going to switch you over to my channel two so you can talk to Black Death."

My switch for talking to Colonel Kroesen was down alongside my collective. I was now able to talk through the radios mounted in the back using that switch. "Black Death, this is Charger niner-four."[12]

"Niner-four, Black Death," he said, his voice hurried over the sounds of gunfire in the background. "In immediate need of a dust-off. Can't raise one. Can you assist?"

"Niner-four copies. Stand by one."

Reid turned us in the direction of Delta Company while I worked the radio looking for an available medical evacuation chopper. I knew it was preferred to have a dust-off crew carry out the mission because trained medics would be able to immediately provide proper care. It took precious minutes as I called and waited for a response from Chu Lai and Da Nang, and every medical station in between that might have a chopper standing by. I had no luck. It was a busy day.

I set my radio to the frequency for Black Death and keyed the switch on the cyclic. "Black Death, Charger niner-four."

"Black Death, go." He sounded excited.

"No dust-offs available. Where are you, and what do you have?"

"We're at 165-180. I've got one urgent and at least three serious."

---

11. Push was another word for frequency.

12. The last two numbers of my aircraft's tail number was ninety-four. For clarity reasons, the military pronounced nine as niner.

I noticed Reid tapping on the instrument panel for me to look. He knew a visual message was stronger than a verbal one. The twenty-minute fuel light had just come on, and it was a fifteen-minute trip back to the closest fuel depot, LZ Baldy.

I took a mental survey of my situation. Reid had us in the vicinity. My fuel was low, so the helicopter was relatively light. With Colonel Kroesen, along with the added weight of the bank of radios in the back, I figured I could take off from an unknown landing site with five wounded. This was important because, while a helicopter might be able to hover with a certain load over a flat surface, it won't hover with the same load over an uneven or sloping hillside. Not being able to hover while out in the field meant not being able to take off.

We circled at least fifteen hundred feet above the green, rolling hills. It looked so peaceful as I looked out my side window. I then realized I had one of my radios tuned to the armed forces radio station out of Da Nang, and they were playing the theme from *The Good, The Bad and the Ugly*. I switched it off.

"Hey," Reid shouted, loud enough to be heard without using the intercom. As I looked over at him, he had a big smile. I keyed the intercom. "The good and the bad are down there. Here comes the ugly."

We laughed as I reached for the intercom button down on my left side. "Colonel, we can pick up five."

When flying C&C missions, many pilots found that their chief passenger ordered them around, sometimes into situations that were unnecessarily dangerous or beyond the capabilities of the aircraft. That wasn't Colonel Kroesen's style.

"Mister Jones, you're the aircraft commander. It's your decision."

Without replying to Colonel Kroesen, I keyed the crew intercom. "I got it."

"You got it," Reid said.

I pulled in pitch and turned a tight left bank so I could see directly below. Somewhere in that beautiful lush countryside, men were bleeding and dying.

"Black Death, Charger niner-four. I'm coming in to pick up at five. Pop smoke."

Black Death sounded unsure. "Niner-four, be advised LZ's hot."

"I copy. Hot LZ. Look, we're low on fuel and have to make a decision. You asked for a dust-off, right?"

"Affirmative."

"Your men ready to load them up?"

"Affirmative." His voice now conveyed confidence.

"All right. Pop smoke." If they were willing to stand in a clearing and load the wounded during a firefight, I was willing to come in.

Black Death reminded me again that it was a hot LZ, but finally reported, "Smoke out."

It took forever to spot yellow smoke drifting up from the edge of a clearing on the western side of a hill, south of where we were circling.

"Charger niner-four has yellow."

"This is Black Death. That's affirmative, yellow."

He didn't tell me the color first, but waited for me to tell him what color I observed to ensure the NVA didn't lure me into the wrong location. More than once, chopper pilots saw red or yellow smoke when the good guys had popped purple. Sometimes, pilots saw two different locations with the same color smoke.

"Black Death, where are the bad guys?" I asked.

"To the east. Come in just north of the smoke."

I keyed the intercom for Colonel Kroesen. "Hold on." I then keyed the aircraft intercom and told Reid, "Get on the controls."

He knew to get on the controls lightly to be ready if something happened to me. Reid also knew the seriousness of the situation. Days earlier, a chopper carrying Lieutenant Colonel Stinson of the 1st/52nd, the unit Delta Company was moving to assist, was on a similar mission when enemy fire killed Stinson.

I lowered the collective and put the helicopter into a steep left spiral to keep the LZ in sight. I purposely kicked in left pedal to take the chopper out of trim, much as I had accidentally done in flight school. The helicopter dropped like a rock in a nose-low attitude, raising the sphincter pucker factor to maximum for anyone on board who had never experienced a high overhead approach. The maneuver was necessary as it limited the time that the aircraft was vulnerable to enemy fire while descending. I timed the descent and turn so we leveled off at the treetops and approached the LZ from the north. I came in hot, flared, and pulled pitch to bring the chopper to a halt. The blades loudly slapped the air.

Several soldiers were crouching in the grass to my left, waiting to load Conover and Taft. The skids had barely touched when everyone went into action. Conover was thrown aboard first and then Taft with Colonel Kroesen's assistance. While Schneider scrambled aboard dragging several others, a lieutenant jumped on the skids and shoved a note through my open window.

I looked over my left shoulder as Colonel Kroesen jumped back in and then hit the intercom. "Clear?"

"Clear," the door gunner and crew chief shouted in unison.

I was barely aware of the sounds of gunfire by the grunts on the ground and was unsure if there were any incoming fire. We hadn't been on the ground ten seconds when I lifted to a hover. I had sufficient power, so I pulled in more pitch, nosed it over, and headed south, low over the trees. Once clear of the action, I climbed to altitude and headed for Baldy. I was going to be cutting the twenty-minute fuel warning close.

Reid took the controls and flew while I looked at the note. They had given me a list of ammunition they were running low on, for M-16 rifles, M-60 machine guns, and M-79 grenade launchers.

Medics were waiting on the Charlie Company, 23rd Medical Battalion helipad at Baldy when we arrived. The colonel went with the wounded, and Reid and I flew the chopper over for fuel. We'd been running a little over twenty minutes since the warning light came on. After taking on half a tank of fuel, we flew over to the ammo depot where the crew chief and door gunner loaded us up with the requested ordnance. I thought it strange that anyone could just fly in and load up whatever ammo they wanted with no one checking. Then I found it curious I'd think of something like that during this life and death situation.

Within minutes, we were back at the aid station to pick up Colonel Kroesen. While sitting at idle, the crew chief checked over the chopper and reported we had taken no hits. *A little excitement today after all.*

On the flight back to Delta Company's location, I dropped low level across the valley before I got close to the hills.

"Black Death, Charger niner-four. Three minutes out. What's your sit rep?"

"This is Black Death." He sounded out of breath. "More wounded, still hot."

"Copy. I'll take five. Pop smoke."

After a few moments, Black Death answered, "Smoke out."

I slithered in below the treetops, and I was fifteen seconds out when I spotted smoke. "I got red."

"Affirmative, red."

This time, a soldier was standing, marking the spot for us to land. *Perfect. Right out of a training manual.* Like a cowboy reigning in a galloping horse, I flared and pulled pitch hard to bring us to a stop. As I set down the chopper, the soldier in front ran off to the left where others were ready to load the wounded. I noticed two body bags lying off to the side. Colonel Kroesen jumped out and helped as two seriously wounded were carried in poncho liners and thrown on the chopper floor. Three walking wounded scrambled aboard. Outside, guns were being fired furiously, and everyone who wasn't loading wounded was laying low in the grass. The scene appeared extraordinarily crisp, clear, and vibrant.

Just as I looked back at Colonel Kroesen to confirm he had climbed back in, there was a massive blast to my left front. It wasn't like in the movies where there's a large ball of fire within the explosion. It was just black and, strangely, eerily quiet. For a moment, it all seemed to be happening in slow motion.

Jesus, what the … ? A shock wave slammed against my body, and, instantaneously, small holes appeared across the windshield. Then it felt like someone had thrown gravel at my helmet and chicken plate. My right leg jumped as I took several hits around the knee. It reminded me of playing cowboys in the orchard as a boy and having rocks slung from my buddy's slingshot striking me. Sound suddenly returned, and there were more explosions. The intense gunfire increased.

Get the hell out of here before they do that again.

I glanced back to insure everyone was aboard before pulling pitch. The blades grasped for air as I brought the helicopter up to a hover. I looked at my escape route ahead through the tress. "Take off now!" an inner voice was screaming.

"Are we green?" I shouted over the intercom to Reid.

I wanted to ensure all the engine instruments were still displaying normal operations and no red lights had appeared, indicating a serious problem.

"We're green."

I felt a slap and sting to my right calf as I pulled pitch, nosed it over, and again departed low level. Once clear of the action, I took stock of our status. My door gunner was wounded and bleeding. Colonel Kroesen had taken hits. Reid and our crew chief were unscathed.

As we headed back to LZ Baldy, I turned the controls over to Reid and pulled up my right pant leg. I noticed a piece of metal about the size of a pebble flush with the surface of the skin and embedded into my shinbone. Pulling the pant leg up farther, I found a nasty two-inch gash on the left side of my calf. On the front of my knee, just below the kneecap, was an entry hole about the size of a pencil eraser. Strangely, none of the wounds was bleeding, and I figured they were all superficial.

Lying on the floor of the chopper, eyes wide open, was Private Vehige. He'd been hit in the neck. He was bleeding profusely, and he couldn't talk. Vehige was afraid that, if he closed his eyes, he'd die.

Once again, they were waiting with stretchers at Baldy. After they unloaded the wounded, including our door gunner, I had Reid move the chopper off to the side of the helipad. My leg hurt, but I walked around as the crew chief began a serious inspection of all critical components. I couldn't believe, with all the holes in the aircraft, that something important hadn't been damaged. The aircraft looked like someone had used it for target practice, and I stopped counting holes at fifty.

I then limped to the aid station to check on the status of the wounded. The inside of the heavily sandbagged tent looked like a scene out of the movie *MASH*, except more chaotic. A heavy anesthetic smell hung in the air.

Numerous shrapnel and small arms holes in my Huey

Moving from patient to patient around the doctors was Chaplain Don Bartley. No one was loved more on Baldy than Major Bartley. A Presbyterian minister from Rockbridge Baths, Virginia, Bartley had been in country since July 1968. He'd overseen the construction of a beautiful A-framed chapel on LZ Baldy where I occasionally attended services. Chaplain Bartley made it a point to be in the aid station when wounded were brought in.

I stood next to someone who appeared to know the situation. "I was the pilot who made the two trips in here. How are they doing?"

"Several are going to be sent on for surgery in Da Nang. The word is, though, they have two KIAs back up there."

My heart sank. Having seen the two body bags, I believed he was right. I immediately began to tell myself that it wasn't the result of my actions or inaction. *Or was it? Could I have arrived on the scene fifteen minutes sooner on the first trip instead of flying circles while discussing the situation and trying to locate a dust-off?* Fifteen minutes sooner on the first trip would have put us back on site earlier the second trip. *Could that fifteen or twenty minutes have made a difference?* Intellectually, I knew I did the best I could. Emotionally, though, I was struggling.

Gary George and Joseph Neske lost their lives. I evacuated ten. Other pilots eventually evacuated thirteen more later that day.

I walked outside the aid station and noticed my knee was swelling and stiffening up. As I sat on a bench, I hung my head low as I tried to picture two mothers receiving a notice of regret.

"Mister Jones." I looked up to see Colonel Kroesen. "You okay?"

"I'm all right. I took a couple hits in the leg. I'll be flying again in a couple days. And you?"

"Just a scratch," he said, minimizing the shrapnel wounds to his backside.

"How's our door gunner?"

"He'll need a period of convalescing, but he'll be fine."

It took an hour before a doctor saw me. After a brief look at the leg, he declared, "Nothing we can do here. I'm sending you to Da Nang."

Before dark, a helicopter took four patients on stretchers and a couple of us walking wounded to Da Nang. Walking, though, was getting more difficult.

Still, I expected a few stitches, a week or two on light duty, and then back to flight status.

Instead, the following morning, I was operated on, woke up groggy, and found myself in a leg cast from the ankle to my hip. Five pieces of shrapnel and fragments of an AK-47 round were taped to my chest. The next day, while heavily sedated, I was on a medevac flight to Camp Zama, Japan.

The hospital at Camp Zama was a seven hundred-bed facility with all the modern equipment of 1969. *Back in the real world.* I was rolled into a small examination room with tile from floor to ceiling. Everything appeared clean and sterile, but smelled nauseously of antibacterial mixtures. I was in a sitting position on my gurney when a tall, stocky medic walked in.

"Good morning, Mister Jones. I'm Sergeant Washington, okay? I'm going to be looking at this here leg." He looked like someone who should be playing professional football.

He had the temporary cast off quickly, and I saw the knee and calf were heavily bandaged.

"Okay, I'm going to lay you back now," he said.

"No, I'm all right."

"Now your operation in Nam was dirty, okay? You haven't been cleaned and sewed up. I think you better lay back, okay?" He started to shift the bed down.

I protested. "No, I want to watch."

"Okay, okay." He smiled big. "So, where you from, Mister Jones?"

We continued small talk as he took off the bandages. I had a small red wound on my shin. The gash to my calf looked strangely like a head of cauliflower was protruding through. Again, I was fascinated that there was no bleeding. He started removing the bandage around the knee.

"So how do I get five pieces of lead with only three entry wounds?"

"They break up after hitting you. Okay, you still got some lead in this here calf, see?" He held up an x-ray showing a piece of metal the size of gravel deep in my calf. "They're going to leave that there. That'll be no problem, okay?"

With the bandage off the knee, I could see the doctors had cut my knee open from one side to the other. The medic had a bowl of what looked like milk and a handful of surgical sponges.

"Okay, I'm going to clean these here wounds up real good before they come in and stitch this here up."

I thought he was going to wash the outside of the wounds. Instead, he lifted what looked and felt like my entire kneecap and started scrubbing inside the wound. The room started to tilt to the left, and everything went gray. I thought I was going to roll off the gurney.

"Uh-huh," I heard a muffled voice say.

I woke laying on the gurney as someone stitched me up. The medic was still in the room.

"Okay, I told you," he said with a booming laugh. "One thing to see someone else's wounds. Something else when they're yours, huh?"

I had to agree, although I wasn't laughing. I felt sick.

A solid cast was applied, and I was wheeled into a large ward with at least forty other patients. After a couple of days, I was able to get around in a wheelchair with my right leg sticking straight out. I was wandering the halls and checking all the different wards for any soldier who may have been with Delta Company, 3rd/21st. Laughter caught my attention from a small ward that held maybe ten patients, so I rolled through the doors and immediately saw a familiar face from flight school. He was still laughing from a story someone just told.

"Hey, Lambie."

He immediately recognized me and smiled. "Jones'y."

"What are you doing here?" I asked, as if I couldn't tell. His right thigh was heavily bandaged.

"Took a round." He looked quite relieved to be out of Vietnam, safe and reasonably sound.

"Where were you?" I asked.

"I flew with the 176th Assault Helicopter Company. I was helping a unit with the 196th out near Tien Phouc."

I interrupted him. "Are you kidding me? I took a couple hits at Tien Phouc on March 7."

"March 9th for me." He laughed.

We talked a while and promised to stay in touch, and I left wondering if I could ever feel as relieved as Lambie appeared to be. Concerned with the status of the wounded soldiers I rescued, I resumed my search, and I was disappointed in never finding any of them.

A week later, I was flown back to the States. It was a miserable experience. They woke us at 0430 for a quick breakfast and, by 0600, had us all strapped on stretchers, covered with double blankets due to the freezing temperatures outdoors. I couldn't roll over or sit up. It took hours, but they finally transported our sweating bodies out to the airport where, instead of immediately placing us aboard the aircraft, they laid us out to freeze on our stretchers on the tarmac in the snow. Only after all the busses were unloaded and we were all spread out on the ground did they begin to load the plane. It was a methodology that only someone with military experience might understand.

I had been strapped to my stretcher for thirty hours by the time I arrived at Fort Travis, California. Although it was 0300, I was told I could request anything I wanted. I ordered steak and eggs, twice. These were real eggs, over easy, not the reconstituted scrambled green stuff served in Vietnam. I then slept for hours and finally made a call home to Susan late in the afternoon. On one hand, it felt good to be home. On the other, I felt like I was getting away with something and I should be back with the troops in Vietnam.

Within days, I was transferred to the army hospital at Fort Ord, California, where, after several weeks, they removed the cast, and I began physical therapy. A month later, I was allowed to go home where I joined a Jack LaLanne health club and made considerably faster progress in gaining full range of motion in my leg than I'd have by sticking to the cautious military rehabilitation schedule. One afternoon I stopped by the hospital where Trent Fair was being treated for his broken neck, and I was stunned to learn that he would be a permanent quadriplegic. *Trent has faith in his Lord, but this certainly isn't the life he hoped for.*

By June, promoted to CW2, I was anxious to get back to work as I felt I was malingering. I was bored with rehabilitation and sitting around the house. I was ready for a new challenge. Vietnam had pumped me with excitement never before imagined, which left a void I was ready to fill. I pushed the doctors at

Fort Ord to release me, and Susan and I were on our way across country to my next assignment, Fort Wolters.

While I had been recuperating, friends continued to lose their lives in Vietnam: Douglas Stover, David Crow, Roger Auld, and Ernest Burns.

At Fort Wolters, I found I was not physically ready to return to flight duty. Not happy with some of my assignment choices, I drove over to the Warrant Officer Candidate Training Brigade to inquire about a job as a TAC. The brigade seemed delighted to see me, as this was a job not normally requested. Within hours, I had a new assignment. Out of the ten different companies, I was back at my alma mater, 1st WOC.

Chapter 5

You Wouldn't Understand

"Candidate?" I said softly so I wouldn't wake his roommates. He was lying on his bunk, with his head at the foot, staring out the window at the string of navigation lights from the helicopters taking off from the nearby airfield. He hadn't seen me approach from behind. When I spoke, he jumped six inches and did the quickest, midair, one hundred and eighty-degree turn I'd ever seen, and he was immediately under the covers.

"Sir, Candidate Eliason, sir," he whispered as he pulled the sheet up to his chin.

"Are you dreaming of when you'll be flying, candidate?" I kindly asked.

His eyes were big and wide, knowing this friendly conversation wasn't all it seemed. "Sir, Candidate Eliason, sir. Yes, sir."

"I bet you see yourself in a flight suit, wings sewn on, aviator sunglasses, white scarf around your neck, flight helmet under your arm, and a big watch on your wrist, don't you?" I didn't give him time to answer as my tone changed and my voice growled. "I suggest that, when I say lights out, you get your ass under those covers and fall to sleep immediately because you've got classes in the morning. Next time, I'm going to eliminate you on the spot, and you'll never see the inside of a military chopper. Is that understood, candidate?"

"Sir, Candidate Eliason, sir. Yes, sir." He immediately closed his eyes and assumed the military position of sleep.

I still got a kick out of the term "eliminate" and had to laugh to myself. I stopped at the door to the room and looked back. My mood darkened as I saw a vision of Ortego talking to Candidate Eliason. *Don't worry. It's only a game. Besides, it's all predestined.*

I felt a heavy burden as I walked down the hall, and I wondered what was in store for Candidate Eliason and the rest of his classmates.

Fort Wolters was graduating six hundred pilots a month in 1969, and new candidates arrived regularly. Pre-flight was now on the "hill," so I was working with candidates straight out of basic training.

As a TAC, my greeting for the candidates wasn't unlike the one I received a few years earlier. After haranguing them for a time, I stood in front of the roughed-up company. I was wearing heavily starched fatigues that were bloused at the spit-shined boots, highly shined brass, and a glossy black helmet adorned with my CW2 bar. 1st WOC sat the highest on the hill, so the candidates could look out behind me and consider the other companies below.

"Welcome to 1st WOC," I said in a loud voice. "You'll be setting the standards on the hill, is that understood?"

"Sir, Candidate (all their names in a jumble), sir. Yes, sir."

"I can't hear you," I sang.

They responded louder.

"In spite of the rumors you've been hearing, you're lucky to be here at 1st WOC." I hesitated to let that sink in. "It's going to take some luck to graduate as an army aviator, and it's also going to take some luck to survive Vietnam. At 1st WOC, we know that luck doesn't care who's right or wrong, but is only concerned with who had the better training. So at 1st WOC, you'll get up earlier, do physical training longer, be louder, study harder, look sharper, and fly better." I then waved my arm toward the companies below. "Better than the rest. Anyone have a problem with that?"

"Sir, Candidate (jumbled), sir. No, sir," they yelled enthusiastically.

"You have your room assignments. One last thing, when you break formation, you'll respond with 'Big. Red. One.' All right. Dismissed."

A roar boomed off the hill, "Big. Red. One." They then took off for their first attempt at squaring their rooms away.

The building was exactly as it had been two years earlier. The walls and windows were bare with nothing to soften the scene. Nothing was allowed to hang on the walls, nor was any other decoration allowed. The floor was smooth cement, which the candidates were expected to keep in a state of high shine. Each room contained three beds, to be made up immediately upon rising in the morning. An army blanket, which was to be wrinkle-free, covered the thin mattress. The sheet was to be folded over at the top at exactly eight inches. The pillow was to be immaculately smooth. The three wooden wardrobes held the uniforms that hung on hangers, each precisely separated, with uniform patches perfectly aligned. The drawer below contained underwear, which was rolled to exact specifications. Civilian clothes were taken away and stored.

The echoes throughout the concrete building were harsh and continuous with the rasp of commands, announcements, and blowing of whistles. To maintain a high shine on the floor, candidates left off their footwear until the last minute. The knocking of hard-heeled boots usually meant the appearance of a TAC and was followed by the sounds of candidates slamming their bodies up against the hallway wall to make room for him to pass. As he did, candidates shouted their names.

I woke them at 0445. Because of my encounter two years earlier with Mother, who was long gone, I still had a grudge against 2nd WOC. They didn't arouse their candidates until 0500, so I marched 1st WOC over and, standing below the 2nd WOC windows, held a boisterous roll call. My candidates loved starting the day that way.

During pre-flight, I was with my flight until lights out at 2200. Between "lights on" and "lights off," it was marching at double time everywhere, to physical training, breakfast, classes, lunch, classes, dinner, and back to the barracks. This time, I got to call cadence.

"I want to be an aviator. I want to live a life of danger. I want to go to Vietnam. I want to kill old Charlie Kong. If I die in a combat zone, box me up and send me home. Pin my medals upon my chest, and tell my momma I did my best."

Life at home was fine for Susan and me. Weekends were demanding in the early stages of the candidate's training, and, when I didn't have to be at the barracks, a parade function or brigade commander's party often required Susan's and my attendance. When I did have time off and was able to get away, we joined other families for picnicking and water skiing at Lake Possum Kingdom.

Susan tried several times at getting us to church, but I wasn't ready to listen to a sermon, for example, from the Epistle to the Hebrews on faith, "the assurance of things hoped for, the conviction of things not seen." *The assurance of things hoped for? Assurance?* What I had experienced was not assurance, but randomness.

Once the candidates started flying, my hours spent at 1st WOC were cut in half. I had the time to get away several times a week for fixed-wing flight lessons in Fort Worth, eventually earning my commercial single and multi-engine ratings along with an instrument rating.

One afternoon, Susan dropped me off in front of the company building and waited as I ran inside, leaving my car door open. As I passed the large boulder painted red, which sat in front of the building, and approached the front door, I noticed the candidate coming out was in my flight.

Upon seeing me, he immediately came to attention and saluted, speaking loudly and confidently. "Sir, Candidate Kimmich, sir."

I returned the salute and noticed he appeared to be hastily dressed and his boots looked like he'd shined them with a Brillo pad.

"God damn it, candidate, what the hell are you doing? I thought I told everyone that they weren't to leave the floor for any reason for the rest of the day."

"Sir, Candidate Kimmich, sir. Lieutenant Swinford is sending me over to 4th WOC to pick up paperwork on a recycled candidate, sir."

I was in his face. "Who's your TAC, candidate? Lieutenant Swinford or me?"

"Sir, Candidate Kimmich, sir. You are, sir."

"And what did I instruct you to do?"

He continued to stand at attention and looked straight ahead. "Sir, Candidate Kimmich, sir. You instructed us to stay on our floor for the rest of the day, sir."

This was one of those situations where I was harassing a candidate in what appeared to be a no-win situation for him. But it gave me an opportunity to watch the candidate react, prioritize, and decide what was important during a stressful situation. Some candidates didn't handle it well.

"So what the hell, pray tell me Candidate Kimmich, are you doing out here, looking like this?" I waved my arms as I circled him.

He quickly responded, "Sir, Candidate Kimmich, sir. I was following the instructions of the senior TAC officer, sir."

Well done. But I wasn't going to let him know that. Not ready to let him go, I looked down at his boots. "Where did you get those boots? They look like hell. Are these the boots you were wearing this morning?"

"Sir, Candidate Kimmich, sir. Yes, sir."

"Your only boots?"

"Sir, Candidate Kimmich, sir. Yes, sir."

When I was a candidate, we had a classmate who thought he could beat the system of keeping his boots in top-notch condition by hiding a second pair in a plastic bag in the brushy area across the street. He'd wear the grungy pair when at the flight line or when he had duties that would get his boots dirty. A TAC caught him, which might have resulted in demerits or losing a weekend pass. That candidate lied about it, though, and he was promptly eliminated from the program since honesty was a top priority.

"Candidate, I can't believe these are the boots you wear for inspection. If I find out you're playing games with me, your ass is out of here. Understand, candidate?"

"Sir, Candidate Kimmich, sir. Yes, sir."

"Carry on, candidate."

I heard him sigh heavily as he ran off toward 4th WOC.

Susan observed and heard the exchange. When I returned to the car and, as Susan drove off, she asked, "Is that necessary?" Her question sounded a lot like mine when I encountered swearing in boot camp and flight school.

"Yes, it's necessary."

Susan and I never talked about my experiences in Vietnam, the lost classmates and friends, the combat, and the bodies of both American and enemy soldiers. I didn't know how to talk to her about Vietnam and the resultant impact it had on me.

"It's part of the training. You wouldn't understand."

"The swearing. Taking our Lord's name in vain?"

"You wouldn't understand."

"I want us to go to church. You're having much more time off now, and there's a Bible study on Thursday evenings."

I didn't respond.

When the candidates were in their last two months of training, the workload for the TAC was light. On average, 30 percent of the candidates had been eliminated from the program by then. Most eliminations occurred during preflight, and those were usually a result of the TAC officers' decisions based on dishonesty, continued lack of attention to detail, or inability to comprehend and follow orders. Many more were lost in the early stages of flight training, and others were failed due to academics. But after three months, the remaining candidates were doing fine, passing flight checks, getting good grades academically, and earning weekend passes.

Susan and I were excited when we learned she was pregnant. She kept occupied working part time on base as a beautician. When I had time off, we spent hours at the local park and even managed to attend a Bible study or two. I bought a BSA 650cc motorcycle and, with other officers who had cycles, would occasionally go for a ride through the countryside.

I couldn't help but be proud of the company as I watched them march off to classes one Friday. Their appearance was up to the strictest military standards, and they were feeling good about themselves. They no longer had to run at double time. TACs weren't accompanying them everywhere, and they'd call their own cadences. This particular day, they marched to their own song. When they got to the end of the cadence, they threw their arms up in the air and shouted, "Whoopee! We're all gonna die."

Hearing them caught me off guard, and I mumbled to myself, "Well, not all. Some of you, though, are destined to die."

They were aggressive, brash, cocky, confident, and intelligent men. Maybe not intelligent enough, however, to realize that they were going to be involved in the most dangerous job there was in Vietnam. Yet they were willing to serve with honor, and I couldn't help but think that they had faith, faith in their political leaders who were sending them off to war and faith in their military trainers. They had faith in me that I was doing right by them. *Was I?*

When they returned from the flight line, they immediately changed into their dress uniforms and formed up with the rest of the company. I met with them briefly before they headed off for a weekend pass. They seemed giddy, anxious to get away.

"Enjoy the weekend. Company dismissed," I said.

"Big. Red. One," they shouted and then quickly departed.

I should have noticed that the barracks were completely empty and not one candidate remained behind. I finished some paperwork. I gave last-minute instructions to the unfortunate candidate who had the officer of the day duty and headed off for my motorcycle to go home. Except it wasn't where I normally parked it.

What the hell? Did I park it out front? I walked around to the front of the building, but it wasn't there either. I walked into the front office and confronted the officer of the day. "Candidate, you know anything about my motorcycle?"

He jumped to attention. "Sir, Candidate Roberts, sir. No, sir."

I eyeballed him for ten seconds. *He's not lying. Damn, someone's stolen my motorcycle.* I didn't want to call the military police in the presence of the candidate, so I walked upstairs to my office. There, two floors up, sitting nicely shined, was my motorcycle. Not a single candidate was around to help me bring it back down the stairs. I couldn't use the duty officer as he was required to stay in the office, so I headed over to 2nd WOC where I knew plenty of candidates would be in the barracks. I shanghaied three, and we safely returned the motorcycle to ground level.

When I saw my flight the following Monday, I said and acted as if nothing had happened, but I had my plans. That week went smoothly, and, as usual, when Friday came around, they were all dressed up for their weekend pass. I wasn't scheduled to be on duty, but I was there.

"Candidates, we have a problem." I held a small matchbox. "In the course of the inspection of your rooms today, I found a dead aviator on a windowsill.

On your way back to your rooms, you'll pass by and pay your respects. In the morning, we'll have a proper burial for this lost brother."

There was a collective moan. Then they marched by, quietly looking in the box in my hand that contained the body of a fly that had buzzed itself against the glass all day, dying legs up. After giving out a few assignments for the ceremonies in the morning, I quickly left. They were angry. I couldn't help but think back to the night in pre-flight when the TAC harassed us into the wee hours.

The following morning, they were in their dress greens. Six candidates were pallbearers. One candidate was assigned a shovel, and he wore fatigues. Another candidate had the task of giving the eulogy, and several other candidates were asked to say something about the departed. We marched across the street to a spot in the wooded field, the six pallbearers lugging the stretcher, which carried only the small matchbox.

It's amazing how soldiers, as a result of their training, will come together even for the most ridiculous of circumstances. The candidates assigned to be pallbearers actually came up with a medic's litter. The eulogy was at least five minutes long and fitting for any soldier. The several candidates who gave remembrances sounded like they had known and flown with the departed aviator for years. The candidate with the shovel had his own little ceremony as he shoveled a bit from each four points of the compass.

The aviator was laid to rest, and the company returned to the barracks with instructions to change into their fatigues. There were moans again as they thought they'd have the rest of the weekend off. What they had no way of knowing was that the TAC officer wives had been busy bringing all the candidates' wives, girlfriends, and family members living in the area to one of the picnic sites on base. The TACs brought beer, sodas, hot dogs, and chips, and all had a fine time. The candidates were ready to graduate on to Fort Rucker.

On June 9, 1970, at Fort Wolters hospital, a healthy Robert Joseph Jones was brought into this world to a couple of proud parents. Susan and I began to discuss whether to make a career of the army or settle down to a nine-to-five job and raise a family in California. A discussion I had with the brigade commander, Colonel Bearden, while attending the candidate's graduation ball, made the decision easier.

One of the last events in the training at Ft. Wolters was the dance, which young women from the college in Denton attended. The vast majority of candidates didn't have prearranged dates, and they stood in line at the entrance to the hall. As the young ladies exited the bus, they took the arm of the next candidate in line and entered the ballroom. The candidates in my flight seemed to be behaving that evening, and I noticed Candidates Kimmich, Sensat, and Smith sitting at a table with their respective dates. One was Phyllis George, who later became Miss America.

Later in the evening, in the midst of the social gathering, Colonel Bearden, who was bearing a friendly smile, approached me. "Mister Jones, I haven't heard of your decision."

The army had recently made me an offer of three choices. I could accept a commission to lieutenant, which would mean going back to Vietnam, I could remain in as a chief warrant officer, which would also mean going back to Vietnam, or I could take an early out and be discharged almost immediately.

I had some desire to stay in as a warrant officer for a second tour as I longed for the excitement again of flying scout missions in the OH-6A. But I still had a bitter taste in my mouth over my short stay with the 123rd AvBn. After I'd been medically evacuated home, Captain Birchenough had closed out my flight records without posting any of my flight time with the 123rd, costing me in excess of a hundred hours of flying time. When they thought they could get away with it, as in this circumstance because I was sent home ahead of my records, it wasn't unheard of for dishonest staff officers to steal flight hours to boost their own flying time toward earning air medals. Then, when my personal belongings arrived home, all items of value, such as five Seiko watches bought at the Da Nang Post Exchange to be given as gifts back home, were missing. I had also learned that Colonel Kroesen had written up Reid and me for the Distinguished Flying Cross, but the staff at the 123rd had trashed the citations.

Although these were not the overriding concerns I had with staying in the military, these petty and contemptible acts bring everlasting grudges. My superiors had violated the principle of doing what was right.

"We need fine officers like you." Colonel Bearden sounded like he had a quota to fill.

"The war is over, sir."

"No, we still have plenty to do over there." He slapped me on the back and then left his arm around my shoulder like he was talking to his son. "You haven't lost faith in our mission, have you, soldier?"

"Our intentions were honorable, sir, but I'm having trouble with the way our politicians are conducting this war."

His demeanor shifted, and he stood in front of me, silent, waiting for further explanation.

"The North is fighting offensively while our politicians are shackling us with a defensive war without an objective."

"So you think we've been defeated?"

"Not by the enemy, sir. Our policy has failed. If we've been defeated, it's been by our politicians who have no will to win. I've lost faith in our ability to complete the mission."

Before turning away from me, he caustically remarked, "I'm not sure that's the attitude we want in our soldiers."

The colonel was right. I no longer had the right attitude. And although I didn't realize it at the time, he was also right in that there was still an honorable mission for helicopter pilots in Vietnam in seeing that our soldiers arrived home safely.

In the fall of 1970, we had a new president who promised an end to the war. The talks in Paris, however, were going excruciatingly slowly. The loss of support for the war was evident in the protests and demonstrations occurring across the nation. I chose to walk away from a war that my candidates would be sent to, and Susan, Joey, and I returned to California.

As I had told my company commander during the inspection in pre-flight, I still considered law enforcement a career choice. Police departments were hiring, and President Nixon had promised us a new war that made sense, a war here at home I felt I could sink my teeth into, the War on Drugs.

Chapter 6

Go Be a Cop

T he police radio sprang to life with the voice of a female dispatcher. "82-10, San Jose Two."

I picked up the microphone attached to the dashboard. "82-10."

"82-10, report of an 11-83 on Race Street, just north of San Carlos."

"82-10 copies."

It was spring of 1971, around 0400. As a police officer in San Jose, California, I was working alone. My call sign was 82-10. The "eight" meant I was working the midnight shift, "two" indicated I was in district two, and the "ten" referred to my beat (B-10). San Jose Two was the communications channel that handled the west side of town, the even numbered beats. San Jose One handled the east side of town, the odd numbered beats.

Responding to an 11-83 meant I was assigned to investigate the report of an "automobile accident with no further details." Neither fire engines nor ambulances would be dispatched until I arrived on the scene and advised what was needed.

I made a right turn on Stevens Creek Boulevard and crossed over the freeway. Traffic was light, and the streetlights had a soft glow from the morning dew that hung in the air. I turned left on Race Street, where I found a vehicle that had run up on the sidewalk and into a telephone pole.

I took the microphone from the dashboard. "82-10, 11-97."[13] I walked up to the left side of the slightly damaged vehicle and could see that the driver had

---

13. 11-97 meant I had arrived on the scene.

smashed his face into the steering wheel. Blood was running from his nose and upper lip. The interior of the car reeked of alcohol. He tried to say something, but his slurred speech, along with the glazed look in his eyes, indicated he was drunk. I looked across the front seat and could see a female passenger who appeared to be unconscious. This was before handheld radios so I had to walk back to my vehicle.

"San Jose Two, 82-10."

"Go ahead," she responded.

"This is a single vehicle 11-79."[14]

"82-10, ambulance dispatched. Do you need a fill?"[15]

I looked around. Heavier than normal traffic for this time of night was passing on Race Street from the direction of San Carlos, but the crashed vehicle was out of the road, so there was no need for someone to direct traffic. The midnight crews were stretched thin across the city, and I saw no need for a patrol unit from far across town to be taken out of service.

"San Jose Two, 82-10, negative on a fill."

"10-4," she replied.

I walked back to the vehicle and had the driver exit. He was too intoxicated to attempt a field sobriety test. I assisted him back to the patrol car and, while searching to ensure he wasn't carrying any weapons, noticed he was wearing a tuxedo. I informed him he was under arrest for driving under the influence of alcohol and sat him on the curb to wait for the ambulance.

As I walked back to the accident, I paid more attention to the passing cars, the drivers honking their horns, and passengers yelling and waving out the windows. They were driving from a large hall, located near the intersection of Race Street and San Carlos, which was occasionally rented for events like wedding receptions.

These two were part of a wedding.

When I opened the passenger door, the female flopped into my arms. I could sense she wasn't unconscious from drinking, but seriously hurt. *Aw,*

---

14. 11-79 meant there were injuries requiring an ambulance.

15. The dispatcher was asking if I needed any assistance at the scene from another patrol unit.

dad gummit. She was wearing a white wedding dress, and the scene suddenly turned surreal. The rotating lights from my patrol car cast a red pulsing glow in the light fog. A celebrating inebriated crowd drove by, horns blaring, and the bride was sprawled on the sidewalk. She was young and beautiful without a mark on her. The passing cars couldn't see her as the lightly damaged vehicle blocked their view, and I assumed they thought I had only made a traffic stop.

The ambulance crew quickly arrived from the hospital only a few blocks away. They promptly loaded her on a stretcher and placed her in the ambulance. I walked the driver over and assisted him into a seat next to her. Santa Clara County Medical Center was close by, and I knew she'd be attended to quickly.

I finished up with the information I needed for my accident report, took measurements, made a crude drawing to be used later for the detailed report, clicked a few photos, and released the car to the tow truck operator.

"San Jose Two, 82-10, put me 10-7 at county ER."[16]

I walked into the emergency room, where I expected to find chaos, doctors, and nurses rushing around to save a young bride's life, but all was calm and quiet. Only the groom was lying on a bed while someone dressed his upper lip.

"Where's the passenger?" I asked.

A nurse didn't even look up from her paperwork. "DOA."

I shook my head. "Geeze maneez." In the months since leaving the military, I was doing better with the swearing. "Dad gum" and "Geeze maneez" had become my favorite expressions.

"She apparently broke her neck," the nurse said.

I motioned over to the driver. "Anyone draw blood for me?"

The nurse picked up a vile of blood and, with a smile, waved it. "He says they had just been married."

"Yeah, they were a block from the wedding reception, and not one person passing by from the party recognized their car."

"Must have been a hell of a party." She sounded sorry she missed it.

"Has he been notified about his bride yet?"

---

16. I was letting dispatch know I was still out of service, but now at the hospital.

"No, we figured he's in custody, so we're leaving that up to you." She pursed her lips as she dragged out the "you." I thought she might have wanted a kiss. For the nurses and doctors, it was just another night in the emergency room.

The driver was still so drunk that there wasn't much use trying to talk to him, but I had to let him know he was in custody. "Mr. Contreras, I'm placing you under arrest for manslaughter as well as for driving under the influence. Deputies will transport you to the county jail."

He stared for a while and then asked in a slurred voice, "Cindy's dead?"

"Yes."

"Oh no," was all he could say as he turned his face away.

How do you live with that? I went to the cafeteria and finished my report on what was to be my first fatality and first felony arrest. With barely two months of experience as a police officer, it was already clear that, although we were in a declared War on Drugs, alcohol was a much bigger problem.

By 0700, I had finished my report and dropped it off, along with the roll of film, at the police administration building. I then drove down North First Street to the Hyatt where meals were half price to police officers. Around 0755, I pulled into the police garage.

"San Jose Two, 82-10, I'll be 10-7 OD."[17]

"82-10, before going OD, traffic investigations would like you to stop by their office."

"82-10 copies."

I had yet to grace the offices of any detective unit, and, still on probation, I worried about what I must have done wrong. I walked across the parking lot and into the police administration building, down to the basement, and to the far end where traffic investigations was located. About six investigators, older men wearing suits, were just arriving for work. They were drinking coffee, reading newspapers, and going through the slow motions required to get up to working speed.

"Someone looking for Officer Jones?"

No one answered, but I saw a hand from a balding detective, deep into

---

17. I was informing communications that I was going off duty.

reading a report, wave me over. A large, grey-haired lieutenant stormed out of his office and met me at the investigator's desk.

"You had a fatality last night?" the lieutenant asked in a raised voice.

"Yes, sir."

"Well, why weren't we notified?"

I wondered how that was supposed to happen. "I don't know."

"How long have you been a cop?"

"Couple of months."

"You're working alone after only a couple of months?" He was clearly exasperated. "Hasn't anyone told you the procedure when you have a fatality?"

"Well," I thought aloud, "I guess not."

"It's a good report," the detective quietly said, still seated at his desk.

"Look," the lieutenant said, "you need to notify this office immediately when you have a fatality. Understand?" His finger was pointed at me as if he were ready to poke me in the chest. "I have investigators on call for this very thing. We have procedures to follow. Have I made myself clear?"

"Yes, sir."

With that, the lieutenant stomped back to his office and slammed the door behind him.

"All you need to do is notify communications from the scene," the detective said. "They'll notify us." Then he added with a smile, "Don't worry about this. You wrote a good report, and the perp's in custody. Not much for me to do except walk it over to the DA.[18] Just the way I like it, Jones." His smile broadened into a big grin.

Briefing the next night went smoothly, and I thought it was all behind me until, as we were all heading out to our patrol cars, I heard my sergeant, Bert Kelsey, call my name. He was the kind of supervisor his team rarely saw unless something was wrong.

"You had a fatality last night?" he asked.

Here we go again.

"Yes, Sarge."

---

18. district attorney

"Why wasn't I notified?" he asked in a growl.

"I didn't know the procedure. I do now. It won't happen again,"

He gave a grunt of acknowledgement and started to leave, but then turned back. "By the way, traffic said you gave them an excellent report."

Two months earlier, after a written test and an oral board, several others and I had been hired. There was no police academy or field training program, and, luckily for me, no psychological examination. I had walked into the office of Ray Blackmore, the chief since 1947, and he swore me in and gave me badge 383. I was told to report on the following Wednesday at 2200 for the midnight shift. I had a gun and a badge, and I was expected to go be a cop.

I was assigned to work with Fred Farnsworth, a soft-spoken senior patrol officer, and the first several weeks were typical: family fights, drunk drivers, false burglar alarms, and minor vehicle accidents. We worked ten-hour shifts, four days a week. I had Sundays, Mondays, and Tuesdays off.

During the first month, if Farnsworth took a day off, I was assigned to a different beat with another partner. One night, I had the opportunity to work with Walt Atkins, a tall, athletic officer. It was slow as we patrolled the east foothills of San Jose, and Atkins was giving me advice as he drove.

"One of the problems with police work is that, if you do your job right, no one will notice."

He had my attention. "I'm not sure I follow."

"Well, it looks good when you make arrests. That's the easy thing to do, and you get noticed for having all those statistics at the end of the month. If you're doing a good job, though, that sometimes means settling the situation peacefully. So that could mean, at the end of the shift, the officer who goes off duty not having made one arrest might have done a better job than the officer who couldn't leave the family fight or disturbance at the bar without booking someone." I remembered that conversation, although I didn't always heed his advice.

After I completed my six-month probationary period, I worked a one-man car as much as possible, preferring B-10. A blue-collar community at the time, I had lived in that area until age seven.

At the end of World War II, my father purchased a new home on Baywood

Avenue, a short street that ran south off Stevens Creek between Winchester and Bascom Avenues. Besides Baywood, the little subdivision consisted of Redwood and Clover Avenues, all of which Hemlock Avenue enclosed. This was considered "in the country" back then, and the rest of the area was orchards.

The southeast corner of Stevens Creek and Winchester, though, was a field encompassing several acres. It was here, at the age of six, that my actions resulted in meeting my first police officer. I had crawled through the tall, dry grass. I made trails and cleared areas for forts so I could battle invading forces. I had also brought along matches. As a novice in experimentation, things got out of hand, but I made it home safe and, I thought, unseen. Mom and I walked over and watched with excitement as the fire department, with all their wonderful red trucks, brought the inferno under control.

When it was over and we were home, safe behind closed doors, a San Jose police officer visited. This was pre-Miranda, so he didn't inform me of any rights to remain silent. Under the finesse of his skillful interrogation, coupled with the color of authority I sensed from his uniform, gun, and badge, I confessed. He left with the assurance from me that I had learned my lesson. As evidenced by my later experiments with high voltage, explosive gases, and homemade gunpowder, apparently the only lesson I learned that day was not to get caught.

Within that first year on the police department, Susan and I were living up on top of the Santa Cruz Mountains in a beautiful home with a view of Santa Clara Valley below. I honored her requests and came straight home after work on Sunday mornings in order for us to go to church at Calvary in Los Gatos where we were active with the young married group. I then had the rest of Sunday off, all day Monday, and Tuesday and didn't have to report back to work until Wednesday night. Susan was working as a beautician at her mom's shop in Los Gatos, and I'd look after Joey during the day. Susan was able to adjust her work hours accordingly so we had plenty of time to spend together and with both sides of the family. I had access to an airplane, and we'd frequently fly to South Lake Tahoe for a day or two. Life was good, and all was well with the world.

San Jose Police Department, with Aussie who joins me later.

On workdays, I arrived at the police station a half hour early and dressed in the locker room. I prepared for battle every evening. My "chicken plate" was now a second-chance vest worn under my neatly pressed dark blue uniform shirt upon which a plain, but shiny, silver star was pinned. After the dark blue pants with white stripe down the side, I put on my highly polished combat boots. I could smell the leather as I swung my heavy belt, containing holster, handcuffs, flashlight holder, extra ammunition, and a nightstick ring, around my waist and secured it in front with a large silver buckle. I checked to ensure my .357-caliber revolver, carrying a fresh scent of cleaning oil, was loaded before I slipped it into the holster. I slid a nightstick into the ring holder. Before heading to briefing, I stopped in front of a full-length mirror and admired myself.

Midnight shift briefing started promptly at 2200 and consisted of taking roll call, discussing crime trends in the different beats, and pertinent administrative matters. A half hour later, we'd drive out to our respective beats and directly into situations everyday citizens would flee from.

It was around 0200 one Sunday when I received a call. "82-10, San Jose Two."

"82-10, go ahead."

"82-10, numerous reports of a 4-15[19] at the farm house at Cypress and Stevens Creek."

The location was a home subject to frequent Saturday night/early Sunday morning complaints. San Jose still had large tracts of undeveloped land, and in the area east of Cypress Avenue was a large walnut orchard. In the middle of this orchard, set back from Stevens Creek, stood an old, two-story Victorian farmhouse. The San Jose chapter of the Hell's Angels had rented this home as a place to gather and party on weekends. Behind the home was a large bonfire pit surrounded by bleachers, which, I suspected, came from a Little League field. When the Angels became too boisterous, played music too loud, cranked up their Harleys, and spun circles out in the orchard, nearby citizens would complain.

I drove down the dirt driveway to the house. As I exited my patrol car, I could see dozens of bikers and their "mommas" sitting in the glow around the fire. Beer cans, whiskey bottles, and empty pizza boxes were scattered around. Seeing I

19. A 4-15 was code for disturbing the peace.

had arrived, they quieted down. A lone biker in dirty jeans and a vest over a bare chest, beer in hand, met me at the car.

Members of the Hell's Angels wore "colors" on the back of their jackets or vests. A skull with wings, known as the "death head," was in the center under an upper rocker, a white patch with the words "Hell's Angels" in red. Below the death head was a lower rocker, a white patch with the location of the club. I had seen lower rockers that said Oakland or Frisco. The back of this character's vest had only a lower rocker with the word "California." Wearing only the lower rocker meant he was a prospect to join the Hell's Angels. Prospects did menial jobs for the members, which included meeting and dealing with the cops.

"Evening, officer, what's the problem?"

I knew his job was to keep me back at the car and convince me that all would be fine so that I'd just leave, so I walked past him and into the backyard where all could hear.

"I'm getting tired of coming out here. This is the last time." I probably sounded like a parent nagging his teenager.

They snickered and taunted, "Like, what are you going to do, Mister Policeman?" or "We're sorry, officer. We'll never do it again."

"Look," the prospect said, "we're only members of a club having a good time. You know, a club like the one you belong to."

He had a point. Bikers and cops belonged to exclusive organizations with similar traits. Membership was a gratifying emotional experience. They displayed fraternal loyalty. Membership involved risk taking and trust in other members. There was a hierarchy where members on the bottom took the greater risks. Members of these organizations each thought that his group was smarter, braver, stronger, and more self-reliant than anyone else was.

"Except for one big difference," I said to the prospect, nudging him back as he was standing too close. "I'm willing to wear my colors into your club and tell you to knock it off."

Hooting and laughter went up from the crowd, directed at the prospect who had failed to keep me back at the patrol car, making him look bad in the process.

Several weeks later, the Angels had another large party. When I received a call from dispatch, I acknowledged it, but never responded. Citing a Hell's Angel for disturbing the peace, my only option, would have been a wasted effort. The only other officer working district two that night and I had plans, though. Around 0400, when all was quiet and I was fairly convinced the bikers at the old farmhouse were asleep, I gave Officer Ray Berrett a call and asked him to meet me in the parking lot of a movie theater on Winchester Boulevard.

We finalized our plan, and then I drove over to the eastern side of the orchard by the Hell's Angel's farmhouse, parked, and walked in through the trees. Berrett drove around to the far western side and walked in. The bonfire had burned down to glowing embers. Many Angels were asleep on the ground, others were in the house, and no one seemed to be stirring. Someone, hopefully the same prospect, was supposed to be on watch. Berrett and I each set four large firecrackers, M-80s, attached to cigarettes as fuses around the perimeter and then hurried back to our patrol cars.

I drove over to the Bob's Big Boy on Winchester where I told dispatch that I'd be off the air because a citizen was waving me down. Berrett dashed up Stevens Creek where he went off the air by making a car stop. Several minutes later, I heard the sounds of the M-80s exploding in the distance. After several more minutes, the call came from the radio.

"All units, report of shots fired Cypress and Stevens Creek."

A call from a lieutenant quickly followed. "All units responding, 10-87 at Town and Country."

I gave it a minute and then came back on the air. "San Jose Two, 82-10 is 10-8. What's the traffic?"

"82-10, shots fired in the vicinity of Cypress and Stevens Creek. Units responding are to meet at Town and Country Shopping Center."

I met the lieutenant at the shopping center, now built on the site where, twenty years earlier, I had set the field ablaze. Four other units from across town finally arrived, including Berrett, who certainly wasn't going to miss the pending confrontation. We then took off in a convoy of flashing red lights.

Dust from the patrol cars speeding up the driveway billowed through the night air, reflecting the flashing red beacons and white spotlights. The confused Hell's Angel in charge already had the half-dressed and hung-over partiers standing in line, and he was giving them grief as he suspected one of them had, in fact, fired a gun.

It was a wonderful sight, and Berrett and I did our best to stifle smiles as the lieutenant took over and placed the Angel in charge in line with everyone else. By the time we left, the house, the motorcycles, and all the personal gear and clothing had been thoroughly tossed in search of a weapon. None was found, no one was arrested, and it was the last time the Angels met at that location. Atkins was right. Sometimes doing the right thing meant settling the situation peacefully without arresting anyone. My solution, though, was probably not what he had in mind.

Early one morning, I was dispatched to take a report of a 2-61A, attempted rape. I pulled up to the address on Cadillac Drive.

A middle-aged woman solemnly greeted me. "Someone tried to rape my daughter Rosemary." She led me into the apartment.

A young teenage girl sat with her face in her hands at the kitchen table. I could tell she'd been crying hard for some time. She didn't seem ready to talk.

"I'm sorry, Rosemary," I said. "Just give me an overview of what happened tonight."

"We were at a party, and this guy offered to drive me home. He seemed nice, but he stopped the car in a parking lot." She paused to collect herself. "He raped me." She then started sobbing.

Her mom's body slumped, and then she wrapped her arms around her daughter. I was momentarily at a loss for words. I went over to the phone in the kitchen and called communications, informing them that this was a rape. APW[20] Sharon Moore was on duty, and I requested they dispatch her to my location.

I then returned to the table. "Rosemary, I have a policewoman coming over. I think you'll be more comfortable talking about the details with her."

Rosemary looked relieved.

"What can you tell me about this guy?" I asked.

---

20. assistant policewoman

"All I know is his name is Donnie."

"Tell me about his car."

"It's a Chevy, I think. Blue."

"Who else at this party would know Donnie."

"Traci. You need to talk to Traci. She introduced us."

By the time Moore arrived, I had plenty of information. Moore would file a supplemental report with more explicit details.

Normally, this would be the end of the investigation for a patrol officer. He'd file the report, and detectives would follow up. The patrol officer would go back in service, ready to respond to the next emergency. I took a different view of the circumstances. This happened on my beat, in territory under my responsibility, and I wanted to personally identify and arrest this asshole.

"Asshole" was the most common adjective in a cop's daily vocabulary. Assholes were the troublemakers and perpetrators of crime. I was learning that, as police officers, we saw ourselves as the blunt tool of righteousness in protecting the community from these punks. As a young, inexperienced cop at the time, on a quest for justice, I tried to treat everyone with respect. But perpetrators of these crimes were assholes.

APW Moore contacted me from the hospital and said an examination confirmed that the victim had been raped and there had been plenty of bleeding. By 0600, I found myself pounding on the door where Traci lived. This was disturbing to the family, even after learning their daughter wasn't in trouble.

"Did you see who Rosemary left the party with?" I asked a sleepy Traci.

"A guy named Donnie. He lives on a street off Payne and drives a blue Chevy."

At 0800 hours, while the entire midnight shift, along with my supervisors, went home, I kept working. I cruised each of the possible streets off Payne: Eden, Lexington, and Essex. I found a 1966 blue Chevrolet Super Sport parked in the driveway of a home in the area. I gave the license plate information to communications, and the registration came back to a Donald who resided at the house where the Chevy was parked. Looking through the windows of the Chevrolet, I could see what appeared to be smeared, dried blood in the middle of the seat.

A cheerful woman appeared at the front door. "May I help you, officer?"

"I need to talk to Donnie."

"He's asleep. Can I help you?" She had a pleasant smile.

"I don't know yet. Bring him out here, or I'm going in to get him." The tone of my voice told her that something was wrong.

If Donnie had been asleep, he did a great job of waking up refreshed. He was charismatic and polite, and he had a good answer for every question I initially threw at him. After an hour, though, he finally confessed. His car was sealed and towed to the police garage. While his wailing mom collapsed on the front steps, I loaded a handcuffed Donnie into the patrol car and headed back to the police department.

"San Jose Two, 82-10, notify sexual assaults that I'm 10-15, 10-19."[21]

I had a sense of accomplishment in arresting him, but the trauma and anxiety experienced by the victim, the mothers, the witnesses, and their families over-shadowed it. It was nearly noon when I dropped off my reports and the suspect to the waiting detectives on the third floor. The bureau of investigations (BOI) was hallowed ground for a young patrolman, and I felt uncomfortable intruding. I was made to feel at ease, though, as they appeared impressed with my work.

"Hey, Jones'y," one called out as I was leaving. "Come on down to Bini's this evening. We owe you one."

I had been working four hours overtime and had to be back at work in ten hours. There was no way I was going to be able to go to Bini's in the evening, but it felt good to be invited to the honored watering hole of those who walked the halls of BOI.

Bini's was a classless, battered bar and grill that had been around since 1932. Located on the northeastern side of town in the old deserted cannery district, attorneys, detectives, and local businessmen who appreciated the rustic atmo-sphere would frequent it at lunchtime. In the evening hours, the detectives would be back, bellying up to the bar with the local bums.

Patrol officers had their own spots for gathering. The swing shift crews, who went off duty at 0200, held their "choir practice" in a chosen parking lot. There they'd drink confiscated beer and swap stories to relax before heading home. The midnight crew showed up by 0830 at a dive called Bruni's. Located south

---

21. I was letting them know I was returning to headquarters with the suspect in custody.

of downtown, it was in an area of rough bars and cheap hotels that rented rooms by the hour. The "midnighters" would have a couple of drinks to unwind before heading home to sleep the rest of the day before reporting back that night.

Whether it was at Bruni's, Bini's, or in the parking lot, cop gatherings always included heated discussions about departmental "bullshit," probably the second-most frequently used word in our gritty vocabulary. As cops, we used our authority on a daily basis, yet perceived the authority from management and supervisors as bullshit. In complaining, it was like whining that our brother was a son of a bitch.

A few days a week, I'd stop by Bruni's. On occasion, when it had been a particularly rough night and we all had plenty of stories to tell, I'd come home late and sleep through the evening, missing dinner with Susan and Joey. I was also finding reasons to avoid going to church.

"Can't you start working the day shift?" Susan asked.

"The best I could get would be Tuesday, Wednesday and Thursday off. I'd be working all day Sunday."

"At least you'd have the evenings off so we could do things with the family. What about swing shift?"

"That's the most popular shift. I don't have enough seniority and would still only have the middle of the week off."

" Well, at least we could go to church." Susan didn't like my work hours or the alternatives. I was happy on midnights.

Work continued to involve the routine tasks of a city police officer. Domestic disputes were common and often dangerous. Once I arrested a husband for physical abuse and then the wife attacked me for removing the family breadwinner. There were suicides, like the pretty thirty-eight-year-old redhead I found days after she had chased a bottle of aspirin with a pint of gin. Fatal vehicle accidents were emotionally difficult, such as the time I had to view the body of a six year old with a freshly stapled "Y" incision down his chest from the doctors' frantic attempt to save his life. Then there were house fires—like the one with the charred remains of the elderly couple who were trapped inside. Alcohol played a role in most of those circumstances. I saw few problems with drugs, and, when I did, the situation usually also involved alcohol.

Foot chases weren't uncommon, and, on a few occasions, someone would want to fight. That usually ended with me getting a chokehold on the suspect, his Adam's apple in the crook of my arm, and squeezing tightly until he passed out. I would then let him drop to the ground. Upon regaining consciousness, the suspect would flop around as he fought to breathe. Police officers referred to this as "making him do the chicken."

And after nearly two years on the department, I began to realize that I was no longer giving people I encountered the benefit of the doubt. I now considered everyone an asshole until he proved otherwise.

On August 18, 1973, around 2300, I was working 85-03, a midnight shift in district five, beat three, just east of downtown.

"85-03, San Jose One."

"85-03."

"85-03, report of a shooting at 652 North Tenth Street. Ambulance has been dispatched."

"85-03 copies." I made a left on Taylor Street and, with lights flashing, headed to Tenth. I turned right, and the address was several homes down. Two agitated females were waiting outside. They led me to a back bedroom where a third female was attending Jasper Turco, a twenty-six year old. He was in bed, leaning against the headboard. His T-shirt was pulled up, and I could see six bullet holes at critical points in his torso. *Oh, this isn't going to end well.*

His belly was extended due to internal bleeding, and he labored to breathe. There was no blood except for a slight oozing from one of the three exit wounds on his backside. *What's with these bullet wounds that don't bleed?*

I knelt beside the bed. "Who shot you?"

"I don't know."

I looked at the women in the room. "Who shot him?"

The young women only gave a series of looks at Turco and me. They knew, but weren't talking. Officer Bob Gummow showed up to assist, and I asked him to remove the women from the room and get their identifying information. When they left, I continued my conversation with Turco.

"I can't get this guy without your help."

He gasped for air. "I'll take care of it."

"Listen to me. This is bad. Your chest cavity is filling with blood, and it's getting harder for you to breathe." I hesitated to let that sink in. "You're going to die, Mr. Turco. Do you understand this?"

He stared at me while struggling to breathe and then simply said, "Yes."

"Understanding that you're going to die, are you willing to tell me who shot you?"

"Yes, it was Columbo."

He had just given me a dying declaration. Ordinarily, I couldn't testify to what Jasper Turco told me because it would be hearsay. By acknowledging he was going to die, though, this meant the statement he gave me, if he did, in fact, die, would be admissible in court.

Police officers are usually focused on saving a victim's life, so they don't have the opportunity or time to properly ask the question. It was also difficult to look a dying victim in the eye and get him to acknowledge that he's in the last moments of his life.

Turco had no further information, and had slipped into unconsciousness by the time the ambulance arrived. Gummow followed the victim to the hospital, and I stayed behind to further question the witnesses. I informed them that Turco had named his assailant, and they seemed relieved and ready to talk. Two of the young women were eyewitnesses to the shooting. Based on their statements, Columbo had been over earlier in the day, and Turco had thrown him out of the house because he was causing a disturbance with one of the women.

I followed up on where Columbo might be while Detectives Arca and Harrison processed the crime scene. They finally identified the suspect as Salvatore Castiglia, who went by the nicknames of Sam and Columbo. Turco expired, and, on September 7, Castiglia surrendered to homicide detectives.

By December, I had forgotten the Castiglia case, so I was concerned when asked to report to Sergeant Bobby Burroughs in the homicide division. Burroughs, short and stocky, had wavy gray hair that was beginning to thin. He was energetic in everything he did, including chain smoking. An old school cop, he'd been with the department since 1957, and he was a legend, with all respecting him. I had only seen Burroughs from afar, and the privilege of entering the homicide unit and meeting with him was unnerving.

"Jones'y," he said with a big smile.

How does he know me? He was gracious as he invited me to sit beside his desk. He quickly put me at ease, and, after some pleasant small talk, he opened a file folder and got down to business.

"Good job on this Castiglia case. Motions in superior court are coming up, and the DA office wants me to follow up on this statement you took from Turco. Tell me about your interview with him." Burroughs was leaning back in his chair with his hands behind his head.

"Not much more I can say that's not in the report," I said.

"The defense is going to hammer you." Burroughs sat forward. "So there's no question in your mind, no doubt, that Turco understood and acknowledged he was going to die?"

I was confident. "No, none whatsoever."

We continued to talk about the case, upcoming testimony, and tactics of the defense. Burroughs was truly caring and kept me feeling comfortable. When I returned to earth, to the patrol division, I had a better understanding why Burroughs was so respected. He certainly left me feeling more secure about future forays up to BOI.

When the Castiglia case finally came to trial, I testified in superior court, and the jury convicted him of second-degree murder.

———————

Terry Moudakas, the "Greek," was an outstanding cop who worked with his canine, Celto. A few years earlier, the Greek and his dog were instrumental in locating and arresting Emile Thompson. The son of an Oakland police officer, Thompson was a political radical and Black Panther sympathizer who stalked and murdered Officer Richard Huerta as Huerta was writing a citizen a traffic ticket.

Huerta didn't "pass away" as citizens might remark among themselves when a loved one died. He didn't die a "glorious death" as historians have written for centuries about those who gave their lives in battle while protecting society. Police officers and soldiers know that's the stuff of Hollywood. Huerta was cowardly assassinated, and it took professionalism and restraint from Moudakas and other officers to take Thompson alive.

Moudakas worked the midnight shift, and he was always willing to work with and give guidance to officers junior to him. So in 1973, when I expressed an interest in working with the canine unit, Moudakas gave me a fully trained German shepherd by the name of Aussie. Working a canine turned out to be excellent duty because, in an effort to keep them available for crimes in progress, canine units were relieved from the more mundane assignments. Whether it was chasing down fleeing perpetrators, searching for hidden burglars, or looking for lost children, working with Aussie was a rewarding experience.

During this time, the department, under the direction of Chief Bob Murphy who had replaced the retiring Ray Blackmore, initiated a field training program for new officers. I was selected as a field training officer (FTO) and had the opportunity to work with many outstanding trainees such as Officer Joe Ireland. One evening, he was driving as we traveled west on Alum Rock Avenue when an ambulance, running red lights and siren, passed us heading east.

"That car's following the ambulance awful close," Ireland said.

He'd already proven himself to be competent, and I was slumped in my seat, not paying attention. *An anxious husband following a pregnant wife to the hospital?*

"Do whatever you think you should."

Ireland hung a U-turn and quickly caught up with the light blue Plymouth Valiant. When he hit the red lights, the Plymouth took off.

I sat up and grabbed the microphone. "85-03's in pursuit. Eastbound Alum Rock approaching King."

"All units, code three traffic," the dispatcher broadcasted. "85-03's in pursuit. Eastbound Alum Rock approaching King."

The chase was on, and we were hitting speeds of ninety miles an hour, weaving through traffic and busting through intersections against red lights as I continued to call out the streets we were crossing. The driver, later identified as Phillip Weber, was a hundred yards ahead when he tried to turn left onto White Road. With his excessive speed, he lost control and slid sideways into the lanes of opposing traffic, which, luckily, were clear. Upon regaining control, he drove behind a closed gas station where he tried to hide. Ireland skidded into the lot and tried to block Weber's exit with the patrol car, which suddenly died.

My adrenalin was pumping, and I jumped out. As I did, Weber floored it and managed to squeak by the left side of the patrol vehicle. Dust and dirt were flying from the gravel parking lot as Weber peeled away. As he hit the pavement, the car spun out in the westbound lanes and stalled. I ran out and stood in the street, fifty feet in front of the car, yelling for the driver to get his hands up where I could see them. Instead, Weber decided to go toe to toe, his vehicle as his weapon. He restarted his car and popped it into gear, and the tires burned blue smoke as the car accelerated forward. *Oh, Jesus. Here we go.*

At moments like this, I was most aware of life. I jumped up and pushed off the front right fender as the car struck my shins, knocking me down. As the car careened by, Weber made a sweeping left turn, crossing into the eastbound lanes before circling back into the westbound lanes where I again stood.

Shit, this guy's trying to kill me.

As the car approached, smoke belching from the spinning, screaming rear tires, I drew my service revolver and fired one shot directly at Weber. I jumped clear of the car's sweeping turn, and, as it continued past me, I fired three more shots at the tires. Weber managed to straighten out and drove off, westbound on Alum Rock. It was suddenly quiet at the scene of the assault as billowing blue clouds dissipated into the night air.

Ireland wasn't able to restart the patrol vehicle. We were now stranded, unable to continue the pursuit. Witnesses who had followed Weber from the scene pointed out the Plymouth to a swing shift unit. Weber had pulled off to the side of a road with three flat tires. He was still behind the wheel, but was close to bleeding to death. The first round I had fired ripped through his upper arm and tore the major artery. Weber recovered and, after witnesses testified that they observed him run me down, was convicted and sentenced to prison.

———•———

While most criminals like Weber were punks and dismissed as assholes, there was another term for the real threatening and dangerous perpetrator, the "bad ass." It was a term spoken in hushed voices and serious tones, with a certain knowing look in the cop's eye. The armed robber was the quintessential bad ass, the guy who could stick a gun in someone's face and demand money. If he thought someone might identify him, he would just as soon blow him away.

San Jose was having a rash of 2-11s, armed robberies, of mom-and-pop stores. The suspects were always two male adults, Afro hairdos, one armed, with no vehicle seen. The robbers were so successful and so frequent that members of the MERGE[22] unit were hiding in selected stores, shotguns at the ready, hoping to catch them in the act.

After midnight, working 85-03, I was driving on Julian Street with Aussie in the back. I was not assigned a recruit this night.

San Jose One suddenly had an assignment for a swing shift unit. "61-07, a 2-11 just occurred …"

I floored the accelerator, crossed over the freeway, and then made a quick left turn across traffic so I could take the on-ramp for northbound traffic on Highway 101. Hot chases might have been exciting, but catching armed robbers was the ultimate achievement in my book. *Maybe these guys are out of Oakland.*

I pulled off to the side of the on-ramp where I could get a fairly good look at passing cars. Shortly after stopping, I had a glance at a passing car with a front passenger who wore an Afro. I punched the accelerator and screamed onto the freeway, taking nearly a mile to catch up.

"85-03, 11-95."[23]

I hit the red lights, and, as the car pulled over, I called communications again

---

22. Mobile Emergency Response Group and Equipment, known as the SWAT Team on other departments

23. I was informing communications that I was making a car stop.

and gave them the license plate and location of the stop. I then flooded the interior of the stopped vehicle with the brilliant white light from my spotlight. I could see three more individuals seated in the back.

Dad gummit. Five people were in the car, leading me to think these were probably not the perpetrators. I got out of the patrol car, circled wide behind it, and approached the stopped vehicle on the passenger side. Everyone in the car was looking around to their left, expecting me to approach the driver's side. I stood slightly behind the right rear window where I could observe that the hands of the passengers appeared normal. No one seemed to be trying to conceal anything or, worse, holding a weapon. I did notice a banana peel on the dashboard in front of the passenger. All five were startled as I tapped the right rear window. The passenger at the window rolled it down.

"Driver, you have faulty tail lights," I lied. "Would you please step back here and bring your vehicle registration?"

He exited and met me back at the patrol car. He didn't have registration.

"Whose car is it?"

"It's Freddy's. He's in the front seat."

I started filling out a three-by-five field interrogation (FI) card on the driver. FI cards were useful to detectives in solving crimes when the patrol officer didn't have the information necessary to make a case in the field. While completing the card, the swing shift unit taking the report at the scene of the robbery came on the air.

"San Jose One, 61-07, two black males came up to the counter to buy a banana ..."

My senses went on high alert, but I acted as if nothing was wrong. I quickly entered my vehicle on the passenger side and turned down the volume on the radio. Luckily, those not used to listening to police communications found it hard to understand.

I also picked up the mike and simply said, "San Jose One, 85-03, make this an 11-96."

Communications knew I was indicating that this was now a car stop where I wanted a fill.

I went back to the driver who was standing in front of my vehicle. "I'm going to ask you to have a seat while I talk with Freddy about whose car this is."

Aussie got out, I patted down the driver to ensure he wasn't carrying a weapon, and I had him sit in the rear of the patrol car. When I closed the door, he was automatically locked in. I walked back to the stopped vehicle.

"Freddy, this your car?"

"It's my uncle's."

"Okay, step back while I write this down."

Freddy got out and walked back where Aussie obediently waited. As soon as he was out of the beam from the spotlight, where the remaining passengers would have a hard time observing while looking into the blinding glare, I immediately cuffed him and placed him in the back with his buddy. I was down to one set of handcuffs with three more suspects in the vehicle, and I was wondering how far away my fill was.

With Aussie at my side as cars zoomed by on the freeway, I removed, at gunpoint, the remaining three suspects from their vehicle. Aussie's tongue was hanging out as she panted, and she appeared to be grinning with anticipation. As each suspect cautiously eyed her, Aussie seemed to be advising, "You have the right to run. Should you decide to run ..."

Aussie was disappointed when no one chose to flee. When my fill arrived, the other officer kept cover as I searched the car. I found the gun and money in a paper bag under the front seat.

As defendants were being interrogated, reports were filed, the banana peel and other evidence was booked, and congratulations were offered from all corners of the BOI.

"Officer Jones."

I looked up from my paperwork. It was Sergeant Larry Darr, a sharply dressed detective who worked the robbery division. Always carrying a military bearing, Darr lived and breathed robbery cases as if they were his sole reason for existing.

"I've been working these guys for a long time. Good job. Friday evening at the Foghorn. Be there. I owe you one."

The Foghorn was an upscale bar and restaurant conveniently located close to city and county administration offices. On any evening, customers from the district attorney, city hall, and county offices crowded the place. Plenty of young women seeking to meet lawyers and detectives also frequented the Foghorn.

That Friday morning, I took several hours off at the end of the shift to get some decent sleep. I rose early in the evening and showed up at the Foghorn. It was crowded at the bar, but Darr was holding court with a covey of young ladies and other detectives down at the far end. Upon seeing me, they made room. Drinks were ordered again and again, stories were told and embellished, and laughter filled the room. I was having a grand time, and it felt good to be included in the camaraderie. My heart, though, wasn't where it should have been, at home with Susan and Joey.

I knew the secret to being an unusually successful cop was to have a reliable informant. As a patrolman, though, I was finding that this wasn't easy. Around 0300, I stopped Donald Ray Signorelli on Vine, a one-way street in an older residential area. From the moment we made eye contact, I suspected he was one bad dude. I had him exit the vehicle, and, while he was getting his driver's license and registration, we watched each other like a cat would watch a mouse, each ready to pounce.

In what might have been an illegal search, I found a loaded handgun in the car. He was a parolee for an armed robbery conviction, though, and whether the search was legal or not wasn't an issue. He was going back to prison for violation of parole, and he knew it.

He decided to talk in return for me not immediately notifying his parole officer and provided information on a recent burglary in which a safe had been broken into. Subsequent arrests were made, and I had now come to the attention of the detectives working in the burglary division.

Signorelli was a true bad ass. He had several convictions for armed offenses and had survived being shot seven times by other gangsters. He later mentioned to me that, had I made one mistake the night I made the stop on him, he'd have shot me rather than risk returning to prison. I believed him.

I continued to hold the gun offense over him, and he continued to work as my informant. He was able to clear up several more burglary offenses, all safe jobs, and later assisted on narcotics cases. He was eventually shot and killed within his own world of violence.

I showed up for work one night in 1974 and saw an announcement that several positions were available for assignment to the narcotics division. A briefing was to be held for those interested.

Despite the so-called War on Drugs, I was hardly aware that we had a narcotics unit. The only time I had heard anything about them was when one narcotics detective, Tommy Perez, mistakenly shot and seriously wounded undercover detective Jim LeRoy. There certainly weren't any recent headlines in the *San Jose Mercury News* about large narcotics seizures. As a police officer, I had yet to see a serious problem with drugs in the community. Alcohol was, by far, the drug that was causing most of our community's problems. National nightly news, though, stressed the War on Drugs, and my interest in narcotics hadn't waned since joining the department. I made a point of attending the briefing.

Chapter 7

They're Just Dopers

Working undercover, I parked my Harley in the driveway at Carter's house and walked in. I was surprised to see "Dirty Doug" Bontempi sitting in the living room all alone. Heavyset and unshaven, he was wearing filthy jeans with a black leather vest over a black T-shirt. He gave me a hard stare as I walked through. I placed a six-pack I had brought into the refrigerator and called out to Carter. No one answered, so I took a beer, popped the top, went back into the living room, and sat down.

"I don't get a beer?" Dirty Doug asked.

I wiped spilt beer into my beard with the back of my hand. "Who the hell are you?"

"None of your business."

I laughed. "Well, none of my business means none of my beer."

He watched as I drank. I motioned with my hand toward the kitchen. "Get your own damn beer."

He just sat. "What are you doing here?"

"Well, aren't we both a bucket full of questions?" I spiced it up with profanity. "I came here to drink my beer."

I took another drink. When I looked back, Dirty Doug was pointing a revolver at me.

Shit, where the hell did that come from? I could see the copper-coated bullets in the cylinder. Past narcotics training started racing through my mind, like why and when you're supposed to have someone backing you up.

It had been a year since I had been to the meeting for those interested in the narcotics division, when working undercover seemed only a distant possibility. Lieutenant Arnold Bertotti held the briefing.

"Good afternoon." He motioned to two men on his left. "This is Sergeant Terry Boone and Sergeant Larry Fernsworth."

Lieutenant Bertotti was stocky with a full head of hair worn in a 1960s Ricky Nelson pompadour style. His thick glasses made his eyes look large. He had a reputation as a hard-drinking, old school cop who stood up for his men. Those who knew Bertotti referred to him as "the boss." Boone, tall and lean, was clean cut with short hair, and he had a reputation as a slow, methodical, and thorough investigator. Fernsworth, sporting a goatee, wore long, unkempt hair to his shoulders. His clothes were tattered, and he looked like the guy I passed on the way to the department that morning, standing at the intersection with a sign saying "will work for food." Before being introduced, I assumed he was a recent arrestee who was there as a prop to show what drug abuse can do to one's body and soul. *He's working undercover, cool.*

Bertotti continued, "As you know, this nation is now in a War on Drugs. The federal government has provided monetary grants to police departments across the nation for equipment and personnel, so we're able to expand the narcotics division by ten men. If chosen, you will be giving up your four-day workweek for five. You'll be working at all different hours of the day and night, and you can expect to put in plenty of overtime." Bertotti informed us of other administrative details and concluded, "If I don't already know who you are, don't expect to be appointed to this unit."

I left the briefing with the feeling I had wasted my afternoon. There was no way that Bertotti knew who I was. I had never made a significant drug arrest, only a few cases for possession of pills like Seconal or Phenobarbital. Other than in training classes, I'd never seen cocaine, methamphetamine, or heroin. When I encountered marijuana on the streets and the suspect didn't fail the personality test, meaning he was polite and respectful, I did what most police officers were doing at the time. I dumped it on the ground and told the suspect that he'd be arrested if I caught him again.

So several weeks later, I was surprised to see my name on the list of those transferring to narcotics. In conducting an internal background investigation, Bertotti found I had a good reputation with the rest of the BOI.

Susan was receptive to the news. "A two year assignment?"

"That's what I understand."

"So you'll have weekends off?"

"Yeah. It's five days a week, though. Some overtime once in a while."

"Well good. At least we'll have the evenings and weekends. We'll be able to function as a family again."

The new fifteen-man narcotics division was organized into three teams: the street team, the buy team, and the major violator team. The men on the street team were clean-cut and wore work clothes such as Levis and collared shirts. Their main duty was to work in unmarked cars and arrest people in possession or under the influence of drugs. They also conducted surveillance, monitored wires that undercover officers wore, trailed suspects, and served search warrants. Officers assigned included Lew Smith, Craig Buckhout, and experienced narcotics officer Bob Grant. Each of these guys was a "cop's cop." Grant was the kind of cop who could spot someone under the influence of a drug while walking down the street two blocks away. Smith could smell a revolver hidden behind a dashboard. Buckhout could spot a postage stamp-sized package of cocaine being tossed from a speeding car as it turned a corner. These guys looked like cops, walked like cops, talked like cops, and, no matter how you dressed them up, the look in their eyes said "I'm a cop."

The goal of the street team was to flip those arrested. Those who flipped, that is, those who agreed to work in exchange for leniency from the DA, were turned over to the buy team. The buy team consisted of undercover officers who created new identities for themselves. Headed up by experienced Sergeant Fernsworth, the team included Dee Avila and Mike Mendez. Fernsworth could infiltrate any group and buy anything from anyone: heroin, cocaine, speed, a stolen tractor, or weird sex. Avila was as nice, gentle, and clean-cut as anyone could be. He just didn't look like a cop. Even in a police uniform driving a patrol vehicle, he might arouse suspicion that he was a kid who had stolen the police car. Mendez was also a perfect fit for the buy team as he had the ability to blend in, infiltrate, and buy drugs from middle to upper-level dealers.

Those who the street team had arrested and flipped introduced members of the buy team to dealers. After a member of the buy team made several purchases, the street team served warrants and arrested the dealers. Drug dealers willing to cooperate and give information on major suppliers were then turned over to the third group, the major violator team.

The purpose of the major violator team, led by Sergeant Boone, was to identify the upper-level drug dealers. By using information from informants and other intelligence methods such as surveillance, phone records, and financial records, the major violator team made cases against those suspected of being sources for drugs. I, along with Officer Dan Gutierrez, was assigned to the major violator team.

It didn't take long for the narcotics division to start making cases with the system working as planned. Grant, Buckhout, and Smith arrested drug users and small-time street dealers and turned some into informants. These informants were turned over to the buy team where Avila and Mendez bought heroin and cocaine.

In the beginning, the informants turned over to the major violator team were providing information on dealers who were selling what we considered at the time to be large quantities, ounces of heroin or cocaine. We developed cases and, with help of the street team, made arrests, searched homes, and seized dope. Through surveillance, informants, and intelligence, I arrested two major heroin dealers who had been evading the narcotics division for the previous couple of years.

We started making headlines in the *San Jose Mercury News* and on TV, where they'd run a picture of a table full of dope, money, and guns. The DA and police department brass would proclaim that the narcotics division had put a significant dent in the community's drug network.

A couple of months into using the new tactics, the narcotics division made the largest drug seizure, at that time, in the history of Santa Clara County. The case started with the buy team making a couple of buys of small amounts of cocaine and then escalated to the use of informants and intelligence. Eventually, we were able to set up, with assistance from the Drug Enforcement Administration, DEA, a purchase of five pounds of cocaine.

During this case, I learned one of the tricks of the trade in dealing with the press. The defendants had agreed to sell us the cocaine for $80,000. The need to show, or flash, $80,000 was the reason we needed assistance from DEA. After the seizure, I sat at my desk and calculated the value of the cocaine. When cut down to 20 percent strength and sold on the street, it would yield $500,000. The press, police department officials, and DA loved those big numbers, so the next morning "$500,000 in Cocaine Seized" was the headline in the *Mercury News*.

One of the fun aspects of working with the major violator team was that I worked not only in San Jose, but all over the state. I was allowed to follow the trail, and it wasn't just ounce quantities anymore. Using transponders and help from FAA flight control, I tracked a planeload of dope and had it seized when it landed at a small airstrip in the California Sierra Mountains. Gutierrez and I impounded boatloads of heroin in Monterey. We were kicking in doors and confiscating multi-pound quantities of cocaine from homes in high-income neighborhoods of Silicon Valley. More arrests, more headlines, more pictures in the paper, and more statements by the authorities that we had delivered a blow to our city's drug networks.

Before long, during those press conferences, when the DA or police officials were making these comments, Buckhout or Gutierrez and I would cut a glance at each other and smile. We knew nothing would change. We knew, because of the amounts of money involved, another dealer was always ready to take the arrested dealer's place in the organization. The more dealers we took off the streets, the more new drug dealers appeared. We felt assured we weren't putting ourselves out of a job.

San Jose Police Department Narcotics Unit

We worked long hours and late nights on many occasions. I did have the time, though, to pick up where I had left off with my college education. Bertotti and I were both attending evening classes, once a week, at the University of San Francisco. We were working together on several studies that became a thesis on the impact of drug use on crime in a community. One of the early conclusions we reached was that 80 percent of the prisoners in the local county jail were in custody for offenses related to the inmate's drug use, such as burglary, robbery, shoplifting, and bad checks.

We were off duty one evening, sitting at the bar in the Los Gatos Lodge, and I brought up the topic of our study.

"Boss, would you be happy if we were able to remove 50 percent of the drugs off our streets?"

Bertotti took a drink and thought for a moment. "Well, yes. It would raise the price of drugs." He paused and then smiled. "You're not going to try to tell me that the demand for drugs would be reduced if prices were raised, are you?"

"No, but doesn't our study show that crimes are committed to pay for drugs? Therefore, aren't more burglaries and robberies committed when drug prices increase due to our drug seizures?"

Bertotti stared behind the bartender at the bottles of liquor and then turned back toward me. "And if prices rise, then it looks like a better business opportunity for another dealer."

"So what are we doing?" I thought I was on to something, but couldn't articulate it.

Bertotti sat in thought. "They're just dopers."

We laughed and tapped our bottles of beer together in a toast. "They're dopers."

Our professor at the university was satisfied with the progress in our research for the thesis, but suggested there was nothing new to our recent discovery. He directed us to statements by Albert Einstein, who had pointed out the rapid rise in property crimes and violence during alcohol prohibition in the 1920s.

———••———

One of the advantages of working the major violator team was that, unlike the buy team, we didn't make quick drug buys followed by an immediate arrest. The case against the higher echelon drug dealer took time and patience, sometimes months. When I wasn't making buys, I'd hang out with drug suspects without other officers providing surveillance. I took advantage of my relationship with Bertotti, a co-student working together on our study, by stretching the rules about when and where I'd work without someone covering me.

My tightly curled hair had the appearance of an Afro. I wore old jeans and a T-shirt that a vest or jacket covered. I was making cases against dealers of heroin, cocaine, and psychedelic drugs. My specialty, though, was buying methamphetamine, the drug of choice of motorcycle gangs. I might not have been working all night, but I came home late looking like a biker and brought home the attitude and language. Church attendance was declining, and I missed many family gatherings.

One of the cases I had developed involved a guy named Carter, who was dealing in everything from marijuana and psychedelic mushrooms to mescaline, cocaine, and methamphetamine. I made a few small buys now and then from him, but, as was my custom in working this type of case, I spent plenty of time at his place without buying drugs. I had intelligence that his supplier for methamphetamine (meth, speed, or crank as it was sometimes called) was a Hell's Angel by the name of Doug "Dirty Doug" Bontempi. I wanted to confirm that and, if possible, meet Bontempi. In the drug world, though, I couldn't just ask, "Do you know Doug Bontempi?" I also knew the Hell's Angels were extremely cautious and placing a big order of meth with Carter wouldn't flush out Bontempi, so I needed to hang around and hope to run into him.

I had two motorcycles at the time. I was riding a new, customized Triumph to and from work and had a beat-up 1962 "panhead" Harley, which I kept at a city maintenance yard. I used the Harley in cases such as Carter's. I'd ride it over to his place, sit around, and have a beer or two. Then I'd make small talk and maybe buy a small amount of speed or other drug offered. I was slowly gaining Carter's confidence, and he was letting me in on his activities. He had rented a warehouse and added indoor growing lights, setting it up as a marijuana nursery. I discovered the location when I helped him fill several truckloads of mulch and took it over to the warehouse. During this investigation, I found myself staring at the gun that Dirty Doug held.

"I think you're a snitch," he said, adding a few expletives to make his point.

His wording was important. He didn't say he thought I was a cop. As a Hell's Angel, if he'd thought I was a cop, he'd have simply gotten up and left. But calling me a snitch was different. A Hell's Angel might kill a snitch and dump the body in some reservoir without a second thought.

I looked at him for a few seconds and then, trying to act calm and cool, took the last swig from my can of beer. "If I were a snitch, this place would've been taken down long ago."

Dirty Doug lowered the gun and placed it back under his belt. He got up, took a beer from the refrigerator, and returned without bringing me one. We talked about motorcycles, as he seemed to be testing my knowledge. Then I decided it was time to go. He had seen me and had a chance to check me out. I was certain Carter had mentioned me to him. There was no sense pressing anything, so I hopped on my ride and left.

Yes, sir. Dirty Doug is the one supplying crank to Carter.

I knew members of the Hell's Angels were the biggest suppliers of methamphetamine in the state. I was determined to build this case, however long it might take.

Ted Sumner, a young-looking officer, had been brought up to the narcotics division to work the high schools. He was successful and even bought drugs off several teachers, but, when his identity was eventually learned as a result of the arrests, a major riot occurred at Del Mar High School. The police brass decided not to infiltrate any more schools, and Sumner was now working with the buy team.

He yelled out as he approached my desk one afternoon, "Jones'y, you brought the fuck'n narcs!"

We laughed. On an earlier case, a small-time dealer suggested to Sumner that he could introduce him to someone who sold large amounts. Sumner took me back to the dealer's apartment and introduced me as his financial backer.

When we arrived, the paranoid dealer cracked open the front door and whispered, "You didn't bring the narcs, did you?"

We assured him we hadn't. After a few beers, it became obvious that the small-time dealer had been bragging and was unable to introduce me directly to any substantial supplier, so Sumner gave a signal to the backup team to raid the apartment with us in it. When Buckhout, Smith, and uniformed police officers stormed up the stairwell, the suspect, eyes wide in shock, let out a string of expletives while crying, "Oh, no! You brought the narcs."

I was still laughing at our private joke as Sumner sat on the edge of my desk.

"Your mamma. What's happening?" I asked.

"Hey, man, I got this gal, Debbie." Then speaking as if he were recording a promo for a new movie, Sumner said, "Debbie Dalton of the Dalton Gang." He then continued in a normal voice. "She says she can introduce us to multi-ounce speed dealers. You like buying speed, right?"

"My specialty. Got a hammer on her?"

"Not really. It's her old man. I busted him on a couple buys, and she wants to keep him out of prison. She knows he's going to do time, but, if we can keep him local, she'll turn us on to a big-time crank dealer. But she won't talk until we can assure her of keeping him out of state prison."

"Where is she?"

Sumner switched to his radio voice again. "Right this way, oh great one."

He led me down the hall where Debbie was waiting in an interrogation room. Debbie had been a real looker in high school, the homecoming queen type. Barely thirty, she was now gaunt with infected needle injection marks on the inside of her arms. Her hair was scraggly, and she looked like she'd been wearing the same dress for the last week. Sumner walked me into the room and then, without an introduction, left us alone.

"Hi, Debbie. How're you doing?" I acted as if she were an old friend.

Debbie started to cry quietly. "You need to help me. Please don't let them take Chad to prison. A year here at the local jail, I can live with that. But, please, not prison."

People would say anything in pleading a case for themselves, but I had never met someone, especially a doper, so emotional in pleading for someone else. I sensed the concern on her part and wanted to take advantage of it.

"Does he want this? Does he know you're here?"

Debbie's face took on a look of pure panic. "Oh, no, he can't know. He'd kill me if he knew I was in here talking to you." She started to cry hard.

I got that she was sincere, scared out of her wits. So it was time to play hardball. "Debbie, this decision needs to be made now. We don't have time to play around with the DA."

Actually, I didn't know enough about Sumner's case with Chad Dalton to know if I could do anything for him. He was on parole, and, since already booked, it might have been out of my hands. I knew, though, that I had a good working relationship with parole officers and the DA's office. So I continued to play Debbie, speaking as softly as I could.

"I need to know who you can take me to and just how much crank he can supply." I reached across the table and gently took her hand. She worked to get control of herself, took deep breaths, and wiped tears from her eyes.

She struggled to speak, a gasp for air following each word. "I ... buy ... my ... crank ... from ... Bill ... Perkey. Do ... you ... know ... who ... he ... is?"

I tried to remain stone-faced. I knew who "Wild Bill" Perkey was. He was the vice president of the San Jose chapter of the Hell's Angels. The Hell's Angels first received notoriety in 1947 during a wild rally in Hollister, California. After that event, law-abiding motorcycle organizations across the nation claimed that only one percent of motorcyclists were outlaws. The reference stuck, and Hell's Angels, calling themselves "one percenters," felt they had to prove it to themselves and others. They rode fast, loved guns, drank hard, and preferred the drug methamphetamine, which allowed them to party longer into the night. Staying up late and partying hard meant more alcohol, which meant more violence.

The president of the San Jose chapter was Phil "Crazy" Cross. In an effort to improve the public image of the Hell's Angels, which had been damaged in the late 1960s and early 1970s with members being convicted of rape, robbery, and drugs, Cross had put up billboards around San Jose that read, "No Hope with Dope."

I didn't know where the Hell's Angels as a club stood regarding drugs, but I had a pretty good idea that Dirty Doug was involved. I now felt confident that, with a little luck, I could build a case against Wild Bill.

Sumner managed to get the DA's temporary approval, pending Debbie's cooperation, for keeping Chad in the local jail. I then began to scheme how I could meet Wild Bill through Debbie. Although Dirty Doug had met me, I wanted a different way to approach Wild Bill. I certainly didn't want to appear to be a street-level buyer, as Debbie was. I came up with the idea of using guns.

The San Jose police department was beginning to consider new Smith & Wesson Model 59 handguns for officers. I knew outlaw motorcycle gangs loved guns and would be most interested in the latest gun to hit the market, so Sumner and I checked out three of the new weapons from the department armory.

Patrick Thorton wanted to be a Hell's Angel, but couldn't afford a Harley. He, like Debbie, bought moderate amounts of meth from Wild Bill and then turned around and sold it off in smaller amounts, snorting up any profits he might have made. I had Debbie inform Thorton that I could supply guns. Sumner, in building his case against Chad Dalton, had already met Thorton. So with Debbie in tow, Sumner and I showed up at a place Thorton was staying on the southwestern side of town. When Debbie introduced us, Thorton, wanting to impress us that he was a man in the know, acted like he already knew me.

When we showed him the guns, Thorton, who was hyperactive without needing a morning dose of speed, started running in circles, gesticulating like a wounded chicken trying to take flight. He shouted, "Oh, wow! Oh, wow!" over and over, and it took everything Sumner and I had to keep from laughing. Once we got him calmed down, we made it clear that the guns were already spoken for, but I mentioned I was going to be coming into another shipment of stolen model 59s and would need a buyer. It worked. Always looking for credibility and wanting to make an impression and boost his standing with the Hell's Angels, Thorton exaggerated to them his past gun business with me.

While hanging out with Debbie Dalton and Patrick Thorton, Wild Bill saw me on several occasions and eventually invited me to meet with him and his friends. There was no talk of drugs or guns. We hung out, drank beer, and talked motorcycles. Dirty Doug was usually present. I worked late on weekends and met them at their favorite bars and dance halls. It was interesting to watch how, as the Angels walked into a bar, people would quietly make way for them, surrendering their tables or place at the bar.

The talk of guns first came up one Saturday evening when I was in their clubhouse's backyard. While sitting around a picnic table and drinking beer, one of the prospects showed me a forty-five-caliber automatic handgun.

"Nice." I immediately disassembled it, showing my familiarity with the weapon.

"Where'd you learn to handle a piece?" someone asked as I was putting it back together.

"Vietnam. Got to handle all kinds."

Another prospect mentioned he had been in Nam and asked, "What'd you do there?"

I gave them a full account of my tour of duty, knowing the soldier in Vietnam loved Huey pilots. It only takes a few questions and answers, and a fellow veteran will know if someone is lying about his combat service.

I could do no wrong for the rest of the evening and picked up my nickname. My undercover driver's license identified me as Joseph Demkowski, and I tried to go by the nickname of "Ski." After hearing my stories of Vietnam, though, the Angels called me "Huey."

While Hell's Angels sat back and listened, a prospect brought the conversation back to the topic of guns.

"So, Huey, Thorton says he did a big gun deal with you."

I chuckled. "I don't think Thorton has done anything big in his life. Never done business with him, but, yeah, he's seen some of my guns."

"What can you get?" asked the prospect.

"Might take some time, but I'll have twenty-four new nine-millimeter Smith & Wessons."

"How much?"

"Two bucks each." That meant $200.

"What if I want to take 'em all?"

Wild Bill, Dirty Doug, and other Angels watched and listened as the prospect tried to bargain.

"Still two bucks each. And I'll only sell them all at once. Too much risk trying to sell one or two at a time."

"Where do you get them?"

I gave a look that said that question wasn't going to be answered, and I changed the subject back to Vietnam.

Later in the evening, the members went inside for club business, leaving two fairly drunk prospects and me in the backyard. One of the Angels left his "colors," his vest with the Hell's Angels patch, on the back of his motorcycle. Always one to start trouble, I put them on and had one of them take pictures. Then an inebriated prospect wanted his picture taken while wearing the vest.

Hanging out with the Hells Angels

Even touching a member's colors was a major violation, not only by the non-member, but also by the member who left his colors unattended. So when a member of the club came out the back door when one of the prospects still had them on, a fight ensued. Hell's Angels love to brawl and prove they're tougher than the next guy is, and the rest of the club streamed out the back door to join in the beating of the hapless biker.

The other prospect, anxious to prove his willingness to go to blows and show support for club rules, jumped me from behind. I quickly put him in a chokehold, and he passed out and dropped to the ground when I released him. The Angels got a kick out of it as he flopped around in the dirt like a chicken with his head cut off, gasping for air as he came to.

We drank hard that night, told war stories, rode our motorcycles over to a small bar, and partied more, and I got home late.

Several months later, I was riding the Harley over to a Hell's Angel's house in Campbell, a town southwest of San Jose. I wore heavy motorcycle boots, dirty jeans with a wide belt that passed through a small chain attached to my wallet, and a black leather vest over my Levi jacket. As I approached my next turn in the residential area, I noticed a Campbell police department patrol car pulling up behind me. He hit the red lights and siren, but I continued with my turn, drove a half block, and stopped in front of my destination. Several bikers at the house came out on the front porch to watch.

I got off the motorcycle, took off my gloves, and proceeded to take out my driver's license and registration. Without saying anything, the officer grabbed and tossed me onto the hood of his patrol car as my paperwork went flying. After cuffing me and throwing me to the ground, he began to verbally instruct me on the proper procedure of pulling over immediately when an officer displays his red light. He recovered my license and registration from the street and ran a background check through communications. He finally took off the cuffs when he received the results indicating there were neither warrants nor outstanding tickets in my name. He drove off with me having said little more than a "thank you" when he returned my paperwork.

With everyone watching from the house, it couldn't have gone any better if I had planned it. It was another great day of bonding, complaining about cop harassment, talking guns and motorcycles, and drinking beer.

The time was also approaching when I was supposed to have the guns, and Wild Bill, anxious for me to supply them, invited me on an upcoming motorcycle ride to Oakland. I certainly wanted to go. Working undercover was what I did. Its allure seduced me, and I wanted to see how far into that seamy, dangerous side of life I could go. I sat down with Bertotti, other supervisors, and a couple of investigators from Alcohol, Tobacco, and Firearms (ATF).

"Can you take someone like Officer Brenda Wells along with you?" Bertotti asked.

"No, not a chance. Only women with fully patched members are treated respectfully. Women guests and girlfriends of prospects are free game."

A supervisor with ATF jumped into the conversation. "Collins is going to be there." He indicated a plump, young, baby-faced ATF agent who was sitting across the table from me. "He's working a firearms case on some Angels with the Oakland club, and he's planning on attending the event through his own connections."

Collins was struggling to grow a beard that, with his blond hair, was hardly noticeable. Wearing a suit and tie, he hardly looked like someone who could be associating with the Angels.

Bertotti wasn't comfortable with the overall plan. But I continued to press my case, and, with the ATF's assurance that they'd be present, the boss gave his approval.

On the evening of the ride, I met up with the Angels at their clubhouse in San Jose. Several Angels from the Gilroy area were there, and we rode off around 2200 with the highest-ranking officer of the club at the head of the group. Riding two by two, the rest of the members, wearing their colors, rode behind. The prospects, wearing their vests or jackets displaying only the lower rocker, rode next in line. Two of us who were guests rode in back. We made stops in Milpitas and Hayward as others joined.

In boot camp, I found marching, with the cadence and the stomp of the boots, exhilarating. Flying Hueys, sensing the thumping helicopter blades throughout my body, was thrilling. On this night, the unique rumble of the Harley engines resonated in my bones. As we thundered along the freeway, my front wheel only inches from the rear wheel of the bike in front, I experienced a sense of camaraderie, and the line between being a cop and a biker began to blur.

By the time we got off the freeway, more than thirty motorcycles were in our procession. Driving through Oakland, when we got to an intersection, several bikers stopped cross traffic as if they were cops, and the motorcade continued through against red lights.

At our destination, a warehouse, hundreds of Harleys were converging. Behind a fence, they were parked in row after row, and prospects from different clubs were assigned guard duty. Inside, there was a long bar with neon lights all around. Large speakers were blaring a song about someone being meaner than a junkyard dog. Clouds of tobacco smoke hung over tables where Hell's Angels from San Francisco, Oakland, and San Bernardino sat. Prospects were running around serving drinks and food to members and cleaning tables when directed. As a guest, I was on my own when it came to getting beer or pizza.

As with any group, there were cliques. The boys from "Frisco" or "Berdoo" were over here. The biker "mammas" were back there. Some small groups were partying hard while others looked like they were quietly doing business. I couldn't believe how big the bikers were. They were tall and heavyset, and many had spent time lifting weights, probably while inside, that is, in prison.

On a couple of occasions, I made eye contact with the ATF agent through the blue haze. His transformation was startling. In his biker clothes, with his size, demeanor, tattoos, and scraggly beard, he fit right in. He always had a big grin and appeared to be having a grand time. On one hand, I was scared. Working a one-man patrol car, the uniform and badge weighed heavily on my side. Working undercover in this situation, I was truly alone. If things went wrong, the ATF agent could only be a witness to, at best, a severe beating and, at worst, a homicide. It wasn't like they suspected me of being a cop. I'd been around Dalton, Thorton, Wild Bill, and Dirty Doug too long. But I still had to be tested, and everyone was checking me out and asking about my past.

Angels took pride in having done time in prison, but that wasn't something I could lie about. Someone who hadn't fought combat in Vietnam couldn't lie about it to someone who had, and someone who hadn't been to prison couldn't lie about it to someone who had. Working undercover in this situation was like flying scouts where things could go wrong at any minute. I hid the fear, though, and fed on the adrenalin.

Around 0300, the raucous atmosphere suddenly became subdued. The music was turned down, and bikers were running here and there, speaking in hushed tones. Many were coming and going from the front door of the warehouse. Curiosity finally got the better of me, and I sauntered out. A steady rain sparkled as it fell through the glow of the streetlights. At least twenty police officers, their black raincoats glistening, surrounded the warehouse. They were spread out on foot thirty yards apart. Prospects paced like wet dogs around inside the fence and wondered what the next move was. Several groups of Hell's Angels were in hushed discussions under the eaves by the front door.

"Huey," someone called out.

I looked around. Wild Bill was standing with a group of other fully patched Angels. He motioned for me to come over. He then threw me a black leather vest with a lower rocker that said "California." He pointed to two bikers walking over to their motorcycles. "Go with those guys, and do as you're told. I'll see you later." He then turned back to the group. I was being tested.

The other two bikers, prospects, fired up their bikes. I put on the vest, climbed on my bike, cranked it, and followed them out the gate. Several police officers standing in the street tried to stop us, but we ignored them and drove through the lines. We didn't make it two blocks, though, before we found a patrol car had blocked our route. Another then swooped in and trapped us as if we might try to run. The cops ran checks on our driver's licenses and registrations and held us for thirty minutes before letting us go. I was relieved and felt like I had gotten away with something when they didn't find my police ID hidden deep in one of my boots.

We drove off and, once back among civilization, pulled into a gas station. We had simply been bait to see what the cops were going to do, and one of the prospects made a call back to the warehouse to inform the Angels what occurred.

We continued south down Highway 17, observing traffic laws, but the California Highway Patrol stopped us. One of the bikers failed the personality test, so he was arrested. The other biker and I were allowed to leave. He exited at Hayward, and I continued, through the rain, southbound through San Jose. As I approached Los Gatos, I noticed another police car following me.

Is this asshole going to stop me? I was anxious to get home and to bed.

When I first became a cop, I treated everyone with respect until someone proved to be an asshole. After a few years, every citizen encountered was an asshole until he proved otherwise. Now, even cops were assholes.

He stopped me. Since I was now alone, I could have identified myself as a cop, but didn't. He physically searched me, checked out the serial numbers on the Harley, confirmed I had no outstanding warrants, and filled out an interrogation card. I took silent pride in the fact that even the cops couldn't discover my identity. I finally made it home around 0500, wet, smelling of booze, and reeking of cigarettes. I knew I would be hearing from Susan about my long and unpredictable work schedule.

At this point in the investigation, I had a methamphetamine case against Wild Bill that I knew would hold up in court. But I was never going to get in a position to make a large buy directly from any Hell's Angel without "taking care of business," completing the gun transaction I had promised. And that wasn't going to be legally possible. Furthermore, the request to ride off through the police lines in Oakland was simply a minor test, and I knew that, if I were going to hang around the Hell's Angels any longer, the next requests would come closer to crossing the lines of legality.

We were in uncharted waters with the investigation. Too much time and money would have to be spent to continue, and the investigation had to end. We had learned plenty, though, that would be useful in future investigations.

I got a haircut, trimmed my beard, donned some clean clothes, and sat down with a deputy DA. In an effort not to disclose information that would be useful in continuing investigations, we decided which cases to charge and which to hold onto for later use. I obtained arrest warrants for Wild Bill Perkey and other suspects, along with search warrants for their homes.

After several days of planning, I held a pre-raid briefing at 0400. Besides members of the street team who would make the arrests and execute the search warrants, there were representatives from the FBI and ATF. I wanted uniformed police officers to be at each residence we were going to, so I requested assistance from MERGE. Just before the briefing began, they entered the room wearing dark coveralls and watch caps, uniforms I had never seen before. They looked like they were getting ready to storm a hostage situation.

I approached Lieutenant Melz, head of MERGE. "What's this?"

"Our new uniform."

"Lieutenant, I need officers wearing uniforms clearly identifiable as San Jose police department."

"Well, you asked for MERGE. This is our uniform of the day for the situation you're calling for."

"I asked for patrol officers. I'm not sending my men, in plainclothes, up to pound on a door at six in the morning without a uniform cop standing there with them. If you can't have your men change into the patrol uniform, I'll have to request a beat cop from the district when we get out there."

Melz was livid. I won the argument, though, since Melz, not wanting patrol officers called to assist when his men were already going to be there, had MERGE change into their regular patrol uniforms.

The search warrants were carried out without breaking down doors or busting out windows, and the arrest warrants were served peacefully. A search of Wild Bill's home resulted in the seizure of more methamphetamine along with scales, packaging materials, and other evidence of possession for the purpose of sales.

Later that day, Bertotti caught up with me in the office. He looked perturbed. "Jones'y, you're causing trouble."

I laughed. "Now what did I do?"

Bertotti stopped and gave me a hard stare through his thick glasses. "Melz is on my case."

I explained my point of view, and he seemed to agree. Bertotti walked toward his office and then stopped and turned in the doorway. "You might have won the argument this morning, but you'll lose the battle. They got new toys. They want to use them."

The boss was right. The federal government, in the name of the War on Drugs, was providing money to police departments for new gear, equipment, and training. Law enforcement looked for opportunities to put it all to use.

Shortly after the arrest of Perkey, while off duty, I was leaving the Ace Hardware store in Los Gatos when I noticed a business card for a mortuary under my windshield wiper. I thought it strange, threw it away, and forgot about it. Several days later, I was having dinner at home with Susan and Joey.

While chatting away at a mile a minute, Susan suddenly said, "Can you believe it? Someone left a business card for a funeral home on my car today."

It took a minute for this to register. "What did you just say?"

"A funeral home, advertising for a funeral home, I guess. They left a card on my windshield."

I tried to act disinterested. "Someone who works in the business thought it was someone else's car. No one would advertise that way."

Susan laughed. "I sure hope not."

"Did you keep the card?" I asked, as if it were an afterthought.

"It should be in the car. I don't know. Here, Joey, eat your potatoes." She wasn't concerned.

I retrieved the card and noticed it was from a different mortuary. Several days later, upon leaving a grocery store, another business card for a mortuary was on my windshield. I gingerly removed it and placed it in an evidence bag. Unfortunately, evidence technicians were unable to locate any readable prints.

The next day, I was sitting in Bertotti's office. "There were three, boss."

Bertotti turned the two cards over again and again in his hand. "You think it's Perkey?"

"Probably a prospect trying to make an impression with the club."

"What do you want to do?"

"I don't think it's a big deal."

I really didn't think it was. Hell's Angels may have had a reputation of violence against informants, but physical confrontations between cops and American flag-waving Angels rarely occurred. There was a sort of détente, based on a shared dislike of long-haired, flag-burning, anti-government agitators. When arrested, most Angels accepted that the cops were just doing their job.

Bertotti glared at me over his glasses and raised his voice. "It's intimidation of a witness, a cop no less." He didn't wait for me to reply. "I've got an idea. I'll let you know."

Several hours later, Bertotti walked by my desk. "It's taken care of."

"What'd you do?" I asked.

Bertotti laughed. "You don't want to know."

Apparently, after a meeting Bertotti had with the DA, one of the deputy attorneys contacted all the private attorneys known to be representing Hell's Angels. He made it clear that any further attempts at intimidation would be too close to home for law enforcement to ignore. Unless the Angels were willing to have the entire US Department of Justice come down nationwide on the entire club, the intimidation was to cease and desist. Contact with the attorneys representing Hell's Angels apparently worked, as the harassment stopped. Not long afterward, Wild Bill Perkey pled guilty, avoiding a trial.

However, the issue with the mortuary calling cards was a bigger deal than I had thought. Two Hell's Angel prospects were arrested in Los Angeles as they kept watch at the home of an undercover cop. In their possession was a machine gun, a handgun with silencer, and binoculars. And not long after my incident, a Solano County deputy sheriff investigator by the name of Zerbe and San Jose police detective John Kracht were each victims of homemade bombs placed near their cars. Zerbe was seriously hurt; Kracht was not, but could have been. The common denominator in their investigations was a nutcase of a Hell's Angel by the name of "Jim Jim" Brandes. A later search of Brandes' home uncovered a file with names, home addresses, and personal vehicle information on police officers and narcotics detectives from agencies all over northern California. Brandes also had police scanners and listening device (bug) detectors. When Brandes was arrested for attempted murder, Dirty Doug was also present and arrested. Neither was convicted in that case, but the relationship between the Angels and the cops had become a personal feud.

During this period of time, the San Jose police department went to a new badge design, starting with badge number 1000 for the chief. The numbering was now in order of seniority, and my new highly detailed star bore the number 1502.

It was another early evening after work, and Bertotti and I were sitting at the bar in the Foghorn, discussing our research and studies. Sumner, also a student at the University of San Francisco who participated in our studies, was with us. He had on his serious face as he explained how he came up with the number of heroin addicts.

"It's the Baden formula. Multiply the number of overdose deaths by two hundred."

"So what's our county's addict population?" Bertotti asked.

"Forty-four hundred in 1973," Sumner said.

Bertotti did the math in his head. "Heroin is killing about two a month?"

"It's not the heroin," I said. "It's the unknown quality that's killing them."

Bertotti laughed and then leaned forward to look across at Sumner on my other side. "Oh, no. Here goes Jones'y again."

"Just like the 1920s, people were driven to hard and adulterated liquor, which killed them. Prohibition was the problem."

"So you want to go back to the days where they could get a pharmaceutical dose across the counter?" Bertotti asked.

I shrugged my shoulders. "It would stop the overdoses and remove the street dealer."

There was a pause in the conversation, and then Sumner, knowing what Bertotti was getting ready to say, replied in his radio voice, "They're just dopers."

We laughed, clicked our beer bottles together, and toasted in unison, "They're dopers."

———————

I loved the job and camaraderie, but was completely blind to what it was doing to my marriage. I was working late and then coming home talking trash and looking like a motorcycle gang member. Or worse, I was getting off work at a normal hour and then, instead of going home and having dinner with Susan and Joey, I was going down to the Foghorn to drink and unwind with the guys and enjoy the attention of the girls who were interested in cops. I always had an excuse for Susan by saying I was working late and had been drinking while undercover on a case. In the course of the job that required I live a lie, deception was becoming too easy.

Playing the role of a criminal meant I was doing well at work, but the toxicity of the job was beginning to overwhelm me. I was working undercover with drug dealers, showing up with large amounts of cash, and never knowing if they were going to try to rip me off. My worries were about gang members willing to place bombs under police officers' private vehicles. When I went home, I'd sometimes find Susan angry over things that seemed trivial in comparison to me, such as the yard needed mowing or I had missed church. We were living in two different worlds.

One evening in December, I was home. The three of us were in the living room. Susan was sitting in a chair by the window, which looked out over the lights of the valley far below. Aussie was lying in her self-appointed spot, guarding the front door. Joey and I were playing on the shag carpet. I was leaning on my elbow, and Joey, trying to be like Dad, was also trying to lean on his elbow, except he was using the wrong arm and he had an elbow sticking straight up in the air. Joey knew he was doing something wrong, but couldn't figure it out, and we were all having a good laugh. I couldn't see that this was how it was supposed to be with family.

"How much longer are you going to be in narcotics?" Susan asked.

I immediately got defensive. "I don't know. Why?"

"You have seniority now, and, when you go back to patrol, you could work something other than the midnight shift and have weekends off. And you'd be back to a four-day workweek."

"I'm not even thinking of going back to patrol. I like what I'm doing."

"You promised that this was a two-year assignment. We have no family or social life. We're not involved in church. We can't go on like this as a family."

"What the hell is that supposed to mean?"

Susan tried to interrupt. "That language is—"

But I continued in a raised voice. "You knew who I was when you married me. You knew I took law enforcement classes in college. You knew I loved flying, the military, and this kind of life, so don't give me any crap."

"Russ, you don't need to use that language with me, and you certainly don't need to use it in front of Joey. And I know who I married." Her voice grew stern. "You're no longer who I married. And I certainly didn't sign up for this kind of life. You have a wife, Russ. You have a son. Okay, you've had your fun with this assignment. Let's get back to a family life that's a little more normal." I didn't respond. "If you're not willing to go back to church, to get involved in Bible study, then maybe we should look at marriage counseling."

"You've got to be—" I caught myself as I almost swore again. "You've got to be kidding. I'm not going to sit and listen to some counselor."

"Well, Russ, you need to understand that I'm not happy."

My world suddenly went still as I went into a brain freeze. Aussie stopped breathing, the refrigerator stopped running, and Joey looked immobilized. Susan might as well have added "young man" to the end of that sentence. Her statement took me back to painful memories of my mother.

Mom was extraordinarily cute. Short, slender, and fair-skinned, she had abundant, curling, reddish blonde hair. She'd been athletic in high school and a star on the women's basketball team. Outgoing and chatty, she was always popular in public. But as wonderful as my mother could be, out of the public eyes and ears, she could be difficult to please. In her desire to see her children do better, she was never satisfied with any household chore, report card, or holiday gift. Her favorite dismissive statement to me was, "I'm not happy, young man." By high school, I had emotionally disassociated myself from her. As a young adult, unwilling and unable to properly communicate with her, our relationship remained distant.

Susan knew my relationship with my mother was strained, but I had never talked about it so she had no way of knowing about the painful memories. When Susan said she wasn't happy, an emotional switch was thrown within me, the same switch that had been thrown years ago in the relationship with my mother.

Within a few months, unwilling to change my lifestyle and work assignment and unwilling to sit down and talk, I walked out of the house and filed for divorce.

I buried myself in the job and worked a case that kept me up over twenty-four hours. I was at my desk one evening when Sergeant Dwyer from the buy team walked in.

I looked up. "Hey, Sarge."

"Jones'y, we busted an attorney and several others on a cocaine buy. The attorney and another suspect are in an interrogation room. Are you going to be around long enough to turn them over to a patrol officer who's on the way to book them?"

"Sure, no problem. See you tomorrow."

The door closed as Dwyer and his team left for home, and the narcotics division was quiet. I continued my paperwork but then suddenly stopped. *Wait a minute. We got an attorney under arrest sitting in the same room with a co-defendant?* I walked down the hall and looked through the small window into the interrogation room. Sure enough, the two were sitting there talking. I went over to a small side room that contained equipment that records conversations held in those rooms. The equipment was usually used for interviews and interrogations, but nothing prevented me from making a recording of two defendants. There was no expected right to privacy in those rooms, and, since the attorney was also a defendant, he had no attorney-client privilege. I started a recording, put on a headset, and couldn't believe my ears as I listened in on the hushed conversation.

The attorney said, "They could call San Mateo sheriff's office and get a search warrant and go to my house."

The other arrestee asked, "They could bust the door right in?"

"Yes, they could. I have to get bail and get out of here. I have to get it out of my house, my boat, and my car."

The uniformed officer showed up. "Sir, I'm here to transport the prisoners."

"I'm sorry," I whispered, holding a finger up to my lips. "They're not quite ready. Can you hold off for a couple minutes?"

I went back to the headphones as the patrol officer sat back and enjoyed a cup of coffee in the hallowed offices of BOI. The whispered conversation went on for some time with one of the final remarks coming from the attorney. "I have got to get a hold of Ralph and get it out of my house."

I had the information I needed, so the patrol officer took the prisoners to the county jail. I then went into overdrive. It was after 2200. I found the paperwork that Dwyer's team left behind and obtained addresses and vehicle information.

"What are you doing here so late?" someone asked.

I looked up. It was Charlie Rosseau, a young-looking, charismatic officer who had been recently brought up to narcotics. "You want to go to work?"

"Sure, what do you have?"

I gave him a quick explanation of what I was doing, what the prospects for the night were, and what he could do to help. I then went back to work.

Relying on an assistant DA at that time of night would have been fruitless, but I had been in narcotics long enough to know how to compose my own search warrants, and, within a couple of hours, I had written up an affidavit for the suspect's home in San Carlos. Rosseau had arranged with the sheriff's deputies working the jail to procrastinate as long as possible on any phone call by the suspects. He also saw to it that any release on bail would be delayed.

By 0300, Rosseau and I met with a county judge, who signed the search warrant. We then contacted San Carlos police and executed the search, finding over three pounds of cocaine and $8,000 in cash.

By 0600, Rosseau and I were back at the police department. I began working on search warrants for the car and boat. The vehicle was located right outside the apartment where the arrest had been made the day before, and we found eight ounces of cocaine. Members of the street team were in the office by midmorning, and I had them head over to the Santa Cruz coast. A search of the sailboat recovered another two pounds of cocaine. Twenty-four hours after I was asked to wait for a patrol officer to come and book two prisoners, I finished my reports. Over $1 million in cocaine had been seized.

After the court case against the attorney and his co-defendants was adjudicated, the evidence was scheduled to be destroyed. Officer Rosseau, though, succumbed to the lure of big money to be made from black market prices as a result of the War on Drugs. He went into the evidence room, took the cocaine, and replaced it with something like lactose. Rosseau knew the cocaine wouldn't be sent to the lab again, and, as long as the evidence weighed the same, there was no chance of someone suspecting something wrong. Rosseau then gave the cocaine to his brother-in-law to sell. But the DEA caught the brother-in-law and turned him into an informant. Rosseau, back working patrol, was arrested right out of his patrol vehicle. I resisted believing that he could have committed the crime, but Rosseau eventually pled guilty and spent time in the federal penitentiary.

He wasn't the first and certainly not the last police officer in the nation to fall for corruption. Just as during alcohol prohibition, while the War on Drugs progressed, individual police officers and entire narcotics divisions were caught and convicted of stealing money from drug dealers, selling stolen narcotics, taking bribes, and submitting false reports to cover their crimes.

— · · —

A few narcotics officers were transferring out of the division, and we gathered at the Foghorn one evening for a going-away party. On the second floor was a room with another bar that was usually reserved for special occasions or rowdy law enforcement gatherings. Sumner and I were sitting upstairs at the bar, waiting.

"Is it just me, or is there more cocaine and meth on the streets?" I asked.

Sumner looked concerned as he gazed into his drink. "I can't believe the amount that's out there. I don't remember cocaine at all a couple years ago, and I don't think I ever saw meth when working patrol."

"We didn't. It was whites[24] back then," I said, as if "back then" was decades ago.

Lieutenant Bertotti walked in and took a place next to me at the bar. He ordered a beer.

"Boss, after marijuana, what was the biggest drug problem on the street when you worked patrol?" Sumner asked.

Bertotti took a couple of swallows and thought it over. "Well, even marijuana wasn't a problem. You can't find one arrest and conviction in this county for anyone driving under the influence of marijuana. The biggest problem we had was pharmaceuticals. Uppers and downers."

"What about methamphetamine?" Sumner asked.

"That's a fairly new phenomenon," Bertotti said, as if it was a matter of fact.

I jumped into the conversation. "It's an unintended consequence of the War on Drugs." Bertotti looked at me as if I were nuts, but I continued. "Since the beginning of the War on Drugs, with the crackdown on the pharmaceutical

---

24. "Whites" was the name for pharmaceutical amphetamines. A mild stimulant, they were commonly prescribed as a dietary aid or for combating fatigue. College students took them to stay up late and cram for finals, and truck drivers used them when on long routes. Young adults who wanted to party into the night would abuse them.

172

industry and doctors who prescribed amphetamines, you can trace the rise in the illicit manufacture of meth."

Sumner knew where I was going. "You can make meth in your bathtub."

"It's like alcohol prohibition," I said, "when people were driven from the softer substance, beer and wine, to hard adulterated liquor. The War on Drugs has driven people from the milder, pharmaceutical amphetamine to the harsher, homemade meth."

"So how do you explain the increased use of cocaine?" asked Bertotti.

Sumner started laughing. "Dennis Hopper. Remember that scene in *Easy Rider* where they're stuffing money from the sale of the cocaine into the gas tanks of their bikes?"

We laughed with Sumner and then I turned back to Bertotti. "I'd make the same argument. Cocaine is the milder stimulant and, for those who have money, the drug of choice for those who are forced to the black market."

"Ah, cocaine." Sumner sounded like a host on a TV game show. "The Dom Perignon of drugs."

I turned to him. "The what?"

"Jones'y, you've been hanging around these bikers and buying too much cheap speed." Sumner placed his arm around me. "Dom Perignon is champagne, the sophisticated taste of the upper echelon of society. You need to clean up and buy a little cocaine now and then."

Bertotti finally stopped laughing and came back to my point. "You're probably right. It's supply and demand. If you restrict the supply of what's wanted, someone will find another way to supply it or provide a substitute. Sounds like another study."

Sumner protested loudly. "Oh, no, not another study."

We all agreed that there would be no more studies. Our statistics were complete, and we only had to write the thesis. Sumner and Bertotti got up to join others at a table downstairs as I took care of the bill.

"Hey, *viejo*[25]," a female voice said.

I recognized the voice before turning. "Hi, Lucy."

---

25. old man

Lucille was a student at San Jose State University. We had met on previous occasions at the Foghorn. She was wearing a tight sweater along with a mini-skirt, and her long, wavy hair rested gently on her shoulders. She had perched on the seat Sumner vacated.

"How are you?" she asked with a pleasant smile.

"I'm fine. Working long hours. We're having a little get-together for a couple guys downstairs."

"How are things at home?"

"Not good. I left."

She raised her eyebrows, and gently placed her hand on my arm. "How are you doing with that?"

I clenched my teeth. "I don't know."

In the background, a female voice on the jukebox sang about not caring what's right or wrong.

Lucy looked concerned. "Would you like to talk about it later?"

"Sure."

We agreed to meet that Friday back at the Foghorn, and I went downstairs. I didn't catch the irony that I was willing to talk about my personal life with an acquaintance, but was unwilling to sit down and talk to my wife.

Chapter 8

La Nuestra Familia

I n law enforcement, there was always humor to be found in the job. Near the end of the year, one of my ancillary duties was taking care of the narcotics evidence that patrol officers had seized. When the evidence was needed for trial, the police officer signed it out for court. Once the case had been adjudicated, I arranged for the evidence to be destroyed.

Around December, I noticed a mouse was eating into the marijuana evidence. Using my finely tuned investigative skills, I set a trap using peanut butter, cheese, or crackers that would catch the mouse alive. I had no luck, although he continued to eat marijuana evidence. I used another mouse in the cage to lure the culprit, again with no success. I managed to get the media interested in the story, and, for the next couple of days, the newspaper carried articles about the elusive antics of "Marty the Marijuana Mouse."

On December 20, one of my buddies, Officer Anton Erickson, suggested planting the trap with marijuana. Sure enough, after placing fresh marijuana in the cage, I showed up for work the next morning, and there was Marty. As a result of the news articles, dozens of citizens sent Christmas cards to Marty. *Newsweek* and even Johnny Carson got in on the act.

On December 24, two defense attorneys went to court and obtained a hearing from Municipal Court Judge Nelson, charging that I had unlawfully detained Marty. At the end of the day, the judge played along and held a formal hearing. Sergeant Jim LeRoy, who now worked the crime scene investigation unit and had an office next to the narcotics division, picked up the phone and was directed to bring Marty into the courtroom. They also tracked me down, and I had to rush over, not understanding what was transpiring. The *Mercury News* reported the court proceedings the following day.

Defense attorney Kramer, who claimed to be representing Marty, charged that Marty's imprisonment was illegal since his arrest was the result of official entrapment. He also claimed that Marty was a minor, no formal charges had been made against him, he'd been held more than seventy-two hours without bail, and I had captured him by the use of illegal drugs and seduction.

"Is this, and I hate to say defendant, being held against his will?" Judge Nelson asked. "After all, he hasn't been arrested."

"He's not being held against his will," said the police department's legal counsel. "He's one of us."

At this point, they had me swear to tell the truth, the whole truth, and nothing but the truth and take the witness stand.

"Is he a special employee or informant?" Judge Nelson asked.

"He's a special employee, your Honor," I testified.

Judge Nelson looked back at Kramer. "One more question, and I'm almost afraid to ask it. You claim he was caught by seduction. What do you mean by that?"

"The second mouse was in the form of Mata Hari," Kramer said. "That represents attempted seduction and entrapment."

Under cross-examination, I denied entrapment, but admitted I had used seduction on a regular basis in the course of my undercover work.

Judge Nelson adjusted his noble robes. Then with great dignity, he declared, "Marty the Marijuana Mouse is to be taken back to the San Jose police department's narcotics division and live happily ever after as a special employee."

Late in the day, on Christmas Eve, we were finally allowed to go home. I fed Marty proper mouse food over the holidays, but, as the *Mercury News* reported, he probably remembered when the grass was greener.

———··———

I continued to involve the newspapers as often as I could. One day, Maline Hazle, looking for a story, stopped by the narcotics division.

"So what's behind this drug problem and kids?"

I simply said, "Parents."

She grabbed a chair, sat next to my desk, pulled out her note pad, and asked me to explain. I hadn't thought this out, but wasn't going to pass up an opportunity to get the press to post another article about our War on Drugs.

"A big part of the drug problem is parents. They're not paying attention to their children's activities. Their kid shows up with a garage full of tools, new bikes, and clothes with no apparent source of income, and the parents aren't curious. Their children start showing personality changes, such as aggressiveness or laziness; physical changes, such as red eyes or constant tiredness; or a sudden change in friends and acquaintances, yet the parents ask no questions. Then when the kid is arrested for drugs, the parents act surprised. Parents aren't assuming the role of being parents."

The next morning, the banner headline in the *Mercury News* blared "Problem Parents" in large, bold print as if war had been declared.

Sumner was a quick study of how to use the press and followed my lead. He had a case where he had purchased heroin from a customer of Ron Gonzales. He asked for my assistance, and, through phone records, surveillance, and informants, we learned Jesse Estrada was the supplier for Gonzales. Estrada never sold drugs out of his apartment, but had Gonzales walk to a drop spot.

After obtaining a search warrant for Estrada's apartment, Sumner placed an order. When Gonzales exited Estrada's apartment and started walking down the street to the drop location, Sumner and I, wearing gym clothes and dribbling a basketball, started jogging down the street. As we passed an unsuspecting Gonzales, we simply surrounded and arrested him. He was carrying the amount of heroin that Sumner had ordered, and the subsequent search of Estrada's apartment yielded more heroin, packaging materials, paraphernalia, scales, a large amount of cash, and a handgun.

Back at the narcotics division, with the evidence on Sumner's desk, the best response I could get from a news reporter was, "So what?" We were several years into the War on Drugs, and they had seen this spread before. They knew we had only created another job opening for a long line of aspiring drug dealers willing to take Estrada's place, risking it all for the money. But Sumner wasn't going to let the reporter walk off without taking our story.

Drug seizure with Officer Ted Sumner

"We used the Alfred Von Schlieffen plan from World War I." Sumner looked serious. "It nearly resulted in the fall of Paris."

It was the first I heard about it. I didn't even know who Von Schlieffen was, but the reporter looked interested, so Sumner continued. "While running down the street, Jones'y fell back, and I ran ahead and passed Gonzalez. We then closed the gap, trapping Gonzales, just as Von Schlieffen had planned to trap the French."

It might have been a simplification of the Von Schlieffen plan, but that didn't matter. The reporter took the story, and, the next morning, the *Mercury News* said, "Historic Plan in S.J. Drug Bust."

—————•·•—————

The following year brought new cases with more arrests, more doors kicked in, and more drugs, guns, and money seized. But something else was going on in the county that those of us in law enforcement couldn't put our fingers on. There seemed to be an increase in murders, robberies, and drug dealing. The street team was getting information that there was an increase in drug rip-offs. The community was falling apart with unexplained crime. Not crime committed by those under the influence of drugs, but by those fighting over control of the drug market.

What the department didn't know was that someone was moving in and taking over the drug business in our community. Someone was filling the void the narcotics division had created by arresting the local dealers. What we also didn't know was that we were going to uncover this through a classic case of our division operating exactly as it was designed to work, although with an unusual twist.

"Jones'y," Grant said as he sat on my desk. "We arrested this guy, Bart. I think you might want to talk to him. The buy team tried working with him, but he absolutely refuses to be involved in a buy-bust." Grant handed me a file. "Same old BS, you know, that these guys will kill him if they find out he's working with us. I think there's more to what he knows than what he's giving us. We just don't have the time to work with him that way."

Bart had been arrested and served time in juvenile hall as a teenager for a shooting. He'd recently been released from the prison at Soledad after serving time for armed robbery. He was suspected of a recent burglary, and he had been picked up several weeks earlier for being under the influence of heroin. I wasn't sure what I was supposed to do with him if the buy team wasn't having success, but Grant had a way of knowing, which certain cops have after years of experience. And if Grant thought there was more to this guy, then I was willing to take on Bart as an informant.

"Do we have a hammer on him?" I asked.

"The best we have is a parole violation. He knows it and doesn't want to go back to the joint."

We walked over to an interrogation room, and Grant introduced me. "Bart, this is Detective Jones. He's agreed to work with your butt, but this is your last chance, you got that?"

Grant walked out, and I looked across the table at a white male in his late twenties, stocky with a wrestler physique, and short, red hair. Tattoos, the kind applied in prison, covered parts of his arms. He had that look in his eyes, a look that only comes with serving years in the penitentiary. I also knew he was a convicted armed robber, a bad ass.

"So what's the problem?" I asked.

Bart sat back and crossed his arms against his chest while thrusting out his chin. "There's no problem, ese.[26] You just don't go in and score from these guys and then bust them. You're gonna get someone killed."

I checked out his tattoos, which clearly identified him with Mexican groups. "You Mexican? I figured you for the Brotherhood."

"No, inside I was with the Mexicans, though."

I figured he was talking about the Mexican Mafia. I knew prisons had three main gangs inside: the Mexican Mafia, the Aryan Brotherhood, and the Black Guerilla Family.

"Okay, who are we talking about here, Bart? What guys? What can you do for me?"

Bart leaned farther back in the chair and looked down his nose. "These guys are new. You don't know them, ese, believe me."

Standing, I leaned forward with my hands on the table. I raised my voice. "Let's get something straight, Bart. I don't believe you. When I see it, I believe it. You got that, Bucko? Now, we either get results or I'm calling your parole officer and you're going back in." I paused to let that sink in. "Have I got your attention?" Our eyes locked, and I acted angry, like I didn't have time for games.

---

26. Ese, pronounced es-say, was Mexican slang for friend, but not always meant in a friendly manner.

Bart sat forward and put his elbows and the table. He still looked cocky. "I'll show you, holmes."[27]

"When?"

"Tonight. Right now. What do you want?"

"What can we do?"

"Chiva.[28] We can score a couple spoons."

I kept my eyes locked on Bart. *I'm not good at heroin. Cocaine and speed I can buy, as I fit right in with those guys, but heroin?* Questions were running through my head. Dealers usually sold heroin in one-quarter teaspoon amounts. A "spoon," or a full teaspoon, was an amount usually sold to a dealer who would break it down into the smaller amounts. My buying a spoon right off the bat from a dealer sounded improbable. *Is this guy trying to game me?*

"All right, you know the drill, Bart. Strip down, and throw your clothes out the door."

One of the rules of working with informants was that you always strip-searched them before going anywhere. A narc didn't want it suggested in court that maybe the informant had brought the drugs with him into the defendant's pad. The narcotics detective also wanted to make sure the informant had no money other than the marked bills given him. It was also nice to be sure that my informant, a convicted robber in this case, wasn't carrying a weapon. This was one of the more unpleasant sides of the job, searching through clothes and then examining the naked body, making sure he had hid nothing up an orifice, by having him bend over and spread his buttocks.

For several nights, I was out running around with Bart without backup or cover. We'd go into a suspect's pad, score some heroin, and then leave. These guys weren't selling to drug users. They were selling to small-time drug dealers, which I was passing myself off to be. And these dealers didn't allow me to sit around and shoot the bull. I took the dope and got out, without a word said.

I'd note the suspect's name, usually a nickname like Pero, Manny, or Flaco, and the address. The narcotic and subsequent report would then be filed under

---

27. Holmes was short for homeboy, another word for friend.

28. Chiva was a street name for heroin.

a case number. License plate numbers, addresses, nicknames from prior arrest records, and utility bills usually identified a drug dealer. Follow-up on these guys, though, brought up nothing. I was having difficulty identifying them.

Late one night, Bart and I had just scored from yet another dealer. I had on my usual Levi jacket over a white t-shirt. Bart was wearing an old army fatigue jacket over a red flannel shirt and a black ski cap. I was driving a tan Volkswagen bug, and we had left some old apartments in San Jose near Senter Road and Monterey Highway. It was the last stop of the night, and we were headed back to the police station. I drove along the back of the apartments, which were fenced off from a gas station and convenience store along Monterey Highway.

"I got a buddy here who owes me money. Can you let me get it?" Bart asked.

"Make it quick. Otherwise, I'll leave your sorry butt here."

Bart hopped out and ran off around the corner. He was back in less than three minutes. I pulled onto Senter Road and then up to the light to turn right on Monterey Highway. I noticed but gave no thought to red lights approaching from far to the south on my left. I turned right and headed north on Monterey Highway, back to the police station. I dropped off Bart at his car, filed my reports in an empty narcotics division office, booked my evidence, and went home.

The next morning, sitting at my desk, I was reading the Watch Bulletin, a daily department-wide report on the crime activity from the previous day. There were a couple of burglaries here, a stolen car there, a hit-and-run downtown, and an armed robbery on Monterey Highway near Senter Road. *What the ...?*

My body flushed as I read the short synopsis of an armed robbery committed the night before at 2250 by an unknown suspect wearing an army field jacket with a full ski mask. No car was seen. *Oh, no.*

I pulled the paperwork on my last case from the night before, already suspecting the answer. My report said my last buy was at 2245. We were pulling out of the apartments, and Bart went to get money from a friend around 2250.

"Oh, shit," I said aloud as I realized I drove the getaway for an armed robbery.

I headed for the robbery division down the hall. "Got a minute?" I asked Detective Chuck Molosky.

"Hey, Jones'y, what's up?"

"What can you tell me about the 2-11 last night on Monterey at Senter?"

Molosky pulled the file sitting right on top of his desk. "Adult male wearing full ski mask, green army jacket, and Levis. Had a handgun. Took approximately $50 and was last seen running toward the apartments behind the store. No vehicle seen or heard."

I exhaled slowly through pursed lips and then took a deep breath. "Well, you're not going to believe this."

I suggested we go into an interrogation room, and I proceeded to lay it out. By the time I was through, we were both rolling around in laughter with tears.

I got back to the seriousness of the situation. "How are we going to handle this?"

Molosky didn't miss a beat. "Oh, from a prosecution standpoint, this has got problems. Besides, the witness has no ID other than the clothes."

I shook my head. "Yeah, but I can verify what he was wearing along with the other circumstantial evidence, like the time and place."

"Did you search him at the end of the day?" Molosky asked.

That would have been normal procedure if Bart had been given any money and made a controlled buy. I'd want to make sure he wasn't skimming any money or dope while working for me. "No, no reason to. He was never given money and didn't make a buy last night."

"Well, any defense attorney will have a field day with this. I'll run this by my lieutenant, but I suspect this will be closed due to lack of prosecution." Molosky started to laugh again. "I do want to talk to this guy, though. And for now, better keep this between ourselves."

I got up. "Bart's due in here around 1500. I'll let you know."

We walked out of the interrogation room to an office full of detectives working at their desks, oblivious to the situation. I headed back to the narcotics division with visions of sitting in the internal affairs office. I didn't see them laughing like Molosky.

It had all been funny when relating the story to Molosky, but the seriousness settled in. Had patrol officers stopped us as armed suspects, it could've had tragic consequences. So when Bart arrived at 1500, it took everything I had to remain calm, cool, and collected and not allow Bart to suspect I was on to him.

"The room in my office is in use." I led Bart into an interrogation room where Molosky worked. "I'm going to put you in here."

Molosky was standing there with a big grin. I closed the door on Bart, leaving him alone for a minute.

"What does your lieutenant say?" I asked.

His demeanor turned serious. "We have to find the gun. Then we'll close this out for lack of prosecution. But we have plenty to revoke his parole."

"I don't want Bart to know that, though. I'm going to get some leverage out of this. Let me say a few words, and then I'll leave."

Over the years on the job, I had my share of circumstances where physical force was necessary, but it was usually in the course of someone resisting arrest. I had never taken anything personally until Bart pulled this stunt. This was personal. He had gamed me. He had crossed a line and went well beyond the pale, and nearly four hours of pent-up anger was ready to vent.

Molosky and I walked into the interrogation room, which, with a table and two chairs, was small for three people. As soon as the door closed, I unloaded on Bart, who had stood as we entered. I grabbed him and flung him into the table. He lost his balance, which enabled me to bang his face off the tabletop with my forearm to the back of his head.

"Pendejo,[29] you've got to be one of the stupidest punks I've ever run across." More profanities flowed freely. "You're worried about going back to jail for being under the influence and yet you pull this?" I tossed him across the small room, slamming him into the other wall. Blood was running from his nose. Molosky decided that maybe he should leave the room until I was done.

"Just how the hell do you think I'm going to be able to keep you out now?" I didn't wait for an answer. "You ready to do another seven years? Sit down." I had him by the throat and threw him into the chair, but he toppled over onto

---

29. Pendejo could mean idiot, or in this case, asshole.

the floor. He got up, turned the chair up right, and sat down. "I suggest you don't give Sergeant Molosky any bull, understand?" I had never mentioned the word robbery, although I assumed he'd figured it out. "I can't believe anyone could be so stupid," I said as I left. I added a few more expletives as I slammed the door behind me.

Interrogation rooms are insulated to prevent someone from hearing an interview or interrogation. But everyone heard that display, and they were standing and staring as I came out of the room. I had gotten myself so worked up that I couldn't bring myself to smile.

"He's going to owe me," I mentioned to Molosky as he slipped into the room.

Less than fifteen minutes, he came back out. "He didn't waive his rights, but said enough for us to clear the case. He had hid the gun in a friend's car there at the apartments. We know where to get it and the money. I made it clear that it was up to you now."

The detectives standing around were still wondering what was going on as Molosky slapped me on the back with a smile. I let Bart sit for a while before going back.

"Start talking." I slapped my note tablet on the table.

Bart started explaining the armed robbery.

"No, I don't need to hear about that. And we're finished with these small-time heroin dealers. I want the names of some serious suppliers, or your butt is going back to Soledad for a long time. You understand me?"

I had no idea if he could come up with anything more, but it was my last attempt. Either way, I figured he was going back to prison for violating parole. I had hand-to-hand sales from the crooks Bart had introduced me to and didn't need him for prosecution.

"You know La Nuestra Familia?" He held his bloody nose with a corner of his shirt.

"No, what is it?"

"It's a gang, ese, in prison. Mexicans. The guys you've been buying from are Familia. They're on the streets now, taking over and running everything like drugs, burglary, and robbery."

What the hell is he talking about? I hadn't heard of the Nuestra Familia. I headed out the door and down the hall to the opposite end and entered the intelligence division.

"Who can tell me about La Nuestra Familia?" Sergeant John Kracht pointed to Officer Art Hilborn.

"That'd be me," Hilborn said.

I sat down across from his desk and started taking notes.

"Like the Black Guerilla Family, the Aryan Brotherhood, and the Mexican Mafia, La Nuestra Familia is a prison gang."

"Why the Familia when you have the Mexican Mafia?"

"The Mexican Mafia tend to be older, better organized, and, for lack of a better word, more professional. La Nuestra Familia is much younger, aggressive, and violent. They're a nasty prison gang."

"What about on the streets?"

"They're only now beginning to be released, and we haven't seen or heard much from them. So there's little to report. Why do you ask?"

I got up to leave. "I'm not quite sure. I'll get back to you in about an hour. Thanks, this helps."

I went back to Bart. "All right, how do you know this?"

"I'm a member of La Familia, one of the few guys who isn't Mexican ever allowed in." He leaned forward on his elbows. Blood continued to drip from his nose onto the table, and he wiped it with his sleeve. "These guys will kill me if they find out I'm snitching. That's why you can't go busting people right after we score."

I grabbed my pen and got ready to write. "Who do you know, and what are they doing? Start at the top."

"This guy Sosa is the general. Then there's this guy on death row, and that's his name, Death Row, and he's next in line. Bruiser's a captain, and he's head of things here. These guys run all the dope in prison, and now they're getting out and taking over on the street. Anybody who resists is killed. They're doing robberies and burglaries. As soon as you get out of prison, you have to do a crime. If you're Familia, you're in for life. Then you have to pull jobs and put money into the business."

"How many are on the streets here, Bart?"

"About thirty. This city is the headquarters."

"Who's the boss on the streets?"

"Like I said, this guy Bruiser, Bruiser Rios. Then there's Nenny Morales. Some of the other guys I know are Alvarez, Cobos, and Tenario."

Bart went on to give information on murders, assaults, and robberies that were probably unsolved. I couldn't believe what he was spilling. I headed back to my office and got Hilborn on the phone. "If you can, grab what you have about La Nuestra Familia and come down to Bertotti's office."

I headed for Bertotti, where he appeared to be tied up with paperwork. He looked up from his desk through his thick glasses.

"Sorry to bother you, boss."

Bertotti rubbed his forehead and sighed, as if I only had bad news when I needed to see him. He leaned back in his chair and motioned for me to sit as Hilborn walked in. I laid out the information I had received from Bart.

"This guy is for real," Hilborn said. "He'll be a gold mine of info for us."

The following morning, Hilborn and I held a briefing. Present were detectives from robbery, burglary, and homicide, parole officers, someone from the bureau of prisons, and the entire narcotics division. Everyone pretty much dropped what they were working on and took assignments.

A couple of days later, officers from the MERGE team were brought in, and we hit the streets with arrest and search warrants. The investigation took on a life of its own, and it was all I could do to keep track of it. The *Mercury News* ran a banner headline proclaiming, "San Jose Hub of Prison Gang."

Within weeks, several dozen Familia members were in the county jail for assorted crimes. One arrest led to another. One search warrant led to another. I arrested a guy named George Tenario. He wasn't ready to go back to jail and immediately agreed to talk to me. I started working with him and found out he was a close friend of Bart's, so I had to go to great lengths to make sure neither knew the other was cooperating. I passed information I received from Tenario to narcotics detective Schembri, and he uncovered a cache of ten rifles and shotguns, along with boxes of ammo.

We were arresting so many Familia members on assorted charges that the sheriff publicly declared a rise in violence within the jail. The *Mercury News* ran headlines declaring that the sheriff's department had lost control of the jail to the prison gang.

Because of all the arrests and search warrants, La Nuestra Familia was in disarray. They began to suspect anyone and everyone of being an informant. The killings began, in prison and on the street. One of the last to turn informant, George Tenario, was one of the first identified on a hit list taken from an inmate in prison. We made arrangements with the US Marshal's office for Tenario to be shipped to Guam where he had family, but Tenario delayed, and I received a call at home from Bart late one night. Tenario had just been murdered. I was up the rest of the night with the homicide detectives of the Santa Clara County sheriff's department. With the information I was gathering from Bart and other informants, we soon knew who made the hit, Jose Cobos and Daniel Ramos.

It seemed, as fast as it had all started, it was over. The investigation had run its course after a couple months, and all the targets had been arrested, fled, or gone underground. Many were returned to prison on parole violations. Court-appointed attorneys pled out most arrested for crimes, so they were returned to prison.

The most notable court trial that remained was that of Cobos and Ramos, and the sheriff's department had built a great case against them. But they had tenacious defense attorneys who weren't going to allow them to plead out to first-degree murder, and the DA wasn't going to allow them to plead to a lesser charge. Pretrial preparations, motions, and hearings went on for months while La Nuestra Familia was still wondering what happened. When the Cobos and Ramos case finally came to trial, members of La Familia packed the courtroom. During the trial, it became clear to all how extensive my involvement in the investigation had been.

One morning before heading over to the courtroom, Molosky called. "Jones'y, we need to talk with Bertotti. Is he around?"

"I'll let you know when I see him."

Bertotti soon came in, a cup of coffee in one hand and the newspaper in the other.

"Boss, Molosky has something important."

Bertotti stopped, raised both arms up a bit, and smiled. "Hey, I just walked in the door. Can't a guy get a chance to read the paper in the morning?"

I picked up the phone and called Molosky. "He's in."

Molosky was all business as we sat in Bertotti's office. "I was on duty last night and took a call around 2200 from a guy who says his son, Flavio, is a member of La Nuestra Familia. He wouldn't give me a last name. Yesterday, a meeting was held at his house, and he overheard some of what they were talking about. This guy said his son was given $2,500 and a gun to kill Officer Jones. He says he saw the cash and the gun. He said he's tired of this Familia stuff his son is involved in and wants it to stop."

"Do we know which Flavio this is?" asked Bertotti. "Aren't there more than one?"

"Two," I said. "But it's probably Alvarez. He's been implicated in the Naples murder."

"At this point," Molosky said, "it's not so much who, but what we are going to do to prevent any attempt. If we focus on who and have the wrong guy, then we leave Jones'y at risk."

Bertotti looked at me. "What do you think?"

"I don't know. Something doesn't sound right. Why would La Familia need to give $2,500 to one of its members? Either way, Flavio Alvarez is one of the gang members Bart is getting info from, so I'll see what Bart knows. And I'll ask intelligence to keep an ear open for anything from their sources. By the end of the day, I'll have a plan for you on what I'm going to do."

Later in the morning, the secretary informed me I had a call.

"This is Officer Jones. May I help you?"

"This is Bart. You're in trouble."

"Why?"

He spoke calmly, as if it were simply a matter of fact. "These guys are going to kill you, holmes."

"Tell me what you know, Bart."

"I don't know much, just that Flavio Alvarez has been given orders."

"Do you think he'll try?"

"He has no choice. If he doesn't, they'll kill him. That's the way it works in La Familia."

"Ask around. See what you can find out, like where he is and what he has planned."

"I'm not asking any questions, Officer Jones. They suspect everyone. You need to get me in the program."

He was referring to a witness protection program. I ended the conversation with instructions to be by his phone in the evening.

I then went down to intelligence. "Hilborn, do you think they'll try to carry this out?"

"Absolutely. These guys will carry out an order and kill a rival in prison in plain view of a guard. So they'll be bold with no regards to getting caught." It was a sobering thought.

That afternoon, I was back in court and on the witness stand in the Cobos and Rios murder trial. Much of my testimony that day was about my various sources of information. During a short recess, with everyone still in the courtroom, I was in a discussion with Ken Robinson, the assistant DA handling the case. I knew La Familia was still paranoid about who was saying what to whom about their organization, so I mentioned loud enough for some in the audience to hear that our informant got that information from Flavio Alvarez. Out of the corner of my eye, I could see heads turn and eye contact made between them. After a few whispers, several people immediately left the courtroom.

At the end of the day, I called Bart.

"Now they're after Flavio," he said.

"Why?"

Bart's voice was beginning to sound desperate. "I don't know. I'm not asking questions, just listening. These guys are crazy, ese. They suspect everyone of snitching. It won't be long before they suspect me. You gotta get me out of here."

Bart was right. I needed to get him in the witness protection program as we were going to need his testimony in upcoming trials against Nenny Morales and Bruiser Rios, the local leadership in La Familia.

I met Bertotti in the hallway. "Boss, I've switched cars with Mendez. Lyle

Rice and I live at the same apartment complex, so he and others there will be alerted to help keep an eye out." Rice, a sergeant in BOI who, along with me and a few other officers, received a reduction in rent in exchange for working security at the apartment complex.

"Besides, I think I took care of it," I said.

"Why? What'd you do?" he asked.

I hesitated as I tried to figure out how to explain that I might have put Flavio on a hit list. Luckily, I didn't have to answer.

Bertotti could read my eyes. "I don't think I want to know."

"No, you don't."

The jury convicted Cobos and Ramos of first-degree murder in the killing of my informant, George Tenario. Ironically, the gun used to kill Tenario was a gun that Tenario had taken in the course of a burglary he'd committed at the direction of Familia leadership.

With the upcoming trial of Bruiser and Nenny, I met each of them in jail. I pointed out that, as leaders of La Nuestra Familia in San Jose, which was now in disarray, they were in grave danger from their superiors if returned to prison. They rolled over and became informants. In retaliation, their family members had homes firebombed, and others were murdered. La Nuestra Familia had been disrupted, but only temporarily. Street gangs and their control of drug dealing had forever changed the streets of San Jose.

We soon found ourselves back to a normal routine. During the course of the three years I had been in the narcotics division, there were plenty of cases that we worked with the DEA. Usually the experience was positive, but there were a few exceptions.

One was a long, drawn-out investigation that started with anonymous information coming to Officer Gutierrez about a local businessman dealing in heroin. Previously unknown to us, he was supposedly importing large amounts and then bypassing all the middlemen by cutting it down and packaging it in toy balloons in quarter teaspoon quantities. The suspect, married with several children, lived in an expensive home on an acre of land in the eastern foothills of San Jose. A high fence enclosed the entire property.

The case got off the ground before daylight one morning. While digging through his garbage cans left on the street for pickup, Gutierrez and I found many empty bags of toy balloons. With nothing else to go on, the case could only continue from intelligence.

Sergeant Boone had taught me Link-Analysis, a method of linking my intelligence together. This was before computers, so it was done by hand. Using information gathered from the subpoenaed telephone records of the main suspect and surveillance of his daily activities, we were able to track and identify other suspects, including some who lived in Mexico. If I knew my suspect's associates, then I was closer to knowing his crimes.

I had a large poster board with circles for each suspect and lines connecting the circles based on the phone calls or other contacts. I later changed circles to diamonds or squares, depending on where we thought someone existed in the chain. I used different color lines to indicate volume of calls between suspects. The case, spread throughout several different counties in the San Francisco Bay area, soon became so large and complex that we called DEA for assistance. Unfortunately for us, the agent who came to assist simply walked away with the case. We never heard of the investigation again until it ended months later when $2 million of heroin was seized and twelve arrest warrants were served.

So in 1978, when I was asked to join a new joint DEA, customs, and San Jose police department drug task force, I had reservations. I picked up the phone and called Agent Dave Wilson at the DEA's San Francisco office. Wilson, who loved research, details, and building cases using intelligence, was a textbook example of interagency liaison and cooperation. In the past, whenever I needed assistance, he always provided what was necessary, yet he never tried to take over or demand to become active in the case. He informed me that he was going to be transferred to the San Jose task force, and, if I accepted the assignment, he assured me we'd be partners.

Chapter 9

RICO

"We'll provide a kilo for $80,000," Denny said. He then took another bite of his steak. Debra had finished her meal, and she was working on a glass of wine.

I knew the going price for quality cocaine. I pushed away my empty plate, sat back, and frowned. "I'm not paying that. Look, $58,000 a kilo. I'll buy half. If I like it, I'll buy the rest. But we do it all the same evening."

I wanted a situation where, when they went to get the second pound, we could trace phone calls, trail someone, seize more drugs, and identify the person behind the drug dealing. I didn't want a case where we arrested only a courier.

"You've tasted it," Denny said.

I took a sip from my Jack Daniels. "That doesn't mean it'll be the same stuff I get next time. Look, it's a lot of money, so understand that I'm going to be a little cautious."

I was now with the DEA task force, and I had flown a Cessna into Watsonville to meet with Denny and Debra Giordano. My hair was shorter, and my beard was trimmed. I was wearing dress slacks and a long-sleeved shirt unbuttoned at the top, exposing plenty of chest hair and several gold necklaces. My fingers on both hands sported diamond-studded rings. As Sumner would've said, I'd moved up into the world of champagne, and into cocaine.

The Giordanos were in the vegetable business, but got caught up in the cocaine trade. They were anxious to earn extra money, and they were willing to introduce me to their source. Both of them were at the airport to pick me up.

When I climbed out of the plane, I discreetly scanned every shadow and looked for whatever might be out of place. I was aware of the cars behind us as we drove into Santa Cruz. When we entered the upscale steak house, I took a seat with my back to the wall in the far corner, where I could see who was coming and going. I made a mental note of who was at each table. *Is that couple over there married, on a date, or is it Giordano's drug connection?* I made note of the emergency exit door and every window. My suspicions and constant mental preparations had become a habit, a way of life.

I flashed a large roll of money, bought drinks, and paid for dinner. Having flown into town in a private airplane, they certainly thought I was a high roller. We had met like this on several occasions before getting down to serious discussions.

We finally settled on $68,000 a kilo. I'd pay $34,000 for the first half. If I liked the product, the second half would be delivered that same day for another $34,000. To control the setting for the sale, I got Denny to agree to deliver the cocaine to my sailboat, which would be moored at the Oakland harbor. Backup officers would be able to monitor the phone booths and watch all foot and vehicle traffic around the marina and back at the Giordano home. I wanted to ensure that we flushed out someone higher in the organization.

Several nights later, everyone was in place for the final purchase, but there was a hitch. DEA insisted that Agent Rich Camps accompany me. It wasn't necessary, and I knew what the result would be.

Denny Giordano and Kenneth Hozian, a Columbian, showed up and completed the sale of the first pound, but any further transaction was dead in the water for that night. With Camps having been introduced, Hozian wasn't about to proceed until he saw that this transaction went smoothly and some time had passed. We couldn't allow $34,000 to walk, so we had no choice but to arrest them when Hozian refused to complete the deal. The investigation was finished. The Giordanos were recreational cocaine users who were beginning to dabble in sales. Hozian was only a courier, and we never were able to identify the person behind the transaction.

It concerned me that narcotics detectives assigned to the task force were often pressured into bringing a DEA agent into an investigation, even when it wasn't necessary and would compromise the case. With three years in the narcotics division at the police department, I had never experienced another detective try to muscle in and become personally involved in a case. So I brought up the topic with Agent Wilson as we sat at our desks one afternoon.

"Dave, what's the deal with DEA insisting an agent get involved in our cases?"

"Getting promoted requires making your supervisor look good. You need your name as a participant on the bottom of that report, and supervisors need to show that their team is producing."

"Sounds like the OER in the military," I said.

Wilson, a former marine, knew the officer efficiency report. "Exactly. With seniority and a good report from your supervisors, you get promoted." Wilson laughed. "It results in the Peter Principle, though."

"Doesn't work that way at the police department," I explained. "You take a test on police theory, procedures, supervision, and administration. Then you sit in front of an oral board held by members from another department who don't have a clue as to your past performance. They rate you based on how well you articulate an answer and your ability to think on your feet."

Wilson thought it over. "So you can be quite average on the job, but be promoted if you're a good test taker?"

"Yeah, just do your job, lay low, go home, and study."

Wilson tapped his pencil on the desk. "Makes sense. Being a good supervisor or administrator doesn't require you to have been a good cop, and being a good cop doesn't mean you'll be a good supervisor."

"I suppose," I mumbled, although I had to agree he had a point. I had a better idea, though, of why DEA agents were so anxious to get involved in other investigators' cases when they didn't have one of their own.

During the time I was working narcotics, I owned an antique airplane that I enjoyed flying to air shows and Lake Tahoe. I kept my technical flying skills up to date with the use of a Cessna 206, which had the latest electronics and navigation equipment. John DuPont, one of the heirs to the DuPont chemical fortune, owned it.

An avid outdoorsman, bird-watcher, skydiver, and athlete, DuPont was also attracted to law enforcement, to which he donated time, equipment, and money. For a dollar a year, he was a sworn special officer with Chester County, Pennsylvania. Officer Moudakas, who met DuPont when he came out to California in search of a police dog, introduced me to DuPont.

DuPont had property and businesses in the San Jose area and kept the aircraft for that purpose. He allowed San Jose Officer Hoen and me to use the aircraft, and we racked up many hours practicing instrument approaches at airports all over northern California.

Although I enjoyed working undercover best, I continued to use my flying skills when needed. One case involved narcotics detective Doug Zwemke, a tall, lanky, brilliant academic who could have had a career as a professor at any major university, but instead chose to chase down and thump crooks. Zwemke had been assigned to the task force and was working his way up the chain of a group who were selling PCP, a malicious anesthetic and hallucinogenic known as angel dust. After making several buys of the drug, he had ordered a large enough quantity that required the suspects to go to their laboratory. Zwemke suspected the lab to be in the Santa Cruz Mountains, and a Santa Cruz county deputy sheriff and I were in the air to assist several undercover cars on the ground with surveillance.

We expected to identify the location within a couple of hours. The suspects, though, started driving north and didn't stop until they reached Bend, Oregon ten hours later. Undercover officers in cars were able to continue the tail while we landed for fuel.

We hadn't expected to travel and weren't dressed for the February temperatures, which were well below zero. We were out of town, though, on a government expense account, and all had a grand time at the local restaurants and bars ... except for the suspects. As I circled above the forest, directing the cars on the ground, the location of their lab was discovered, five were arrested, and Zwemke seized over fifty pounds of PCP estimated to be worth nearly $7 million.

Nearly ten years into the War on Drugs, we were seizing record amounts of heroin, cocaine, methamphetamine, and drugs like PCP. George Halpin, western regional director of the DEA, and William Hunter, US attorney for Northern California, were making statements that the drug networks were being disrupted and dismantled. Yet we obviously weren't making a dent in the illicit business. Drugs were cheaper, stronger, and more plentiful than ever.

While working other cases, I continued my investigations into the activities of Hell's Angels members. I had boxes of phone records, surveillance reports, and intelligence. I also had agreements with the major chemical supply businesses, and, when someone suspicious ordered chemicals used in the manufacture of methamphetamine, I tracked the delivery.

On the wall above my desk was a Link-Analysis chart, with circles and connecting lines. Names in the circles included "Dirty Doug" Bontempi, "Sir Gay" Walton, "Jim Jim" Brandes, and "Dirt" England. Two non-Hell's Angels who I had on the chart were Ronald Lopez and Sheri Prince, self-styled chemists who I suspected were involved in the manufacture of methamphetamine. In Arizona, they had recently purchased a chemical called phenyl-2-propanone (P2P), which was necessary to produce methamphetamine. They had been tailed after the purchase, but we lost them in the Ben Lomand area of the Santa Cruz Mountains.

Months later, while searching suspects' phone records, an address on Figone Lane in Ben Lomand came to my attention. Renters, who had used false names, had recently vacated the home, and the owner gave me permission to search the property. This type of follow-up was similar to looking for a needle in a haystack, but I was relentless. I grabbed Zwemke on a slow day, and we headed into the Santa Cruz Mountains.

At the home, we found glassware, precursor chemicals used in making meth, and a press with punches used for producing tablets. We had found a lab, but, at that point, we had no strong evidence to tie it to anyone.

One of the items I recovered was an old newspaper with a mailing label to a home on Alba Road, also in Ben Lomand. I found that a renter named Ron Stefenel had recently occupied this home. The landlord indicated that Stefenel was no longer occupying the residence and gave me permission to search. At that residence, I found evidence consistent with the home also having been used as a meth lab. Although Stefenel had been the renter of record, I uncovered evidence that a Hell's Angel had lived at the Alba Road address, as well as at the Figone home. Previously off my radar, his name was Alan "Altamont Al" Passaro.

Back in 1969, the Rolling Stones had given a concert at the Altamont Speedway in Livermore, California. The Hell's Angels were hired, at a modest salary of $500 worth of beer, to provide security for the Rolling Stones to protect them from the three hundred thousand concert attendees. Although peaceful at first, over the course of the day while other bands played, both the crowd and the Angels became progressively intoxicated and violent. By the time the Rolling Stones took to the stage in the evening, the mood between the Angels and the mob had become downright ugly. Several Angels had armed themselves with the heavy end of pool cues and even motorcycle chains. Hell's Angel motorcycles were knocked over, fights ensued, and concert attendees were beaten.

At one point in the evening, an eighteen-year-old man named Meredith Hunter tried to climb onto the stage, and the Angels forcibly removed him. Hunter's girlfriend tried to move him back into the crowd, but Hunter, under the influence of alcohol, moved back toward the stage while producing a gun. Hell's Angel Alan Passaro immediately stabbed him to death.

The entire concert was filmed as a documentary entitled *Gimme Shelter*, and it contained the scenes of Hunter pulling the gun. Passaro was tried for the murder of Hunter, but, when the jury saw the documentary, they acquitted him. Among the Hell's Angels, Passaro's nickname became "Altamont Al."

When a case like the Ben Lomand meth lab begins to come together, like a jigsaw puzzle, the pieces fill in rapidly. With the evidence I had obtained from both residences, I added more circles and names to my chart, which phone records, receipts, and other evidence further connected. Using forensics on the punch set, the DEA lab was able to identify and connect the meth tablets to others previously arrested for possession. Those defendants gave information further implicating Passaro. By the time the results of the fingerprint identifications came in from the lab equipment I had seized, I had a solid case against Lopez, Prince, Stefenel, and Passaro.

Stefenel was allowed to plea to a misdemeanor, and Lopez and Prince pled guilty to conspiracy to manufacture. Altamont Al decided to fight the charge, and he was found guilty of manufacturing methamphetamine. He was sentenced to prison for a term of five years.

Years earlier, while undercover, I had observed a Hell's Angel named Black Bill Solano deliver heroin, leading to his conviction. More recently, I had convicted Wild Bill Perkey. I could now add Altamont Al to my roll of Hell's Angels that I had sent to prison for drugs. Elusive Dirty Doug was still on my list.

I received a phone call one afternoon from San Jose Police Sergeant John Diehl. He'd recently been with the field training program, supervising the downtown district. Chief Joseph McNamara, who had replaced Chief Murphy in 1976, had been receiving citizen complaints about late night activities downtown, and directed patrol units to put pressure on the prostitutes working the area. Diehl, feeling his officers had better things to do, directed his officers to spend time on what he felt were more pressing issues. The chief promptly removed Diehl from his responsibilities as FTO sergeant.

Diehl was now calling me from the Caribbean, where he was on an extended vacation while the issue settled down. While hanging around St. Maarten, Diehl, an avid sailor, made friends with Robert Lafferty, who owned a home and boat there. In the course of getting to know Lafferty, Diehl learned that Lafferty owned a restaurant and several airplanes, including a multi-engine King Air. Nervous about whom he was associating with and not wanting to step into something soft, Diehl suggested I check him out.

I ran Lafferty's name through all the data systems I could. I only found the sale of an aircraft to a drug suspect in Albuquerque by the name of Rodriguez, but there was no information indicating Lafferty knew he was selling to a drug dealer, so there was nothing of interest.

Several days later, Rick Dunigan, the special agent in charge of the task force, came into my office. Dunigan was a large, easygoing man who I rarely saw except when we went to lunch together for seafood at Race Street Fish and Poultry, a restaurant down the street from where I took my first fatal accident report. He was working a toothpick in his mouth as he ushered two men in suits into my office.

"Couple guys from the FBI would like to talk to you," Dunigan said before he left.

One showed me his credentials. "I'm Agent Johnson."

The other agent also showed me his FBI identification, but I didn't catch his name. Johnson, clearly in charge, handed me a business card indicating he was with the FBI's Atlanta office. "We're working a special project out of DC. What can you tell me about Robert Lafferty?"

"Not much." I immediately wondered what Diehl had stepped into.

"Our records indicated you ran a background on him, and he's of special interest to us. Can you elaborate?"

"A year ago, I had a case where a load of cocaine, out of Florida, was being driven to a liquor store in Campbell. While passing through Albuquerque, its driver made contact with a Rodriguez. It then proceeded on through town, but a city patrol car stopped it for a traffic violation. The traffic cop suspected something, searched the car, and found pounds of cocaine. Our case, of course, was blown, and we never confirmed where the drugs were headed. I look into the case now and then to see if there's anything new. I recently had information that led me to a Robert Lafferty, who had an aircraft business transaction in Albuquerque with a Rodriguez. There's no evidence it's the same Rodriguez."

"This source of information, is this someone you can go back to for more info?" Johnson asked.

"I'll see what I can do." I looked at Johnson's card and noticed he had hand-written in another number.

"I'm currently TDY from the Atlanta office. That number on the back will reach me in DC."

I put the business card on my desk. "I'll get back to you."

We shook hands again, and they left. I couldn't help but wonder what was so important about Lafferty that they'd travel all the way out to San Jose instead of simply picking up the phone.

A few days later, I was able to reach Diehl by phone. "I don't have the slightest idea what they're looking for, but they want more info."

"Well, come on down. I'll introduce you to him."

"I'm not for sure that's what they had in mind, but I'll let you know."

Part of me was anxious to make such a trip, but I had concerns. It seemed so out of the ordinary. Suspicious and paranoid, I purposely placed a call to Agent Johnson at the Atlanta phone number on the card. The receptionist politely referred me to the same DC phone number Johnson had written on the back. I felt better. The DC office referred me to the FBI's San Francisco office, where I was able to leave a message.

"How about if I can meet him?" I asked when he returned my call.

Johnson sounded enthusiastic. "Meet Lafferty? That'd be great. We'll meet you at your office Monday morning."

I briefed Agent Wilson about my phone call from Diehl and subsequent contact with Johnson. Then I obtained his assurance that he'd be in the office on Monday.

Johnson showed up alone. He had a few questions. "You need to understand that this isn't a drug case. In fact, we don't want DEA involved."

I looked at Wilson. Johnson then looked at Wilson, as if he had just realized someone else was in the room.

"Don't worry about me." Wilson laughed in his deep voice. "Unless someone asks, I'm not saying anything."

"If this isn't a drug case, what are we looking for?" I asked.

"I need you to find out whatever you can about Lafferty. Where he lives, what he does for a living, and what he's doing with his airplanes. We're finding him elusive, so whatever you can learn will be a big help."

"So how is this going to work?" I asked.

"You'll go on our dime. We'll reimburse you. Can you take vacation or—"

"Between vacation and time off for overtime, I can arrange it."

After Johnson left, Wilson, appearing peeved, shook his head. "Interagency rivalry. We should have cooperation and consolidation of effort from the FBI. Instead, we have these games that lead to animosity."

I let Wilson settle down. "Johnson didn't ask one question, like who my source is."

"He doesn't have a clue about undercover cases," Wilson said. "Don't worry about it. Looks like you have a paid vacation to the Caribbean."

I scheduled the time off and, within a couple weeks, headed down to St. Maarten. A fellow San Jose police officer and boating enthusiast, Chuck Seaton, accompanied me. He was ready for some time away from work and looked forward to a vacation in the Caribbean.

I found Robert Lafferty to be large and charismatic with two fingers missing from one hand. He was an aggressive and superb pilot who had been an officer with the marines in Vietnam. When Diehl introduced me as a former army pilot who also saw combat with the marines, Lafferty and I immediately bonded. Seaton and I stayed on his boat, a large commercial vessel anchored off the town of Phillipsburg, and we visited his modest restaurant in the same part of the island. After a few days in paradise, Seaton headed back home, but I stayed on.

Lafferty and I flew his King Air all over the Caribbean where we met numerous individuals who lavished us with fine food and spirits. They all seemed to be from Latin America, they certainly had dubious careers and lifestyles, and they indicated they had plenty of money to buy large aircraft. The way they carried themselves and the look in their eyes told me that these were clearly dangerous individuals, and I felt the presence of evil.

One of our stops was at Norman's Cay in the Bahamas, an island that Carlos Lehder had taken over by force with the consent of bribed Bahamian officials. At that time, I didn't know that Carlos Lehder was co-founder of the Medellin Cartel. The island eventually became the Caribbean's main cocaine smuggling hub and tropical playground for the Cartel, earning Lehder multimillions.

When it was time for me to return from St. Maarten, Lafferty flew me to Florida. On the way, we stopped in Puerto Rico where we cleared customs back into the United States, therefore avoiding having to land in Miami. It was past midnight when we reached Opa Locka. I had been flying, but Lafferty took over and made a perfect landing at the dark and desolate airport. Not a soul could be seen. He pulled off the runway, taxied to a parking spot, and shut down the engines. The cockpit lights were still on while we continued shutting down the aircraft equipment, and it looked black as ink outside.

Suddenly, the lights of four vehicles came on, and I realized we had been secretly surrounded. Then law enforcement agents, armed with automatic rifles, appeared. Lafferty remained calm.

"What the hell is this?" I wondered aloud.

Lafferty continued turning off switches. "Happens all the time. You'd think they'd know me and my planes after a few times."

"There's nothing you want to tell me before we step out there?"

"No, we're fine. Let's go."

With our passports in our raised hands, we walked down the steps off the plane to waiting DEA agents. Under the direction of the agent in charge, we laid face down on the asphalt, still hot from the heat of the previous day. As another agent was taking our passports, I could hear a handheld radio.

"Cancel that mission," someone said over the radio to the DEA agents.

The agent in charge went over to the radio. "We already have them in custody, so we'll go ahead and search the plane."

"That's a negative," was the reply in a raised voice. "Drop everything you're doing and cancel. Copy?"

The agent in charge turned to his team. "I don't know what's going on, but we're done here. Let's go home, guys."

They dropped our passports on the tarmac, got in their cars, and left. As quickly as it had started, we were suddenly alone again at the quiet and dark airfield. But I had just experienced a slight sense of what it was like to be on the receiving end of the DEA. By not having to identify myself, I again felt as if I had gotten away with something.

From my short trip, I was able to learn that Lafferty was an airplane aficionado who knew everything about long-range, short-field, heavy-load capable aircraft, perfect for smuggling. He was earning vast sums of money by selling such planes to persons of questionable backgrounds.

Back in San Jose, Johnson excitedly took notes as I described the trip. When I got to the part about landing at Opa Locka, Johnson said, "Yes, I know. Sorry about that. Our office in Miami was following you, and they were a little late in calling off DEA."

I was impressed. *These guys are good. They knew when I researched Lafferty through the system, and they knew when I landed in Florida.*

———·•·———

Not long after the Caribbean trip, I learned the US Attorney's office was planning an indictment of members of the Hell's Angels. I was called up to San Francisco on several occasions to discuss with federal prosecutors aspects of my investigations that hadn't been disclosed in earlier prosecutions. The true scope of the indictments, though, was not being disclosed. A few DEA agents from the San Francisco office, sensing the case was going to be big and looking to play a role, started coming down to visit the task force.

My working relationship with most DEA agents was positive. But the agents coming down from San Francisco weren't looking to cooperate. They wanted into my Hell's Angel files so they could know sources or be introduced to my informants. Like dogs, they were sniffing around the perimeter of my cases to see how close they could get. They tried to assert authority, but I wasn't about to submit, and I starting making enemies.

A meeting was scheduled one morning at the US Attorney's office in San Francisco, and a DEA agent suggested we meet an hour beforehand at his San Francisco office. As the only law enforcement officer involved from the task force, I drove up alone. To enter the DEA's offices, I had to show my ID, as I had done countless times before. On this occasion, though, the receptionist informed me that the policy had recently changed, and, until a DEA agent escorted me in, I'd have to take a seat in the room where visitors and snitches waited.

I knew I was being screwed with, so I left and went straight to the US Attorney's office. An assistant attorney walked into the office reception area directly behind me. He was carrying coffee, donuts, and breakfast burritos.

"Ah, good morning. Jones, right?"

"Yes, sir."

"Come on in. Have a seat. Can I get you anything? "

"No, thanks. Just had breakfast."

He seemed rather excited for so early in the morning. "So do you know what we're doing here?"

"Not yet. I've been kept in the dark, so to speak."

"RICO," he said, as if out of breath. "You know what that is?"

"Racketeering." I was unsure of the rest of the acronym.

"Yep, Racketeer Influenced and Corrupt Organizations Act. Mark Webb out of DC is going to be working with William Hunter, the US attorney. They think a Hell's Angels case will be the ultimate test of RICO."

Sounds good to me. What do I know about a RICO prosecution?

The attorney shuffled through some files before finding the one he wanted. "On your end, we already have Solano, Perkey, and Passaro. Now Bontempi. I think we have enough for a search warrant, so let's pull together what you have."

DEA, FBI, and ATF agents walked in the door. The lead DEA agent, seeing me having my own private conference, glared.

I stood to leave. "I'll get working on this," I said to the attorney.

As if an afterthought, the attorney added, "And Walton, Brandes, whoever else you've been looking at."

U.S. Department of Justice

United States Attorney
Northern District of California

16th Floor Federal Buiding- Box 36055
450 Golden Gate Avenue
San Francisco, California 94102

Branch Office:
675 N. First Street, Suite 508
San Jose, California 95112

March 10, 1981

Mr. Robert Jones
Post Office Box 26066
San Francisco, California 95159

Re: <u>United States v. James Brandes, et al.</u>
(The R.I.C.O. Trial)

Dear Mr. Jones:

On behalf of the United States Attorney's Office for the Northern District of California, we would like to express our thanks and appreciation for your participation in the trial of this case. Some of you testified as witnesses for the government, others lent their counsel and advice, and still others were there when we simply needed a sounding board for ideas or problems.

All of you played a vital role in the prosecution of this case. We did not take lightly your sacrifice of time, effort and in some cases, sleep. The trial was long and difficult to present in a logical, cohesive manner. We perservered only with your cooperation.

Thank you.

Sincerely yours,

ROBERT S. MUELLER, III
Assistant United States Attorney

SHELLEY B. WHEELER
Assistant United States Attorney

MARGO D. SMITH
Assistant United States Attorney

CHARLES B. BURCH
Assistant United States Attorney

"You need to coordinate with me on this," the lead DEA agent said through clenched teeth as I passed by.

I ignored him and walked out.

After meeting several more times with members of the US Attorney's office, in June 1979, thirty-six members of the Hell's Angels were indicted for violating federal racketeering statutes. Sweeping simultaneous raids took place across the San Francisco Bay area, resulting in twenty-two arrests, including Ralph "Sonny" Barger, founder and president of the Oakland chapter of the Hell's Angels.

Of those I had investigated, Passaro, Bontempi, Brandes, and Walton were indicted, although Brandes, charged with murder by another jurisdiction, escaped arrest for some time. Besides the arrest warrants, searches were executed, and everything related to the Hell's Angels club—banners, posters, photographs, clothing, records, and paperwork—was seized.

Shortly after the early morning raids, I ran into Lieutenant Trujillo at the San Jose police department. Bertotti had been transferred back to patrol, and Trujillo was running the narcotics division.

"Jones'y, are you stirring the pot?" He grinned.

I smiled back. "The only way to know is to be the one stirring."

With his hands in both pockets, he rocked back on his heels and laughed big. "You can't get along with those guys or what?"

"A few of these feds remind me of some officers in Nam. They were more interested in their careers by getting some combat and resultant decorations than they were in the mission. And if they couldn't do it on their own, they'd horn in on your action. It's the same thing with a few of these guys. They can't make a case on their own and try to elbow in on mine."

Trujillo suddenly looked serious. "Maybe it's time to come back to the PD."

Trujillo wasn't one to beat around the bush, and he didn't make idle suggestions. It was time for me to leave the task force. He was probably right, as I was the last original San Jose officer still assigned there.

"Let's get this trial over with first," I said.

In the course of preparing for the RICO trial, I got a better idea of the prosecution's case. And I didn't like what I saw. Although I was being pressed to provide it, I had no evidence that could tie the individual actions of Solano, Bontempi, Perkey, or Passaro to the Hell's Angels as an organization. Nor could I see the connection with the cases that any of the other agents brought.

Before the trial began, I was at odds with the US Attorney's office. In their pursuit of a RICO conviction against the Hell's Angels, I believed they were applying the law loosely to crimes already on the books and, in some cases, to defendants who had already been convicted of those crimes. I felt a loss in this case would only strengthen the Angels' organization.

The first phase of the RICO trial involved eighteen defendants, and a harbinger of events was seen in the pre-trial motions, which bogged down as the US attorney dealt with eighteen defense attorneys, each making his separate motions, arguments, and objections.

Then the trial turned out to be a circus in spite of Judge Samuel "Slammin' Sam" Conti's hard work. It lugged along as each of the eighteen defense attorneys cross-examined prosecution witnesses, many convicted career criminals, and, more often than not, admitted drug users. Every time there was a sidebar, the attorneys, along with a prosecutor, shuffled as a mob up to the bench and then back to their table, creating a scene right out of an old Keystone Cops movie. The atmosphere seemed to be uncontrollable and juvenile, as when someone in the audience clapped in response to a statement.

Judge Conti slammed his gavel. "Who clapped?"

"I did," said Sonny Barger.

Then other defendants joined in and said they were the one who clapped. Conti knew it was someone in the audience and quietly sat, waiting for an answer. After a few moments of silence, a voice in the back finally said, "I did."

Conti immediately ordered the spectator to leave, and a one-armed biker stood. The courtroom, including members of the jury, erupted in laughter. Conti stormed off the bench for a recess.

During the course of the trial, Conti suffered a heart attack. He recovered, the case continued, and, a year after the trial had begun, the US attorney made his closing argument. Then all eighteen defense attorneys made their closing arguments, and the jury was overwhelmed with charts, diagrams, and relentless hammering at the government's failure to connect the individual criminal actions of the defendants with the Hell's Angels.

After seventeen days of deliberations, the government's case collapsed as an exhausted jury was unable to convict the defendants on the RICO charge. A few days later, the government dropped the case against the Hell's Angels. It wasn't a completely lost cause as some of the defendants, such as Dirty Doug, were later convicted on individual drug or firearm charges.

The nation was ten years into a War on Drugs that was supposed to reduce deaths, disease, crime, and drug use. Yet by the DEA's own statistics, we were losing the battle on every front. The nation was experiencing more deaths due to overdoses caused by impure products of uncertain strength. Diseases such as hepatitis were on the increase due to unsterile and contaminated drug paraphernalia. Crime was rapidly rising due to dealers who were in constant street battles, inflicting death and injury as they sought to control and expand their territories. Drug use was up because drug dealers were using multilevel marketing techniques. Drugs were cheaper, more potent, and more plentiful. Law enforcement was arresting a half-million people a year for drug violations, and 70 percent of those were for simple possession. It was like body count in Vietnam, and I again felt we were shoveling sand against the tide.

I was discouraged at what the nation was doing to itself in the War on Drugs. I believed the laws behind the war had resulted in more snooping, sneaking, prying, informing, entrapping, corruption, and violence than any other act of Congress. If arresting armed robbers and rapists was the purest form of police work, I had concluded that arresting drug offenders was the lowest.

At the time, other matters were also weighing me down emotionally. One was another shooting. To rebuild my finances after the divorce from Susan, I worked extra jobs, which included teaching at the community colleges and providing security at the apartment complex where I lived while constructing a new home. I often worked with Gordon Silva, a San Jose officer who had several off-duty jobs at department stores. Gordi and I were good friends, and he used me on occasions when a particular store was experiencing problems with suspected drug users passing bad checks or shoplifting.

One night after a store had closed, a parolee named Rizo cornered me in the back parking lot as I was leaving. He was there to challenge me for questioning his brother who had tried to cash a check. In the back of his Chevrolet El Camino pickup was a Doberman. Rizo gave a signal, and the dog attacked. I drew my revolver to shoot it, Rizo went for my gun, and a struggle ensued. Moments later, he lay on the pavement. A shot to the left side of his head had severely wounded him. Rizo survived, and investigators found the shooting to be justified. But I knew it had been a situation that might have been handled differently, peacefully.

Another matter on my mind was that I was not spending time with my son as planned and I always had an excuse—too busy with work, extra jobs, and building a new home.

The final issue was with my personal life. Lucy and I had dated, lived together, broken up, and moved back in together. We eventually married in a large ceremony in her hometown of Selma, California, and then moved into the new home I had built in the Santa Cruz Mountains. But as Yogi Berra said, it was "déjà vu all over again." I was still carrying the baggage of Vietnam, still working undercover in an environment of deceit and deception, still unable or unwilling to talk things out, and I was divorced again in eight months.

With all this eating at me, I left work one evening and headed over to Bini's, hoping to catch up with detectives from the police department and restore some of the old camaraderie. As I entered the back door, I could hear someone singing from the jukebox about how a drink would ease all his pain.

Bini's was vacant except for Molosky. Sitting at the bar, slouched over his glass, he didn't see me. At that moment, no bartender was there for him to commiserate with, and no beautiful woman was engrossed in his legend. I saw no other detectives there for him to trade war stories with. He wasn't even forty years old, yet he looked old, alone, and sad. For a moment, I had a vision of myself, and I quietly left. I headed to an empty home, and, in preparing for bed that evening, I looked in the mirror ... and saw an asshole.

Chapter 10

We're Gonna Bomb 'Em

"Jones'y, line two," someone yelled from down the hall at the task force office.

I looked at the beige phone, punched the blinking square button, and picked up the receiver. "This is Jones. May I help you?"

"Jones, Johnson here."

I paused and tried to think of who Johnson was.

"Agent Johnson, FBI," he said, filling in the dead air.

"Oh, yes. Sorry. What's happening?" The Caribbean caper seemed so long ago.

"You have someplace we can meet? I can be there in an hour or so."

I understood his question to mean he didn't want to meet at the task force office. I looked at my watch. It was only 0930.

"If I don't eat lunch around 1130, I start getting light-headed. How about at a place called Original Joe's, South First Street at San Carlos?"

"See you in two hours," he said.

Established in 1956, Original Joe's was an institution, a downtown staple. The Italian restaurant had its own flair as waiters wore tuxedos and were slightly abrupt as they tossed your plate onto the table. I liked to sit at the counter and watch the cooks prepare a meal over the open flame grill. The food was excellent, and the thought of the OJ special, a combination of ground chuck, spinach, eggs, and mushrooms, would make me drool like Pavlov's dogs.

Johnson was there when I arrived. Someone I hadn't met accompanied him, and we took a booth in the back. Before Johnson had a chance to introduce me, the other gentleman offered his hand across the table.

"I'm Benjamin Siegel," he said.

He looked like Woody Allen without glasses, but any further resemblance ended there. He was well manicured and exquisitely dressed in a fine suit. When he talked, his soft-spoken words were measured. When I talked, he was completely attentive and appeared to look into my soul. I knew, without it having to be said, his name was Benjamin. Not Ben and certainly not Benny.

They followed my cue and ordered the OJ special.

Then Siegel wasted no time getting down to business. "Is it Russell or Robert?"

"Russ or Russell, please. The only one who calls me Robert is the IRS."

Only Johnson seemed to appreciate my attempt at humor.

"I understand you flew helicopters for the military. How many rotary wing hours have you logged?"

"Twelve hundred," I said.

Johnson sat and listened. Siegel was in charge of this meeting. "What would it take to get you current in the Hughes?" He was referring to the Hughes 500, known in the military as the OH-6A. I could tell by his questions that he was knowledgeable in the subject.

"Ten hours."

"And your fixed-wing status?"

"Two hundred hours with commercial, multi-engine, and instrument ticket, all current."

"What would it take to get your instructor's license?"

I smiled. "Money."

Johnson laughed. Siegel, all business, didn't. I felt like he was interviewing me for a job. Siegel changed subjects and asked about working in covert operations, the subtleties of using informants, and my ideas on cultivating and keeping special employees. Siegel wasn't asking because he was curious. He was testing my knowledge and working habits.

Lunch ended with me not having a clue as to what the purpose of the meeting was, and it was the last time I was to see Johnson. But certain factors were at work that would ultimately affect the rest of my life.

———◦•◦———

Several days later, Siegel, who was no relation to DEA Agent Bob Siegel at the task force, called and requested we meet at a tire shop in east San Jose.

We sat outside at a table under the trees while his silver BMW was on the lift. Siegel was dressed in a fine tailored suit with a beige shirt and maroon tie. He wore an unobtrusive watch and a plain wedding band.

"Russell, I work for the State Department." He showed me his identification. "In the last four years with President Carter, our intelligence community has been decimated. With the new administration, we're going to be building from scratch." Siegel spoke as if the election of Ronald Reagan were a certainty.

What the hell does the State Department have to do with intelligence? What I didn't know was that the State Department had its own intelligence function, primarily research and analysis. And, as with all large bureaucracies, it had internal factions with their own political agendas.

"The FBI highly recommends you," Siegel said. "With your flying skills, you're a candidate for a position I need to fill. Your real assignment, though, will be my eyes and ears on the ground."

Siegel certainly had my attention. The idea of getting back in the cockpit of the Hughes was appealing. And although it was unsaid, he was correct that I was a perfect match. Besides the qualifications as a pilot with covert work experience, I was recently divorced and single. I was dissatisfied with the War on Drugs, and I wasn't looking forward to going back to the police department. That would mean returning to patrol, being closely supervised, and expected to follow rules of dress and etiquette. I suspected I'd have difficulty reintegrating back into those duties.

Siegel began asking open-ended questions. "What's the role of a covert intelligence agent?"

"To gain trust so information can be gathered in such a way that they don't know what you're really after."

"If you were assigned an overseas mission where you'd essentially live a lie twenty-four hours a day, months on end, what would be your greatest challenge?"

"The isolation and complete separation from friends and family could lead to anxiety, maybe depression."

Siegel rarely followed up on my answers, but moved on to other topics. "Working undercover in law enforcement involves dealing with criminals. What might be your challenge when working covertly on a political mission?"

I had to give that some thought. "Not being criminals, yet betraying them. That might lead to feelings of guilt."

"How would you respond if you observed a United States government official committing illegal acts and knew that reporting it would compromise the mission?"

"I'd report it to you."

Tough questions.

Apparently, Siegel had no problem with my answers. "You don't need to make a decision right away, but I want you to consider taking a position as a pilot in Costa Rica." Siegel's eyes then bored into mine. "This conversation and your contacts with me go no further than between us."

His eyes stayed locked on mine while I assured him that I'd keep our conversations private, and we left with the understanding that he'd contact me later. He gave me a phone number to an answering service in Oakland, California, if I needed to contact him. *Strange.*

Siegel and I met again a few weeks later, this time at a tire shop in Fremont, the city in the East Bay area where I had obtained my glider's license. He said he was having his tires rotated.

"Costa Rica," Siegel started to explain, "is an oasis of tranquility among countries in conflict due to threatening communism: Nicaragua, El Salvador, Guatemala, Honduras, and even Panama. It's a well-functioning, multiparty, Western-style democracy. In Costa Rica, some clandestine operations challenging the leftist movements will be organized. So that's why I need you there, and what better position for you to observe what's going on than as a pilot." He talked as if I had already made up my mind. Siegel looked out at the hills for a moment before turning back to me. "You'll have no cover story and no cover assignment. I'll lead you in the right direction, but it'll be up to you to get the flying job. And except for not disclosing the fact that I'll be your contact, your story will have to be completely true. You're a former military combat helicopter pilot and a former cop. No lies or deceit since the people you'll be consorting with will have the means to completely check your background."

It sounded simple enough to me. But Siegel's eyes displayed the seriousness of his instructions. "You can't disclose this to anyone. Don't get caught. If you do get into trouble, handle it. Don't call me. We won't know you and will have never heard of you." He was beginning to sound like the movies.

There was no one to talk to about whether to take this job except myself, but I always came up with the same answer. *How can I not?* I was drawn into the planning.

"How about I sail down there on my sailboat?" I asked.

For the previous couple years, a new adventure had been my sailboat. The San Francisco Bay was the perfect place with its winds, currents, and tides to learn all aspects of sailing. I was an avid reader of *Cruising World*, a monthly magazine covering the lifestyle of sailing across oceans in small yachts. The sea as a frontier had piqued my imagination, and the boat had become a receptacle of my dreams. Jim Roorda, a San Jose police officer who had recently retired early for medical reasons, had a boat that he was planning to sail down to Panama, through the Canal, and into the Caribbean. We had talked of buddy boating down to Panama.

"How long would that take?" Siegel asked.

I took a guess. "About three weeks."

Siegel stared off into space. His mind shuffled through his mental files. He always took his time and thought everything completely through. He made eye contact again. "The problem will be the boat. Are you going to abandon it at a harbor or marina? I'm not sending you down there to vacation in some exotic anchorage. I want you in northern Costa Rica, on the Nicaraguan border, far from the coast."

He had a point. Boats, especially those kept in saltwater, required lots of attention and maintenance. We went back to plan A, which was to fly into the capital of Costa Rica, San Jose, where the people I needed to meet would be.

Planning seemed to drag on. Every time I met with Siegel, he was at a tire shop somewhere: Milpitas, Fremont, Hayward, and Oakland. I never saw someone have his vehicle's tires rotated so often. By November, the election of Ronald Reagan was a foregone conclusion. I resigned from the police department and had a contract to sell my home.

I hadn't given up on the dream of sailing and had come to an agreement with Roorda to sail with him on his boat to Central America. Siegel had signed off on the plan, and Roorda and I spent several months in the planning. When we sailed out under the Golden Gate Bridge, we had Roorda's son and an Oakland fireman to crew with us to Cabo San Lucas, Mexico.

Each of us had already made several offshore trips down the California coast, so Roorda and I had a fairly easy week of coastal navigating to Mexico. Our two crewmembers returned to California, and Roorda and I spent a couple of weeks hanging out in Cabo. Although it's now a thriving tourist destination, at the time, it was a dusty village whose industry was centered on a commercial fish processing plant at the harbor.

For whatever reason, Siegel got word to me that he preferred that I not show up in Costa Rica until August, so I did my best to delay us in Mexico. With other boaters in the area, we passed the days playing volleyball and spent the evenings drinking margaritas at the thatched roofed huts on the beach. Hurricane season, though, dictated when we'd have to leave, and we weighed anchor and sailed for Costa Rica by June. After three weeks of enduring everything from a two-day gale to three days of doldrums, we successfully pulled into Puntarenas, Costa Rica. I found it a seedy port, with streets and buildings in disrepair, struggling to fight off an encroaching jungle.

I settled into a hotel in downtown San Jose and began hanging out at the local country-and-western bar. Siegel had informed me that this was where I'd most likely make contact with people working at the US embassy or expatriates living in Costa Rica who had an interest in stopping the spread of communism from Nicaragua. Instead, in less than two days, several Cubans were wining and dining me. They were concerned with the mounting storm clouds over Central America as leftist guerrillas were on the verge of toppling several governments. After dinner one evening we met in a hotel room where they emphasized the problem Castro was creating by smuggling arms and ammunition into Nicaragua.

Sailing to Costa Rica

"He is also supplying arms to the communist rebels in Honduras and El Salvador," Roberto said.

"You see," Luis said, "we'll never have a free Cuba if his kind succeed anywhere in Central America."

"Are you guys associated with Felix Rodriguez?" I asked.

There were a few furtive glances between them. "You know him?" Luis asked.

I shrugged my shoulders. "I know of him. Cuban American, CIA, worked with Bolivians in the killing of Che Guevara."

"He passes through here occasionally," Luis explained, "but he's based in Miami."

David quickly changed the subject and began complaining about the CIA in Costa Rica. "While Castro is proactive, everything here is in a constant planning stage. We have access to a helicopter you can keep current in, but nothing we can put to real use yet."

"We're optimistic," said Luis. "But we're cautious. We're veterans of the Bay of Pigs. We already know from experience that we can't depend on the United States."

They could tell I was disappointed to learn that they did not as yet have helicopters to fly missions. "Don't worry," David said as he poured me another drink. "We'll have plenty for you to do."

I sat back in my chair and looked at the Cubans who were sitting on the edges of the hotel bed. I was on their side with regards to fighting for a free Nicaragua and Cuba, but I was covertly infiltrating and gathering information from them for my government. *These are proud men, Bay of Pigs veterans, willing to face prison, torture, and death. They have hope for their country and faith in their cause. They are dangerous to those they perceive as the enemy.*

I spent the next several years, 1981 to 1985, going back and forth between San Jose, Costa Rica, and San Jose, California. The Cubans greased plenty of wheels. For Honduras and El Salvador, they provided me with military visas and often arranged for me to take military flights out of Florida. For Costa Rica, they provided me with a multiple entry, business visa.

In Honduras, where an American presence was developing in the form of Task Force Alpha, the Cubans introduced me to many Nicaraguans who had fought against the Anastasio Somosa regime and were now dissatisfied with the new communist establishment there. In Costa Rica, they introduced me to Bill Crone, an American who had several investments there. Crone drove me all over northern Costa Rica and eventually introduced me to John Hull, an American who owned several thousand acres of cattle ranch that lay along the San Carlos River. Hull worked for the CIA. He seemed primarily concerned with preparing to aid casualties in a coming war between Nicaragua and the anti-communist Nicaraguan fighters who were called "Contras," short for counterrevolutionaries.

After learning the lay of the land, I began staying in the town of Cuidad Quesada, a dusty farm town of fifty thousand located about fifty miles from the Nicaraguan border. I found it had a fun Wild West atmosphere as it experienced a financial boom from the cattle business. In Cuidad Quesada, Hull introduced me to Dr. Pacheco and showed me their plans for making the city the base for treating the expected war casualties. Yet there were no physical preparations in progress.

Hull explained that the Cubans had plenty of Nicaraguan-trained helicopter pilots for the medical evacuation missions and seemed delighted that I'd be available to transition those pilots into the Hughes 500. The reason for needing someone to transition them went beyond just familiarizing them in a new aircraft. It would be more technical because Nicaraguan pilots had been trained in Russian helicopters. Russian helicopter rotor blades rotate clockwise, the opposite direction of American helicopters. Without proper training, the results could be disastrous for the pilot and aircraft.

The problem for me and for the Contras was that a single reliable Hughes 500 was unavailable for the training. I had flown the only one they had a few times out of Tobais Bolanos Airport, but the Contras had somehow lost it in a political struggle with the Costa Rican National Guard. I was beginning to notice an amateurish disorganization of everyone involved with the Contras.

Siegel called one day after I returned from a trip to Central America, and we met at a tire shop in San Leandro, south of Oakland. We were alone in the waiting room.

"Anything to report?"

"Still no helicopters there for me to fly. I'm getting frustrated. Anyway, I've been spending time with John Hull. We've been flying around in his Cessna 180 looking for landing zones. I'm meeting American, Cuban, and Costa Rican ranchers who all seemed concerned with what they perceive as an ever-growing threat from Nicaragua."

"Landing zones?" Siegel wasn't concerned that I wasn't flying helicopters as initially proposed. He was content that I was successful in getting around and observing.

"Yes, different ranches all over northern Costa Rica. He's looking for level pastures with enough room to maintain grass landing strips."

"To be used for?" He sounded like he knew, but just wanted my opinion.

"Logistics: guns, ammo, uniforms, food, and medical."

Siegel leaned forward with his forearms on his knees and sat quietly for a moment. "I need to know where these supplies are coming from."

That's a strange question. You work for the government. I know the Reagan administration is having problems getting congressional funding, but the government has sources. Don't you know the logistical network?

"Supplies not coming out of Florida are from Panama, Chile, South Africa, and even Taiwan. But why wouldn't we already know where this stuff is coming from?"

Siegel ignored my question. "What about the AKs and grenades?"

"I don't know. Hull has introduced me to a guy named Bruce Jones. He's CIA and works directly with the Contras. When I get back, I'm going to do more running around with him along the river where the Contras are based. Hopefully, I can confirm something for you."

"I want hard proof of where the small arms are coming from. When do you go back?"

"I'm flying into Ilopango at the end of the month."[30]

Siegel looked surprised. "I'm not sure I want you in El Salvador. That's a good place to disappear from."

He was right. When the Salvadoran military or police found people to be "persona non grata," they often simply vanished.

"It's the way it worked out. Besides, Ilopango is a waypoint for much of the supplies for the Contras. The Cubans tell me Felix Rodriguez is involved there. If you want to know where this stuff is coming from, then Ilopango is part of the trail."

I didn't tell Siegel that, based on talk from characters I was hanging out with in Costa Rica, I suspected people associated with the Contras were flying drugs out of Ilopango to the States. At the time, I decided not to tell him until I had something more concrete. Siegel wasn't interested in gossip or rumors.

With assistance and contacts made with the help of the Cubans in Costa Rica, I was able to catch a military flight out of Florida into El Salvador. Although Ilopango was an international civilian airport, I was across from the

---

30. Ilopango was the airfield that sat just outside of San Salvador, the capital of El Salvador.

main terminal in an area that the military used exclusively. While there, I met several pilots from the United States and various Latin American countries who were able to display ID cards associating them with DEA, CIA, or both.

I was looking to meet a pilot named Rene, and I was finally able to sit down with him in a shabby office in one of the aircraft hangars. He was already aware of who I was and explained an operation they were thinking of.

"*Que Piensas?*"[31] Rene leaned forward on the edge of the worn couch, anxious for my answer.

I was perplexed. "Why are you asking me?"

"Because you were a combat pilot."

I carefully leaned back into my wobbly chair as I threw my arms out. "I was a helicopter pilot!"

"And you're fixed-wing, multi-engine qualified."

"Civilian, Rene. I fly civilian fixed-wing. Why are you thinking of doing this?" I was frustrated.

"We're gonna bomb 'em," he said excitedly. "Nicaragua needs to know we can strike at their heart."

"Are you people nuts or what?" I wanted to cry out.

"Rene, I don't know anything about dropping bombs, but I have a real problem with mounting them on civilian aircraft and subsequently changing the aircraft's aerodynamics."

Rene had explained to me how the Nicaraguan Contras were planning to mount bombs on aircraft such as a twin-engine Beach Baron, and he was looking for advice. I wanted to ask, "Who are you people?" But I held my tongue. Hull had told me that Rene worked for the CIA and, from what I had seen in the last couple years, I wasn't surprised.

———•·•———

In my next meeting with Siegel, I still didn't have the hard proof he needed as to the source of small arms and weapons.

---

31. What do you think?

"What else do you have for me?" he asked when I was finished describing the improbable plan Rene had laid out to me.

"I have good reason to believe that they're running drugs out of Ilopango." Everything I had done so far seemed so insignificant, and I was looking forward to getting into something much bigger. Siegel looked away for a while and then slowly turned back. He waited for me to continue. "The pilots flying Contra supplies into Ilopango are running cocaine on the return trip to the States. As the plane approaches offshore at a low altitude, the drugs are dropped off to waiting high-speed boats. The plane then lands in Florida empty. These pilots, bragging they work for DEA or CIA, imply the money from the drugs is being used to finance the Contras."

"You think they're DEA, CIA, or military?"

"No, they're probably contract or subcontract employees. I don't know where they're getting the IDs, but they're certainly not DEA agents. Either way, we're not talking about a kilo or two." My voice betrayed my enthusiasm. "I'm talking planeloads of the stuff and—"

Siegel raised his hand to interrupt me. "Russell, you're not a cop anymore. We're not interested in this."

"Benjamin, you have to at least let me pass this on. From what I can tell, this isn't a couple of rogue pilots. There's plenty of evidence that this is happening with the knowledge, if not the complicity, of people in our government."

Siegel stuck with his original argument. "We're not in the business of law enforcement."

"Fine, I understand. But that doesn't mean I shouldn't pass the information to customs or DEA. I'm in a position to introduce an agent, and then they could carry the ball."

"And how would you explain how you came into this knowledge?"

Siegel had me with that question, and I began trying to think of a plan. He didn't give me time though. "Look, give me what you know, and I'll see it gets passed on without compromising your position." I never found out if he did.

On September 8, 1983, Senators Gary Hart and William Cohen were on a US military plane headed for Managua, Nicaragua, on a fact-finding mission. Also headed for Managua were three small, twin-engine civilian aircraft that had taken off from Ilopango. The planes were laden with a couple of bombs each. Their mission, endorsed by the CIA, was to fly low level into Nicaragua and bomb the airport.

One Beechcraft Baron had engine problems and returned. A second Baron dropped its bombs from a safe altitude in the vicinity of Managua, but far from the target. A Cessna 404 swooped in low over the Managua airport as planned and dropped its two bombs, damaging a hangar and military vehicles.

As Rene had suggested, the Contras wanted to show they could reach out and hit Managua, but the entire mission was militarily inept and politically foolish. Not because, as I had suggested, carrying bombs had compromised the aircrafts' ability to fly, but because the bombs were armed to explode on impact.

When dropped from an aircraft, a bomb continues forward for a time, following the aircraft as it falls away. Therefore, when a bomb is released at low level from a slow-moving aircraft, it's still right behind the plane when it strikes the target.

In this case, the bomb went off right behind the Cessna, bringing the aircraft down and killing the pilots. The wreckage gave Nicaragua incriminating evidence pointing to CIA and US embassy officials. The political damage was compounded by the fact that the flight carrying Senators Hart and Cohen had to be diverted from a physical danger that CIA-sponsored action perpetrated.

On my next trip to Costa Rica, I was running around with Bruce Jones. He and his Costa Rican wife lived with their three children on the outskirts of Ciudad Quesada. Banana and mango trees surrounded their modest farm home, and they had a large, beautiful, semi-tame parrot that roamed freely.

As with many farm and ranch owners in northern Costa Rica, Bruce believed Nicaragua was becoming an outpost for terror within Central America by giving sanctuary to Castro and Soviet Union agents.

"You're going to find these guys a little rough around the edges," Bruce explained as he drove us out to a Contra camp. "I've been working with them on small unit tactics."

"That's your job?"

"Actually, it's liaison with CIA, but I also work with them on communications, logistics, and health care."

"So, logistics. Where are the supplies coming from?"

"Who knows? It's arranged by the CIA and drops out of the sky by parachute."

"The weapons?"

"I think Israel. I guess they seized a ton of weapons when they were fighting the PLO and Egypt."

What no one knew at the time was Colonel Oliver North, General Secord, and the Israeli government were running a secret operation called Tipped Kettle. The plan called for Israel to ship small arms seized from the PLO to the Contras.

We stopped at a Contra camp set up in a clearing in the jungle along the San Juan River not far from the Nicaraguan border. There I found a ragtag company of what I'd loosely call soldiers. Their military bearing suggested their education, training, and abilities were severely deficient. The state of their camp indicated their supplies were sorely lacking.

Off to the side of the camp was a stack of newly arrived wooden crates freshly marked, in Spanish, "Medical Supplies." The contents, though, were AK-47s and ammunition. Given that Bruce had already told me that he thought the small arms were weapons that Israel originally seized in their recent wars, I assumed the older markings on the crates were Arabic.

An AK-47 from operation Tipped Kettle

While Bruce was talking to a unit commander, I took a soldier's entrenching tool, a short, folding shovel, and began to bust up one of the boxes. I threw the pieces of wood into the back of our vehicle. No one paid attention to what I was doing. When Bruce saw it, I explained I needed to build a box to carry a rug home that a Costa Rican girlfriend had given me. He didn't seem to mind and asked no questions. It was that simple.

I carried the busted-up wooden pieces home in my luggage and presented the reconstructed box to Siegel.

"Is that what you wanted?" I asked as we sat in a tire shop in Milpitas.

"Yes." He rotated the box around. It was the only time I momentarily caught the faint hint of a smile cross his face.

———•———

By 1985, it was apparent that the Southern Front, as the Contra effort out of Costa Rica was called, was in further disarray. A resupply plane, attempting to parachute equipment to the Contras in Costa Rica, crashed with the loss of all crewmembers. When supplies did get delivered, the Costa Rican Rural Guard, whose job included ensuring that its territory wouldn't be used to launch attacks against Nicaragua, often seized them.

Civilian refugees seeking food and medical care were beginning to gather in camps on the Costa Rican side of the border, yet I saw no system of logistics in place. None of Hull's plans had been put in operation.

There were internal conflicts within the Southern Front, culminating in an attempt on the life of Contra leader Eden Pastora, also known as Comandante Cero. At a press conference at his camp in La Prenca, a bomb hidden in camera equipment exploded. Three died, and seventeen, including Pastora, were severely wounded.

It was time for another briefing. Siegel and I were sitting at a table outside a tire shop in Los Gatos.

"Whatever funding the Contras are receiving," I said, "it's not evident in Costa Rica. I don't see the Contras winning anything."

"I'm not sure they're supposed to win," Siegel quietly said.

"Geeze maneez. Vietnam, the War on Drugs, now the Contras." I couldn't see a bigger picture. All I saw was more money, personnel, violence, and death. It was shoveling sand against the tide again. "So what's the goal?"

"The Sandinistas are Marxists-Leninists who've tied their fortunes to the Soviet Union. That can't stand in Latin America. If the communist Sandinistas are to ever negotiate, the vehicle will be the Contras."

He was talking in a realm of politics above my head. We sat silent for a minute before he continued. "I think, politically, things are going to hit the fan down there. I'd rather you not be there when it does."

With expenses being paid, though, I couldn't resist a few more trips into Costa Rica. Siegel's only assignment for me was to keep abreast of progress during the construction of a large airstrip in the northwest region of the country, called Santa Elena. But when Costa Rican authorities arrested several foreign mercenaries at Hull's ranch, I began to get nervous. Then, when a report was leaked to me suggesting the CIA, including contract employees such as John Hull, was involved in the La Prenca bombing, I decided things were hitting the fan.

In my world, things were supposed to be simple and neat, with the good guys distinguishable from the bad. Here I no longer could tell who was who, as Contras were killing Contras, employees of our own government were apparently running drugs, one department of our government was spying on the other, and the US Congress was battling the president. The good guys were supposed to win, but who were the good guys?

Whether the allegations about the La Prenca bombing were true or not, being in neutral Costa Rica without official cover while associating with anti-Nicaraguan government activists such as the Cubans and John Hull was too risky, so I decided to terminate further expeditions. Siegel concurred, and, in our last meeting in California, he left with a final suggestion.

"Disappear, and stay away from the press. It can only be negative."

As much as I loved tweaking the media, I sensed he was right. So my girl-friend and I sailed to Mexico on a sailboat I recently purchased and based out of La Paz, Baja California. We spent the better part of a year in the Sea of Cortez, far from contact with the real world.

When I returned, I found out what hitting the fan really meant. A CIA sponsored airplane parachuting supplies to the Contras in Nicaragua had been shot down and one crewmember was captured alive, setting off a chain of events resulting in the whole Iran-Contra affair being disclosed to the public. In conferring with Siegel by phone, he suggested it was too soon for me to be surfacing, so I purchased a twenty-five-acre gentleman's ranch in rural northern California, a few miles south of the Oregon border. The closest town was Yreka, with a population of less than six thousand. From my front porch, I could watch snow skiers at night on the slopes of Mt. Ashland. From my back porch, I could sit and view Mt. Shasta.

Susan had remarried and was living in Oregon. A five-hour drive would get me to Joey's high school wrestling matches and other functions. The isolation of Yreka, though, finally drove me back to Los Gatos and Silicon Valley.

No sooner had I surfaced than someone out of the Christic Institute, a public interest law firm with offices in Washington DC and San Francisco, contacted me. The institute first gained notoriety when they represented a case made famous by the movie *Silkwood*. They were now looking into the charges by journalists Martha Honey and Tony Avirgan that the CIA, John Hull, and others were involved in the fatal La Prenca bombing. After several phone calls, I was able to convince the caller that he had the wrong Robert Jones, I was never in Costa Rica, and I was simply a real estate agent who recently moved from Yreka.

The Christic Institute eventually brought a massive racketeering charge in court against the CIA. They exaggerated their case and chased too many conspiracy theories, and the case was thrown out. In dismissing the lawsuit, the judge ordered the institute to pay the defendants $1 million, thereby bankrupting the firm.

The next caller to track me down, representing California Assembly member Maxine Waters, was more informed. He knew my background with the police department and that I was a court-recognized expert in the field of drugs and narcotics, so I had a more difficult time convincing him that I hadn't been working in Central America. Later, I was to hear more from the office of Maxine Waters when she was a member of the US House of Representatives, and her staff was looking into allegations that government operatives were behind the crack cocaine epidemic. Even Gary Webb of the *San Jose Mercury News* tried to drag me into his investigation, entitled "Dark Alliance," in which he alleged CIA knowledge of drug smuggling into the United States by government operatives.

During the time I was in California, I kept busy as a consultant in the field of drugs and narcotics. It had come about quite unexpectedly as I sat in the offices of Homeland Properties, part of the San Jose law firm of Miller and Hinkle. Stan Miller and John Hinkle were two former San Jose police officers. Ron Rose, a successful attorney who specialized in drug cases, tracked me down and called me there.

"Hey, Ron, what can I do for you?"

"Do me a favor. Give me a quick explanation of what causes tracks on a drug user's hands and arms."

"Repeated injections of an unsterile product with unsterile needles. This causes the scarring and tattooing effect."

"Does it make a difference if it's heroin or methamphetamine?"

"No."

"Would you testify to that in court?" Rose asked after explaining the fee for forensic experts.

As a narcotics officer, I had become a court-recognized expert in many aspects of narcotics enforcement. After obtaining my bachelor's degree, I completed my master's, which included a thesis and training program for instructing law enforcement officers in the recognition and documentation of the symptoms of drug use and abuse. The prosecutor's office then used me as a forensic expert on the psychological and physiological effects of alcohol, drugs, and narcotics.

In this instance, to prevent any bias, Rose didn't give me the facts of the case. The superior court judge quickly recognized me as an expert, and I testified in front of the jury as to what causes needle tracks. I later learned a narcotics officer had erroneously testified to the jury that the defendant didn't have tracks on her arms because injecting methamphetamine didn't leave them. The fact she didn't have tracks, yet was supposedly injecting meth, had somehow played an important role in the case against her and other defendants. Once

I left the courtroom, Rose cross-examined the officer. The prosecution's case fell apart based on my testimony, and the jury found the defendants not guilty.

Because of that verdict, I began to get three or four cases every week from defense attorneys all over the state. Prosecutors from counties with small law enforcement agencies and a lack of qualified experts were also sending me reports to review. My opinions usually agreed with the point of view of law enforcement, and, in those instances, the defense attorneys would convince their defendant to take a plea bargain. Sometimes, though, my opinion disagreed, and, if the case went to trial, I'd be called to testify. These proceedings not only involved drug offenses, but ranged from rape to homicide where drugs or alcohol played a role.

In 1982, shortly after I started taking cases as a forensic expert, I stopped by Bertotti's home in Los Gatos.

"For crying out loud, boss," I said as I walked down the hallway toward the kitchen. "I can't see a thing."

The house was dark as all the curtains and shades were drawn with no lights on. I took it upon myself to open a curtain in the kitchen area where sunlight exposed several empty beer bottles laying around the table.

"Want a beer?" Bertotti popped the cap on one for me without waiting for an answer.

I took a cold gulp. "What's new?"

"Well, I'm waiting to hear it from you," Bertotti said with a slight chuckle. "I hear you're causing trouble again." He sat down and waited for my reply.

I leaned back in my chair. "What are you talking about?"

"I heard you've been testifying in court and losing some cases for the boys in narcotics."

I laughed. "Ah. Well, yes. Except I'm not losing them. They are." I explained some of the cases I had recently testified in.

"They can't do that, especially if the court's recognized them as an expert. If they lose credibility once, it'll follow them to the next case."

"It's a result of this War on Drugs," I said.

Bertotti sat back and threw his arm across the back of another chair. "How so?"

"We call it a war. A war has enemies. We're making a broad segment of our society the enemy, and, when you have an enemy, you demonize him. You do what it takes to convict, even if it means stretching your police report and testimony on the stand. The rules of arrest, search, and seizure are being compromised, and the constitution has become collateral damage in this failed policy."

Bertotti sat still for a minute and watched as I drank. "So you think it's a failed policy?"

"Boss, since we started this in 1970, drugs are cheaper, stronger, and more available. We have more deaths, more drug use, and more violence. By any and all measurable standards, this is a failed policy."

"Don't we need to continue to curb the violence?"

"Come on, boss, you're on the streets as a supervisor. You know the violence is from dealers trying to control or expand their territories, a result of prohibition. It's the same as the Valentine's Day Massacre during alcohol prohibition. When's the last time we had a drive-by shooting between Coors and Budweiser?"

Bertotti laughed. "Back in the days of Al Capone."

"Right, and these drug gangs today are nothing more than modern-day Al Capones."

"So you don't think there's violence due to the use of drugs?" Bertotti asked.

"How far back do you have to look to find me a report filed at the police department that says something to the effect, 'After another beer, he proceeded to beat the hell out of me'?"

Bertotti leaned forward on the table and laughed. "Last night. Yeah, but that's alcohol."

"So how far back would we have to search to find a report that says something to the effect, 'After another puff of marijuana, he proceeded to beat the hell out of me'?"

Bertotti continued to laugh. "You couldn't find one."

"Not at San Jose or any other police department across this nation."

"So what about this new stuff called crack?"

I tapped my finger on the table for emphasis. "Crack is simply another form of cocaine. It looks like the black market found a cheaper and easier way to transport and sell it. Another unintended consequence of the War on Drugs."

"You made that argument with meth years ago," Bertotti said, as if reminding himself.

"And I stand by it today. Prohibition drives people to the harder drug. Alcohol prohibition drove people to hard and adulterated booze. Drug prohibition drives the user to harder drugs, meth and crack."

"But we have violence with those," Bertotti said, as if making a point.

"When the dust settles around this crack hysteria, we're going to find that the violence associated with crack is between drug dealers, and you know as well as anyone the experience I have with meth users. The meth doesn't necessarily cause the violence. The user just stays awake and parties longer, which means more drinking. Booze is the only commonly abused drug, legal or otherwise, that causes someone to lose his better judgment, resulting in violence."

Bertotti sighed. "I don't know." He seemed to be running out of arguments. "So what about the kids?"

"Well, when is the last time you heard of Marlboro hiring a twelve year old to run tobacco from one street corner to another?"

Bertotti laughed again.

"When is the last time you heard of a street gang running a still and selling bootleg alcohol to kids in the back alley?" I continued before he could answer, "You don't because they're regulated products, and, as long as they remain reasonably available to adults, there's no financial opportunity for the gangs. What we have today is young kids seeing the easy money, the expensive tennis shoes, and the fancy cars around drug dealers. They get started as runners and lookouts for a few bucks."

Bertotti turned the palm of his hand up. "Look at the problems we have with alcohol."

"Yes, but, absent harm to others, we handle alcohol as a health and social issue because we learned prohibition didn't work. Our alcohol policy isn't perfect, but it's better than the alternative."

He smiled. "Well, I'm not necessarily convinced. So what's the answer?"

"Fight this war economically by ending prohibition. Eliminate the black market." I raised my beer in a toast. "Keep thinking about it. That's all I can ask, boss."

He clinked his bottle against mine. "They're just dopers."

We forced a laugh because it wasn't funny anymore.

"It's hard to admit you were wrong, isn't it?" he asked, as if wondering aloud.

"Nah, I've been caught up in wrong policies before. I think Vietnam was a failed policy. When I realized it, I walked away even though there was more I should have done to help my fellow soldier as we retreated from that mess. The War on Drugs is a failed policy, but I'm not walking away this time. We need to ease out of this chaos. The vast majority of arrests are simple possession, a youthful indiscretion. All we're doing is destroying the lives of those citizens by saddling them with an arrest record that follows them for the rest of their lives."

"Anyway," I said as I got up and opened the sliding glass door for some air. I was ready to change the subject. "What's new with you?"

Bertotti looked as if he were struggling for words. "They're not going to give me the MERGE team." I sat down again and waited for an explanation. "They think I drink too much," he finally said with a forced chuckle.

The room suddenly got quiet as that suggestion sunk in. I didn't know how to respond. I knew that being the commander of the MERGE unit would require being on call twenty-four hours a day, meaning the end to any alcohol use.

"So," I started to ask, stammering a bit, "they don't think you can lay off the booze when you're on call?"

"I can," he said with confidence, "but they apparently don't believe it."

I could tell it bothered him. "Well, hell, boss. I'm sorry." I knew he'd been looking forward to the assignment. It had become uncomfortable, and I got up to leave, promising to drop by again soon.

"Let me know," he said as I left. It was one of his expressions.

"You'll be the first."

It was the last time I saw Bertotti. Several days later, late at night and off duty, he was driving alone and, at forty-five years of age, died in a single car accident.

By 1987, except for what I was hearing on the nightly news, I had put Costa Rica and Iran-Contra out of my mind. I thought it was behind me until I received a call from Siegel asking I go out to Washington DC so several attorneys preparing for hearings could depose me.

The unnamed building I reported to was, on the outside, indistinct. Upon entering, I found that the dimly lit hallway had exposed pipes along the ceiling. File cabinets and boxes cluttered my approach to a door that had no sign to indicate what transpired behind it. I entered and found a room painted in a faded government green. The well-worn floors were tiled in brown linoleum.

I was seated at the head of a long 1950s-era metal table. On my right sat three young attorneys, all male and looking fresh out of law school. They asked questions first and treated me politely. They established for the record that I was working for Benjamin Siegel and then asked questions about my activities in Costa Rica. They wanted to know about the private airfields, Cuidad Quesada, and my associations with Bill Crone, Bruce Jones, John Hull, and the Cubans. They focused on the humanitarian efforts in supporting refugees and logistical work in supporting the Southern Front. The lead attorney for this team made the point that I had no direct evidence, only suspicion and hearsay, of any employee or contract employee of the US government involved in smuggling drugs.

To my left sat four young attorneys whose questions were focused only on trying to show that government agents, and therefore members of the Reagan administration, were in fact smuggling drugs to raise money for the Contra effort. A stern lady with the first name of Margaret was in charge of this team.

She started speaking slowly and deliberately. "So, Mr. Jones." She then glared. "Would you redirect your attention to the map behind you?"

The legs on the metal chair screeched as I turned sideways so I could refer to several maps and an aeronautical chart behind me.

"Please point out again the different airfields you visited while in Costa

Rica." This could have been objected to as having been asked and answered, but this was a deposition where everyone was supposed to be cooperating.

Starting with the airstrip on John Hull's ranch, I proceeded again to point out six or seven areas in northern Costa Rica, ending with the location of the airstrip at Santa Elena. Margaret then asked me to explain how many times I had been to each. After I did, she just sat and gave me a silent stare.

She finally spoke. "Bringing your attention back to the secret airfield on CIA Agent John Hull's ranch—"

"Objection!" one of the attorneys on my right interjected. "Maggie, there's no evidence that John Hull is a CIA agent. By allowing Mr. Jones to answer would suggest that Mr. Jones knows him to be CIA. He's already testified that he has no direct knowledge that John Hull was a CIA officer, agent, or asset."

Margaret sighed. "All right. Mr. Jones." Her tone was dripping with contempt. I was beginning to realize that, from her side of the table, I was being considered a hostile witness. "How many times and at what hours of the day were you present at the secret airfield on John Hull's ranch?"

"Dozens of times, at all hours of the day, but never after dark."

"Mr. Jones," she said again. I guess she liked saying my name. She then slapped her hand down on a stack of files on the table. "We have witness statements that C-123s, King Airs, Cessna 402s, and other such aircraft regularly flew cocaine out of this secret airfield. Do you mean to sit there, with your background in narcotics enforcement, and testify that you never saw drugs smuggled out of this secret airfield?"

"Yes. I never saw any evidence of drugs being flown out of John Hull's ranch." But I wasn't going to limit my reply to her question. She kept referring to the secret airfield, and I wanted to clear that up. "Before you continue with this line of questioning—"

Margaret interrupted in a raised voice, "Just answer my questions, Mr. Jones."

"Maggie," one of the attorneys on her side of the table quietly said. "This is a deposition, not an inquisition. Let him finish."

Margaret, looking irritated, sat back in her chair and motioned for me to continue.

"I'd suggest you consider a few things before you continue this line of questioning. First, there's no secret airfield at John Hull's ranch." I pointed to the spot on the map. "It's preprinted on every aeronautical chart as an airfield recognized by the Costa Rican government." I stood, took a copy of an eight-by-ten photograph of an airplane sitting on a grass airfield at Hull's ranch, and slid it over to the attorneys on my left. "These are grass strips in the middle of a farm intended for a rancher's small, single-engine, light private aircraft such as this Cessna 180 that I flew there. These airstrips required a plane with short takeoff and landing capabilities. I had to fly low over the fields and chase off the cattle. If it rained, the fields were muddy, which prevented me from landing. It's my experience that these pastures aren't suitable for landing the type of aircraft you're suggesting." I sat back down and, using a pointer, directed their attention to the map of Central America. "Cocaine is coming into the United States from the likes of Bolivia and Colombia through Panama. From Panama, flown in large planes as you indicated, it's suspected that one of the next stops, besides Mexico and the Bahamas, is El Salvador. What would be the logistical or any other reason for the drugs to be detoured through a small grass strip in Costa Rica?"

Margaret, her neck lost in her shoulders, sat and waited for me to continue.

"I'd advise that, if you're interested in learning about drug smuggling, you look at Ilopango and the pilots who flew out of there. And I can't help you with that."

After some thought, Margaret asked, "So it's your testimony that, in Costa Rica, the CIA, DEA, and their contractors weren't involved in running drugs to raise money for the Contras?"

"No, I didn't say that. They might well have been, but I have no direct evidence that anyone was."

One of the attorneys sitting with Margaret interrupted. "I have a few questions."

Margaret graciously allowed him to continue.

He cleared his throat, squirmed in his chair, and looked at the floor. Then, making a steeple with his fingers, he looked at me. "Is it possible that a small plane from Panama off-loaded supplies at one of these private Costa Rican airstrips, refueled, and then continued on to the United States or Ilopango with cocaine?"

"Sure, that's a probable scenario with smaller aircraft."

"Did you ever see planes unloading supplies?"

"No. While I was there, to the best of my knowledge, all supplies were air-dropped."

He searched through his notes. "Let me switch gears a bit from the airfields. Are you familiar with Frigoríficos de Puntarenas?"

"Yes, it's a processing operation in Puntarenas that exports frozen shrimp."

"Were you ever present there?"

"Yes, many occasions."

"Why?"

"John Hull was using the company to bring humanitarian aid, provided through our State Department, to Nicaraguan refugees."

"Did you ever meet a Louis Rodriguez while there? I believe he's Cuban."

"I don't recall," I said. "Most of the Cubans I met in Costa Rica, though, went by the last name of Rodriguez at one time or another."

"Did you see any evidence that drugs were being shipped out of Frigorífi-cos?"

"No. While there, I wasn't in a position to have observed anything like that."

"It's clear that the question of drugs wasn't the focus of your work in Costa Rica. Do you think, if you could have pursued that avenue, you'd have found evidence that cocaine smuggling was going on?"

My mind immediately flashed to the conversation I had with Siegel on this issue. I decided to keep my answer simple. "That would be speculative."

"That's okay. We can speculate here."

I gathered my thoughts. "Look, we've spent the afternoon talking about drugs. In Latin America, if you want to secretly move weapons, the drug runners own the established networks. Those networks lent themselves to the purposes of the Contras." I wanted to end the discussion about drug smuggling. "I think subsequent investigations into this matter will reveal that, possibly with the knowledge of our government agents, not at their direction but with their knowledge, individuals within the Contra effort took advantage of their positions and were smuggling drugs to raise money for the effort. Maybe for their personal financial interests as well. I wish I could help you more, but I can't."

Margaret jumped back in. "So why do you feel it wasn't at our government's direction?"

"You asked me to speculate. I guess it's the faith I have in my government." That was no longer a truthful answer.

Everyone on my right began gathering papers and files. It was late in the afternoon, and the attorneys on the left took the cue and prepared to leave. Everyone except Margaret thanked me, and I left. I found Siegel waiting for me in the cluttered and dim hallway.

"Damn it, Siegel."

"What's the matter?" he asked as we headed out of the building.

"You have me spend all that time in Costa Rica chasing the source of small arms, and no one asked me one question about it. They spent the entire time asking me about drug smuggling, the one area you prevented me from getting involved in."

We walked outside to a bright afternoon and stopped under the shade of a large, densely leafed tree. Siegel took a deep look into my eyes. "Drugs. Some see an issue here they can exploit." He then looked out across the city and added, with a hint of disgust in his voice, "It's all politics."

"You think the means justify the end?"

"Absolutely not." I noticed a bit of anger in his voice at the suggestion. "You zero in on the problem and correct it, but don't destroy the mission, in this case preventing totalitarianism in Central America, in the process."

We sat down on a bus stop bench. Siegel appeared deep in thought. "Do you know who General Donovan was?"

The name seemed vaguely familiar. "No."

His voice was hushed in a tone of respect. "Wild Bill Donovan was awarded the Medal of Honor in World War I. In the Second World War, he was the founder and head of the OSS, predecessor to the CIA. After the war, Donovan admitted that, during the war, the OSS relied on the Mafia, who organized resistance against the Fascists and Nazis. Donovan knew at the time that the

Mafia was funding their resistance against totalitarianism through drug smuggling." Siegel, his arm thrown along the back of the bench, raised his eyebrows as I took in this information. "Based on that knowledge, should political opposition have argued to abandon our involvement in that war?"

I smiled. "But that was the good war."

"It was a war against aggression and totalitarianism, as is this fight in Central America. Why do we have to wait until millions die before we get involved and then call it a good war?" Siegel paused as he searched for the right words. "No, we can't condone drug smuggling. But we also can't throw the baby out with the bath water. Too many in Washington purposely look at an issue through the wrong end of the telescope. It's an unintended problem with our system. Politicians don't look forward to see what the consequences might be decades down the road. All they care about is the next election, not the next generation." He looked away again, as if in thought. He turned back and placed his hand on my shoulder. "Don't think for a minute that what you did in Costa Rica wasn't relevant. But the Israeli connection is, politically, a delicate subject that both sides of the aisle aren't about to make public or exploit. Not yet anyway."

We departed separate ways to our respective vehicles. I never saw Siegel again, and it was the last time anyone contacted me regarding the Contras.

———•◦•———

Back in California, I continued working as a forensic consultant in the field of drugs and narcotics. I also reentered academia, writing and implementing a drug rehabilitation program to be used specifically for court-mandated drug clientele. Classes, each involving thirty students for thirteen weeks, were taught in Alameda, Santa Clara, and San Mateo counties. I conducted several studies as I facilitated the programs and came away with two observations.

First, the majority of the attendees were not addicts, but were there for the offense of simple possession, no different than if we sentenced citizens to an alcohol rehabilitation program simply because they were in possession of wine with their groceries while on their way home.

Second, those in the program whose background did indicate a substance abuse problem showed characteristics of someone with underlying psychological issues or conditions. Whether the fault of private health insurance or lack of government programs, they were falling through the cracks of the mental health care system. It was clear that some of the court-referred clients were self-medicating with alcohol and drugs, and they needed professional help above and beyond what could be provided in any thirteen-week court-mandated group program.

I was reminded of the hazards associated with untreated, self-medicating mentally disturbed individuals on an afternoon I attended the San Jose North Rotary Club. I was there to address them about my concerns with what our country was doing to itself in the War on Drugs. Pat Dwyer, a Rotary member who had been one of the sergeants in narcotics, looked distraught as he came up to me before the meeting started.

"Did you hear the news? Two officers have just been shot. One's DOA. The other in surgery."

I let out a heavy sigh. "Oh, no. Do you know who?"

"Gene Simpson and Gordon Silva. Silva's in surgery."

I knew Simpson only as a fellow officer. Gordi and I, though, had stayed in touch since I left the department, occasionally meeting for lunch to talk real estate and girlfriends.

I muddled through my talk to the Rotarians and then rushed over to the hospital to join the concerned crowd of police officers. I learned from them that Simpson had been called to a donut shop to deal with a mentally disturbed homeless man. A struggle ensued, and Simpson lost his gun, resulting in his being fatally shot. Silva had responded to the scene along with other officers. When the gunfire was over, the perpetrator had been killed, and Silva lay on the sidewalk shot in the stomach. Before he could get out of surgery, Gordon Silva died of his wounds.

Chapter 11

The Wheel of Dharma

"Who are these guys?" I asked my interpreter.

"KGB," he said, showing no emotion.

I waited for further explanation, but he offered none. We just stood there and looked at each other in the freezing night air. We were standing between our respective beat-up two-door sedans, which were pulled over to the side of a country road thirty miles outside of Moscow. The two young KGB agents, attired in blue-collar clothes, shuffled nervously about on their feet. They had flagged us down from behind by flashing their headlights.

"So what do they want?" I asked.

"Their car broke down. They want us to tow them."

I was suspicious. "Tow them where?"

"Their job is to follow you, so we'll tow them if it's okay with you."

"If it's okay with me?" I could hardly believe what I was hearing, *Why am I in charge?*

I looked at the two Russian narcotics officers I'd been working with that day. They were waiting for an answer from me and shrugged their shoulders as if this were an everyday occurrence. I wanted to laugh, but thought better of it. *Certainly the KGB is more sophisticated than this.*

"If they don't stay with you," the interpreter suggested, "they'll be in trouble with their bosses."

I figured I had finally seen it all. "Okay, let's tow them."

They took a large rope from the trunk of our vehicle and tied it between the cars. With the KGB securely behind, we slowly pulled back onto the highway and toward our destination.

It was 1989. Through the Office of International Criminal Justice at the University of Illinois, I joined a group who had been invited to the Soviet Union. This delegation, primarily law enforcement officers, was to travel throughout the Soviet Union and consult with their law enforcement officials. As a group, we met with dignitaries and high-ranking law enforcement officials. Individually, we traveled and observed within our own specialties. I worked with Russian narcotics enforcement officers.

I found the Soviet Union to be a dreary society in which everyone lived at a low socioeconomic level. Everything—buildings, housing, roads, and public transportation—was in a state of disrepair. A central authoritarian government in Moscow controlled work, transportation, commerce, and local government right down to the petty details. I saw the results at the largest department store in Leningrad, the most consumer-oriented city in Russia at that time. Two square city blocks wide and two stories high, this store was virtually empty except for a supply of shoes that recently arrived. Customers, waiting in a long line, were allowed into the store one at a time. They could buy one pair of shoes as long as they didn't care what size. Outside, those who had bought shoes exchanged with each other to get the sizes they needed. With the Iron Curtain beginning to crack, the citizens were aware that their system wasn't working as promised. I learned this from the attitude of a discouraged public.

"The politicians lie," my interpreter said. "We know they're lying, they know we know they're lying, but they keep lying anyway, and we pretend to believe them. As long as they pretend to pay us, we pretend to work."

Official from Ministry of Interior, Moscow

Head of narcotics, Leningrad

That work ethic included police officers. Layers of bureaucracy stifled initiative from beginning an investigation to making an arrest. It was better for a police officer to go home at the end of the day without having brought anything to the attention of his supervisor who, in turn, wanted to go home at the end of the day without involving his superiors.

Behind the façade of a classless society, members of the communist party and officers in the military, including law enforcement, enjoyed benefits unavailable to the worker who the bureaucrats claimed to represent. This was most evident in the food. For general consumption, eggs, potatoes, bread, cucumbers, and cherry tomatoes were readily available. Instead of butter, lard, which was plentiful, was served. Meat was of poor quality. In contrast, my hosts, higher-ranking police officials, were always able to serve meals of fresh fruits and vegetables along with plenty of fresh meat.

On the night we towed the two KGB agents around, they sat in their car in freezing temperatures while we partied away the night with several high-ranking military and police officers. We dined on roasted pig, a salad of fresh vegetables, dark bread with real butter, and plenty of vodka. One Soviet army colonel, who thought little of the waiting and watching KGB, repeatedly went outside and raised his voice and glass of vodka in a mocking toast to the hapless pair. Hours later, the two KGB men were still huddled in their car, waiting to be towed, when I was driven to where I was spending the night.

On the way back to my hotel, I considered that, although the Soviet Union was still oppressive, it had become weak, a society not to fear but to pity. Little did I know it was soon to fall, collapsing the Iron Curtain around Eastern Europe.

While in Moscow, we met with the director of the Ministry of Interior. I worked with narcotics officers there and in other major cities such as Leningrad and Yalta. I saw drug dealing on the streets like one would see in San Francisco or New York City. I went on a search warrant where they seized a methamphetamine lab. I visited drug rehabilitation programs where I interviewed patients recovering from substance abuse or dependence.

On the flight back to the United States, one question kept running through my mind. *If the Soviet Union, still behind the Iron Curtain, is unable to control drugs through prohibition, how is the United States, a free country, ever going to?*

In 1990, I attended a criminal justice conference in Chicago. During a break, Harlan Ledger, a large man whose head seemed to protrude through an overly tight collar, approached me. His round eyeglasses and name gave me the impression of a small-town accountant. He had an air of dignity about him, although he kept closing his eyes as he spoke. I thought he was going to fall asleep.

His nametag included an ambiguous government department that gave me no clue as to who he worked for. When I asked for more details, his answer was vague. I finally steered the conversation around to the State Department.

"Sure, I know many of those lads. Like my work, they're involved in research and analysis." He casually looked around the room as he talked. "INR they call it, the Bureau of Intelligence and Research."

"How many at INR are TDY from other government agencies?"

"Many." He then turned toward me, stood a bit more erect, and proudly stated, "I myself am career navy."

"So while TDY, where do your loyalties lie? With your temporary assignment or the navy?"

He showed a slow, knowing smile. "With the United States."

I smiled back as I knew he wasn't going to give me a true answer. I knew agencies within our government had their own agendas and power struggles. And I always wondered whom Siegel really worked for.

"Which brings me to your trip to Tibet," he said, catching me off guard.

The Office of International Criminal Justice was preparing to send me to China, including Tibet, with a delegation similar to the recent trip through the Soviet Union.

"I haven't mentioned China."

He gazed across the sea of people in the conference room and turned back with a smile. "No, you didn't. But I heard about it through OICJ." He looked at me through heavy eyelids. "What do you know about Tibet?"

"Not much more than I read in the newspapers."

The session was ready to resume, and Ledger motioned for us to step out of the room. After getting drinks at the bar, we took a seat in the lounge.

"Tibet is a country where the truth has been swept aside." As he talked, I could sense that Ledger was a wealth of information. "As late as the 1950s, Tibet had no political ties or diplomatic relationships with any other country. Tibet ignored the world, and the world ignored them. Including China. No Chinese lived in Tibet. No one spoke Chinese there. No Chinese military was present. So when Mao claimed Tibet was part of China, the world washed their hands of Tibet. Furthermore, the United States, England, and India refused to allow Tibetans to steer their own course by preventing their representatives from traveling to the United Nations to argue their case for being independent."

I knew Ledger was giving me a brief overview, but I felt as though he was leaving something important out. "Why would we wash our hands of Tibet just because Mao made this claim?"

"Because, before Mao, we were supporting Chiang Kai-shek. And in support of Chiang Kai-shek, we agreed Tibet would fall under the influence of China. So our hand was already played when the communists came into power."

"Well, we dropped the ball there. Sounds like what we did to Poland. World War II was started in its defense, yet, when it was over, to appease the communists, we prevented Poland from self-determination and allowed Russia to dominate it."

Ledger looked deep in thought and then said solemnly, "Tibet was a failed policy from the beginning because we never understood the people. That sent ripples that lapped on the shores of Vietnam, where we failed to understand the patriotism of the Vietnamese and their desire for a united country free from foreign interference."

There's no act that's not the source of an infinite series of lasting effects.

We ordered another round of drinks, and Ledger went on to talk about modern Tibet, China's denial of a military presence, and an oppressed people. "I can't stress enough the opportunity you have been given to take this trip. Do your best to get away from your escort and learn what you can about China's military presence."

"So you had an agenda when you approached me this morning?"

"Ah, well, we all have an agenda now, don't we? Didn't you have an agenda when you asked what department my loyalties lie with?"

We laughed. He was comfortable to be around.

Official from Ministry of Interior, Beijing

I found China to be a mixture of autos, trucks, bicycles, pull carts, rickshaws, and throngs of pedestrians. All appeared to be moving in a motivated expectation of the day's commerce. Police officers who weren't given to coddling offenders kept the order.

In Beijing, I met with officials from the ministry of justice. They assured me that there wasn't a drug problem in China. In Shanghai, while with professors of criminal justice at the university, I learned differently. The drug of choice among businessmen in their city's financial districts was cocaine, as in any major city in the United States. Among the poorer class, the drug of choice was opium.

In Guangzhou and Chengdu, I learned the focus of narcotics enforcement throughout China was on traffickers, usually corrupt government officials. They smuggled heroin through China to the port cities of Shanghai and Hong Kong. I sat through the criminal trial of several defendants accused of property crimes. I was fascinated by the fact that, under China's rules of law, the concept of having a right to remain silent was nonexistent. Furthermore, a defendant and his attorney would never consider offering a defense or another side to the prosecution's case without evidence to back it up. It was a non-adversarial system in which both sides seemed to work at coming to the truth.

I toured several prisons. By our standards the prisons appeared to be a joke, as the cell doors were open during the day while all inmates worked at the prison factory, the only source of revenue for the institution. In the evenings, the inmates attended classes on civics, the law, and personal responsibility. The walls around the prison were no more than ten feet high with a single strand of barbed wire along the top. To attempt escape would be dealt with most harshly, often with the death penalty.

One afternoon, I was notified, with excitement on the part of my host, that I was invited to attend an execution of nine drug dealers. I declined to attend the ceremonies, but learned the death penalty wasn't unusual for drug offenders. As strict as the laws and punishment were in China, prohibition wasn't working there either.

At Chengdu International Airport, where I was to board the flight to Lhasa, Tibet, my experience in China suddenly became bizarre. With ongoing construction at the main terminal, we were relegated to an aged, freestanding concrete building sitting on the airfield far from the main terminal.

There was no air-conditioning, and the musty room's dirty windows were closed. The green tile floor hadn't been cleaned in years. The room was bare except for one portable counter. A female airline employee wearing a smooth white blouse with a blue pleated skirt, which extended comfortably below the knees, staffed it. Appearing clean and fresh with a gentle smile, she looked out of place as she stood quietly with her hands behind her back. To her side, mounted on the wall, was what appeared to be a suggestion box. Below the Chinese characters, the English translation said, "Accusation Box."

I stood in line with an odd assortment of people in various forms of dress and costume. In front of me was an elderly lady, her graying hair in a large bun adorned with chopsticks. Her teeth were black from years of eating lychee nuts. She was wearing a gray Mao suit that looked like it had been cut from an old quilt. She spat on the floor. Several people behind me in line stood a man in an old suit with a goat at his side on a leash, like an obedient dog.

The main terminal had been hustling and bustling with chattering businessmen and tourists, people greeting or saying good-bye, but I sensed the tension build as we were herded into the neglected structure. The Tiananmen Square protests, known in China as the "June 4, 1989 Incident," was recent history, and this assembly of Chinese and Tibetans was uneasy and quiet. No one dared to step out of the queue.

Our plane arrived and was ready to board. With my black gym bag as a carry-on, I trudged across the tarmac under steamy, cloudy skies and climbed the stairs to board the Air China flight.

I worked my way down the aisle and passed a man holding a small wooden crate full of chickens in his lap. I took a seat next to a balding Tibetan man wearing bifocals. His face sported a mustache and goatee. He wore a red cloth with thin blue stripes around his head. A necklace of white beads interspaced with a few red baubles accompanied his yellow, sweat-soaked, short-sleeved shirt. He didn't acknowledge me. Across the aisle sat the older woman with the gray Mao coat. She leaned over, spread her legs, and spat softly on the carpeted floor. The gentleman with the goat passed by with his animal dutifully following behind. I was curious if the goat got his own seat, but decided not to turn around to check.

As the plane crossed over the Himalayan Mountains, providing stunning views of rugged peaks covered with snow, I stood to stretch in the aisle and observed more of my fellow passengers. A middle-aged man with short hair wore a grimy brown robe with a red sash. I assumed he was a monk. Another group of men wore small, broad-rimmed hats that seemed to perch on top of their heads, similar to what I'd seen Indians wear in South America a world away. A smiling, young Tibetan woman wearing a fresh red silk blouse with a yellow circular design had her black hair parted in the middle with a flat, three-inch round gold ornament on top. Strands of yellow and blue beads were braided in and holding her hair back. A few Chinese businessmen wore rumpled suits and ties. The goat stood quietly at the back of the plane as if he'd been chalking up frequent flyer miles for years.

The looks in the passengers' eyes seemed to speak to me. "Welcome to our world. While with us, you'll see that the Accusation Box is appropriately labeled."

The airport at Lhasa had no terminal, and a sound truck blaring loud Tibetan music met us. Our small group's visit seemed to be a big affair, as tourism had been curtailed since China imposed martial law in 1987 and had been nonexistent since the Tiananmen Square riots.

Lhasa, a city of forty thousand, sits at twelve thousand five hundred feet. To accommodate Chinese business travelers and government officials, along with the few tourists who were beginning to visit, hotel rooms contained oxygen connections with masks to ward off altitude sickness.

In walking the city with my Chinese escort, I found the people of Tibet dark and leathery due to the harsh sun at those altitudes. Their brightly colored clothes were dirty because they were forever flopping themselves prostrate in the dust as they approached or passed a temple.

China had been exceptionally clean, but Lhasa was poor and littered with dogs, dung, and garbage. Hawkers, beggars, sheep, chanting monks, spinning prayer wheels, fluttering flags bearing written Buddha petitions, and strange odors overwhelmed my senses. The earthen buildings, low-lying with white-washed walls, appeared to be in disrepair. Little money, if any, was being spent on community needs.

In the bazaar, the only place I was allowed to go unescorted, I was offered both hashish and opium. At other times, men in rumpled, dirty suits pressed a folded piece of paper in my hand without saying anything or making eye contact. The notes asked I carry a message home, "Tibetans are occupied and oppressed."

I had two meetings with the Tibetan Ministry of Justice. The director was from China, and his Tibetan counterpart was with him. The Chinese were clearly in control, and nothing of substance or anything that might shed a negative light on the region was disclosed.

One afternoon, they had me scheduled for a meeting with the head of a community program for young misdemeanor offenders. I begged off, complaining of an altitude headache. An hour after my escort left, I walked out of the hotel and hired a bicycle-pulled rickshaw. I used a tourist map and showed him the location of the meeting I was to attend, but directed him to take a circuitous route on the highway around the city. If caught and confronted, because I was unescorted, at least I could claim I was attempting to make the meeting.

As the bicyclist pedaled away and the stain of sweat on his back began to grow, I couldn't help but think of our fortunes in life. I knew he felt lucky to be hired that day, yet I knew I could never convince myself of that.

No sooner had we pulled out on the main road surrounding the city than a Chinese military convoy, going the opposite direction, passed us. The first couple of cars certainly carried high-ranking officers. Armored personnel carriers and then large trucks carrying troops, all standing in the back as if on parade, followed them. The number of soldiers was significant, and I estimated the movement to be of brigade strength. My years in uniform had taught me the importance of caliber in a military unit, and these were true professionals. They were also soldiers of a dictatorship, designed to frighten the senses and suffocate the soul.

I returned safely to the hotel having never been missed, amused by how simple it went. That evening, as my escort waited at the bottom, I climbed with great effort, due to the thin air, the thirteen stories of steps to the Potala, the principal palace in all of Tibet. The entry hall was several stories high, illuminated only by light wells from courtyards above. The aroma of juniper, rhododendron, incense, and yak butter soothed my senses. I continued my struggle up within the multilevel palace and passed through chambers with massive wall paintings to more stairs. I visited shrines with altars and gold Buddhas and then climbed more stairs to prayer rooms with brightly colored statues. There were hallways painted red with gold trim lit only by sunlight, more stairs, more statues of Buddha and sculptured art, and more stairs.

Prayer wheels at the Potala, Tibet

I finally stepped into the cold evening air and onto one of the rooftops. Prayer flags fluttered in the breeze around the two-foot cylindrical prayer wheels that lined one side of the rooftop. A mantra was written on each wheel. According to Tibetan tradition, spinning a prayer wheel will have the same meritorious effect as if I orally recited the prayer.

I walked to the edge of the roof and looked out over the Himalayas. I felt I had stepped back hundreds of years in time. I was certainly as far from my world as I could physically possibly be.

Yet I couldn't get away from my memories. As I spun a large prayer wheel clockwise, turning the wheel of dharma, I sought a hint of enlightenment. My mind searched for meaning in my life and in the lives of friends such as Gerald Ortego, Gordon Silva, and Trent Fair.

Chapter 12

For Those You Grieve

While walking across an intersection in Chicago's Su-Hu district, a car rushed toward us against the red light. "Sally!" I put my arm out and pulled her back from its path. As the car passed, I reflexively kicked the driver's door. The driver locked up the brakes, and the car skidded, cockeyed, to a halt in the middle of the intersection. Smoke drifted from its tires. Sally looked in shock as I calmly asked her to keep walking and meet me in half a block. The male driver in his twenties left his vehicle in the middle of traffic and stormed over to where I waited on the corner.

"You just kicked in my door," he said in a raised voice, implying I was responsible.

It had been ten years since I'd been a cop, but, once a cop, always a cop. I instantly assumed a cop's attitude. "Yes, I did, and you'll get back in your car and leave. Now."

A female Chicago police officer standing a few feet away surveyed the scene and then looked the other way.

"No, you're going to pay for that door," he insisted, getting angrier.

"I tell you what. You can get back in your car and leave, or I'm going to bust you for nearly running down my lady. I'll have that officer call for a wagon to take you to booking." I motioned with my hand toward the uniformed officer. "She'll tow your car, I'll continue on to dinner, and you'll spend the night in jail." I was sounding self-assured.

He looked at the officer as she glanced over. She might have been one of Chicago's finest yet, in spite of the traffic jam, she wasn't going to get involved. He didn't know that, though, and I could see the wheels turn in his head. My bluff was working. His tone weakened as he again argued that I had kicked in his door.

I lowered my voice and took a softer stance, sounding like I was now offering advice. "Look, you've been drinking. Get in your car and leave before I have to arrest you."

I didn't know if he'd been drinking or not, but he didn't protest. He looked at the police officer, back at me with resignation, and walked to his car.

Sally, her mouth wide open with a look of terror as she watched, was waiting in front of an art gallery. "What were you thinking?"

"It's no big deal. Let's go." I began to walk toward the art exhibition as if nothing had happened.

Apparently, this was a big deal to Sally, who had never experienced anything like this with men she'd dated. She stepped in front of me with her blonde hair blowing in the wind and her hazel eyes wide. "What if he were some gang member who wanted to fight?"

"I would've choked him out and made him do the chicken."

Sally's earlier look of horror returned as she realized she was talking to a psychopath. She would know. She was finishing her PhD in clinical social work and had a full-time practice as a counselor.

It was 1990, and I was living in Florida on my sailboat. I had traveled to Chicago for several reasons. First, I was to discuss with the OICJ the possibility of an assignment to teach American criminal justice at a law university in Shanghai. Second, I was to attend a gathering of Vietnam helicopter pilots.

At the reunion, I saw many I hadn't seen in over twenty years, Walt "Sugar Bear" Henderson, Tom Andrews, and Carl Kimmich. The wife of another pilot, who had been a candidate at 1st WOC when I was there as a TAC, was Sally's cousin, and she invited Sally to lunch at the reunion. There they introduced us.

In spite of the incident in the Su-Hu district, Sally felt I might be redeemable with some effort on her part, especially after learning I could cook. Working full time as a therapist, coupled with attending classes for her PhD, the restraints of time over the years had reduced her diet to Burger King for breakfast, lunch, and dinner. So we continued to date.

I packed a picnic basket with my broiled game hens stuffed with apple dressing, along with grapes and a selection of fine cheese. We enjoyed it with an exceptional bottle of wine, all spread out on the lawn during a symphony concert at Ravinia Park.

That fall, I sailed to the Bahamas. For Christmas, I flew back to Chicago and baked a goose, preparing the skin with a rub of brown sugar, bay leaves, and peppercorns. I then stuffed it with chestnuts, oranges, lemon, and onions. I served it with roasted fall vegetables, wild rice, and a rhubarb pie for dessert.

Sally visited me on the boat in the Abacos one weekend, and I seared grouper that I had marinated in sesame oil, soy sauce, garlic, chopped green onions and then sprinkled with lemon juice. I served it on a bed of fresh greens with a side of mashed garlic potatoes. Le grand finale was a flambé banana in raspberry sauce.

Upon finishing her PhD, we gathered in Wimberley, Texas, close to her mother's. There, in the heart of the Hill Country, along the green banks of Cypress Creek and under the shade of tall trees, Sally Hill married a cook. I married a psychotherapist.

Although we were both offered a position to teach at the university in Shanghai, I was then consciously under the influence of the events in the life of my father who had recently passed away. Having worked hard all his life building his business and dedicating his evenings and weekends to the church, he had looked forward to traveling when reaching retirement. Instead, at the age of fifty-nine, he was diagnosed with Parkinson's and lived the final ten years of his life in desperation. I now wanted to quietly travel without any work commitments, and Sally and I decided to take off time and live aboard the boat.

We spent the first winter sailing from Sarasota, Florida, across the Okeechobee, through Key Largo, and then on to Key West. That summer in Annapolis, Maryland, in preparation for sailing through the shallow waters of the Bahamas, we purchased a thirty-two-foot catamaran. The previous boat was named *My Way*, but now, no longer a lone wolf buying drinks for divorcees at Tiki huts in the Caribbean, I was ready for a paradigm shift. We christened the new boat *Harmony*. We then explored the Chesapeake, visiting historic places such as St. Michaels and Jamestown.

In the fall, we started down the Intracoastal Waterway (ICW), visiting Elizabeth City, Ocracoke, New Bern, and both cities named Beaufort. Savannah and Charleston, with their beautifully restored historic buildings, were our favorites. During the trip, we enjoyed the availability of soft shell crabs, oysters, clams, and fresh Atlantic fish. As we continued south, we dined on dishes such as Southern fried chicken accompanied by okra gumbo, buttery cornbread, and black-eyed peas.

St. Augustine, founded in 1565, welcomed us back to Florida with a lunch of blue crab claw meat, breaded and fried. We then continued on to Miami where we anchored in Key Biscayne. After a short trip into Miami for a genuine, made-to-order Cuban sandwich, we readied *Harmony* to cross through Angel Creek and into the Gulf Stream to the Bahamas.

Besides airplanes and flying, I always loved boats. Like Ratty in *The Wind in the Willows*, I believed "there was nothing, absolutely nothing half so worth doing as messing around in boats."

My first ocean boating experience was in 1957 when, at the age of eleven, my family shipped to Brazil on a Japanese vessel named the *Brazil Maru*. We sailed out of Los Angeles and down through the Panama Canal before our first stop. We then continued toward Caracas, Venezuela, but encountered a major gale en route. All other passengers were sick in their cabins, but, as the ship rose and fell, listed to port, and then rolled to starboard, I made my way to the bridge where the crew was surprised to see anyone moving about. They allowed me to stay and watch the waves crash over the bow of the ship as it plunged ahead into cresting waves. I loved it.

In the 1970s, I sought the open ocean experience by sailing my boat out of San Francisco Bay and around the Farallon Islands, which lie thirty miles from the Golden Gate Bridge. From the berth in Alameda and back would sometimes be a twenty-four-hour expedition. Sailing out under the Golden Gate, leaving the safe and the familiar, I passed through the Potato Patch, a shoal thirty feet deep. Depending on the tides, all the water in the Pacific was either trying to get into or out of the bay, creating swift tide currents over that shallow area. No matter how calm the ocean was otherwise, the Potato Patch was a cold, wet, and wild ride in frothing seas. It was never a setting conducive to euphoria except to a masochist willing to go toe to toe with the ocean. The sea could not only challenge with brutal violence, but also with oppressive calm.

I experienced both lessons in 1981 on the trip to Costa Rica. Four hundred miles offshore from Central America, dark squalls appeared on the horizon. The thirty-seven-foot boat lost its predictable pattern of motion as it rose, heaved, and dropped over mounting waves that swamped the deck. The lightning and thunder were unnerving because the metal mast was the tallest object around.

With sails reduced to the bare minimum, the wind screamed through the rigging, grabbing words out of my mouth. It was too warm for foul weather gear, yet, without it, the rain, blown horizontal, struck my body like pellets from a gun.

Down the face of a wave, the vessel raced with a shudder as the sea chased, only to lose the pursuit at the bottom when the breaking wave caught up from behind. That wave lifted the boat up where it wallowed in the foam at the crest before it appeared to slide backward as the wave passed beneath. When the next hissing wave loomed from astern, the boat again surfed down its face, only to repeat the action as the wave caught up and passed beneath. At times, a green mass of ocean swirled across the decks, overwhelmed the scuppers, and spilled into the cockpit. The water was inescapable. My attempts to move around during the storm resulted in being violently thrown about. This scene repeated itself into the night when the following sea couldn't be seen and every fifth wave sounded like the one that would surely take us under.

Within a couple of days, the wind eased, the sea settled, and the motion of the boat again became predictable. The gray skies parted, the wet deck was awash with sunshine, and the sky was quilted in blue and puffy white as a rainbow radiated to the east. We again sailed along in paradise.

Then we were be-calmed. For three days, the ocean, scorched by a hundred degrees, was flat as a billiard table with not a whisper of air. The excessive sunlight was brutal as it glared off the water. Unable to motor, since precious fuel would be necessary when we entered Golfo de Nicoya, unable to talk to anyone by radio due to our distance from land, and unable to sleep in the oppressive heat and humidity, we could only sit, swelter, and silently wonder just how long the fresh water would hold out if the doldrums didn't lift. Being hundreds of miles offshore in these situations, I didn't contemplate insignificance. I experienced it.

In 1986, my boat was a full keel, cutter-rigged, heavy displacement cruiser. When sailing to Mexico, I was again answering the call of the sea. We sailed from San Francisco and followed the wind and currents. We went along with the sea and obeyed. But on coming home, by the nature of our destination, we committed a deliberate act against her. We went against the tides, currents, winds, and waves, and she finally let us know when we reached Point Conception, just north of Santa Barbara, California. The weather in this area, due to topography and sea currents, could go from windless, flat seas to thirty-knot blows with square waves in minutes.

We anchored south of Conception at Cojo where I was able to catch a good nap until 2200. The fog had lowered over the sea like a heavy shroud, but the weather report indicated light winds with low swells so we weighed anchor and sailed off to round Conception. We were past my self-determined point of no return when the wind started driving foam off the tops of waves. I had the mainsail double-reefed and the jib dropped and secured along the lifelines, and we were motoring through with the wind right off the bow. As the seas and winds increased in the black of night and as the bow began to plow into oncoming seas, I realized I had made an earlier error. I was going to have to go forward, bring the jib back, and stow it.

Wearing a full set of foul weather gear with my safety harness on the outside, I clipped on a jack line that ran along the deck. I then worked my way forward, crawling as the seas continued to build. Something that would take only minutes in fair weather took a half hour in the raging sea. While I was lying on the foredeck, gathering in the sail, the bow bored into every fourth wave, plunging me beneath as dark water swept the deck. The bitter cold

Pacific surged through my foul weather gear and, like an enema, into every orifice of my body.

Over the howling wind, while the waves crashed over me, I thought I heard a Mayday transmission from a boat named the *Jack Junior*. The radio was then again silent. With the jib finally secured in a locker, I stood in the cockpit, soaked and shivering, and stared into utter darkness. I tried to raise the *Jack Junior* on the radio, but received no response.

I gripped the tiller and looked at the time. I calculated that we reached a position where I was able to change the heading toward shore. And as fast as the wind and sea had built, it began to calm. Soon we were safely anchored in Avila as the morning sun fought to break through the fog.

After several hours of sleep while a small diesel furnace mounted on the bulkhead warmed the cabin, members of the Coast Guard woke me. A fishing boat named *Jack Junior* had been off the coast the night before, and it was missing. The Coast Guard was searching for information. I later learned that, in the dark of night, during the height of the blow, the *Jack Junior* sunk, and all aboard were lost.

By then, I knew all too well that, in going toe to toe with the ocean, one could never win. The ocean can become a relentless enemy from which there might be no escape. For some, the ocean will win. In that case, the sailor will lose his boat or, worse, his life. The best a sailor can ever hope for is a draw.

As Sally and I prepared *Harmony* to cross the Gulf Stream, those previous days of trials and tribulation were distant memories. They were war stories about dragons of the deep to be embellished later with other sailors. I was now making plans for this adventure. As Sally stowed and secured everything below deck, I plotted waypoints on my nautical charts. At 2300, with Sally at the starboard bow to assure we stayed in the channel, we crossed through a pass in the reef and into the open sea.

Mahi-mahi

Sally was excited. Her first ocean voyage was becoming a reality. She took her position as first mate seriously, yet, upon sailing onto the open waters, she had an overwhelming urge to climb into the berth. As the gentle motion of *Harmony* joined the rhythm of the water sweeping along the hulls, she fell fast asleep. Behind me, the sliver of land began to fade as twinkling lights ashore slowly and magically sank, leaving only a dark horizon. Soon only the universe above, lit with distant galaxies, accompanied me. *Harmony* rode over long, smooth, invisible swells. The only evidence left behind were two iridescent trails of phosphorescence.

Dawn was painted with a bright yellow glow off the port bow, and, by 0800, right on schedule, I saw Bimini dead ahead. I trailed a fishing line in the water and quickly caught a mahi-mahi, which I cleaned, cut into steaks, and placed in the refrigerator. By 0945, with Sally fully refreshed and up on the bow, we crossed from deep cobalt waters between the islands of Bimini and into the light blue and shallow waters of the Bahama Banks.

The wind was barely a breeze as we coasted toward our next waypoint, Chub Cay. With the shallow water crystal clear, we were sure we'd strike the tops of the mustard-colored brain coral. By 1600, it was evident that, if we continued, we were going to be passing out of the banks too late in the day. I set the anchor and found the water shallow enough to dive down and confirm it was secure. For three hundred and sixty degrees, there was neither sight of land nor evidence of civilization. Sally and I were the only two people alive in a universe of gin-clear water poured over glistening sand.

I went into the galley and cut up some of the raw mahi-mahi into quarter-inch pieces, added chopped tomatoes, onion and garlic, oregano, a little cilantro, and several dashes of Tabasco. I then added lime juice and placed it in the refrigerator to marinate. It would make a fine ceviche for lunch the next day.

After a quick swim and fresh water rinse, I grilled the remaining mahi-mahi steaks for dinner, served them on a bed of asparagus with a side of brown rice, and matched it all with a Sauvignon Blanc. We enjoyed dinner while watching a large sun pass through fiery clouds and set into a tranquil sea. A female voice from the CD player was softly singing about a sailboat "in the moonlight with you."

The following morning, we continued across the banks, through a break in the reef, and into the deep blue waters of Providence Channel. By noon, we were safely anchored in the shallow waters that separated sparsely inhabited Chub Cay from uninhabited Crab Cay. That afternoon, six monohull sailboats joined us, but, due to their draft, all anchored in deeper, exposed water. The radio was all chatter between them as a winter front was expected to blow in that evening.

That night, sitting in our berth, we could see the swinging anchor lights from the boats a hundred yards in front of us at the mouth of the channel. The wind picked up, and, while we were experiencing no waves between the two islands, the other vessels began to rock, bob, and roll. Sally smiled and snuggled up. It warmed the cockles of our hearts knowing we were safe, secure, comfortable, and together.

In the morning, not wanting to spend another night at a rough anchorage, the other boats left, and Sally and I were left to explore the islands on our own. When it was time to think about dinner, I went looking for lobsters. In the Bahamas, you can legally take lobster and fish only while free diving, not with scuba gear. Since lobsters live at ten feet or deeper, under coral ledges, outcroppings, or in holes, I had to hold my breath for extended periods of time during the hunt. For someone who had difficulty with stamina during soccer, water polo, and marching, I had an uncanny ability to hold my breath for up to two minutes while gently swimming down, locating, and maneuvering a lobster to the point where I could grab or spear it. Among boaters in the Sea of Cortez, and later throughout the Caribbean, I was sought after for lessons.

At Chub, as Sally hovered above in the dinghy, I drifted down to the multi-colored reefs. Sunbeams of light danced around as I carefully peeked into the broken glass-edged coral. A barracuda, several feet above and to my rear, monitored my progress like a cobra gunship. I then laid my cheek in the sand as I peered into the gloom under a ledge. There I saw the tip of a lobster's antenna slowly waving about, monitoring its environment. I slowly floated over the top of the coral and, with my spear, began lightly tapping on the ledge.

The lobster hadn't sensed my presence and started to walk out. He was trying to use his antenna to discern what was occurring. The more it walked out, the more I tapped. I kept movement on my part to a minimum so as not to alert the lobster and to conserve oxygen. With patience and perseverance on my part, the lobster eventually exposed its body, and I speared it. With my lungs burning, I shot up and startled Sally as I breached the surface like a dolphin, gasping for fresh air through my wide grin. Sally laughed with delight as I dropped the lobster over the side and onto the floor of the dinghy. I then slipped beneath the surface, scouted out, and found another.

Lobster

For dinner that evening, after allowing the boiled lobsters to cool, I cubed and tossed them with small slices of mango. I covered it all in a light cream mixed with honey and lemon juice and served it chilled over a bed of rice.

As we sat on the foredeck that evening, I couldn't help but notice the absence of noise. Not the absence of sound. We heard the breeze, the water lapping against the hull, and the night birds. But otherwise, there was a complete absence of the incessant noise of civilization.

Several days later, we sailed to the Exumas with a stiff northerly wind behind. The spray off the bows sparkled like gems in the sunlight. A school of dolphins stampeded by. Many crisscrossed and played at the bows. As *Harmony* surged ahead of the waves, she remained flat and stable.

The first stop was Norman's Cay, where Lafferty and I visited a decade earlier. Sally and I found the island virtually abandoned with empty homes. Weeds were growing on the airstrip I had landed on. A sunken twin-engine cargo plane, a remnant from the island's drug smuggling days, lay on the bottom of the inner harbor. I wondered if this were a plane Lafferty sold them. We quickly sailed on the following day, as the island had nothing more to offer.

Warderick Wells was undoubtedly the most beautiful, idyllic place either of us had ever seen. Except for a park ranger on the north end, the island was uninhabited. We were the only boaters in the small, tight, and protected anchorage that swirled with aqua blue currents that hurried in and out. The unusual flow of water resulted in an abundance of sea life, all protected because the area was a national park. The surrounding gentle rolling hills offered hiking trails that took us from one side of the small island, through a tropical paradise, to the other. Two days later, we continued through the protected waters on the banks while deeper draft vessels traveled through the choppy sea on the eastern side of the island chain.

At Staniel Cay, we found a small village. Many boaters gathered here due to the good anchorage, water from a community well, and a bar at Happy People Marina. We spent Christmas and New Year's at Staniel Cay along with *My Bonnie* from England, *Windsong* from Oregon, and *SeaQuence* from Minnesota. Of course, we knew their personal names, such as George and Venetia, from South Africa, on *Calicoco*, but boaters referred to everyone by the names of their boats.

"We ran into *Caper* this afternoon," someone would say.

Ralph, a WWII RAF pilot, and his wife Marion sailed her, so they were simply *Caper*. I took silent pleasure in the knowledge that boaters referred to Sally and me as *Harmony*.

We moved on and promised to meet everyone again in Georgetown. Sally and I spent a week at Rudder Cut Cay, where we had good protection from the weather as another winter front blew through. We read books, swam, took walks on the isolated beach, and played Scrabble. We had fresh lobster or grouper every day we wanted.

One culinary diversion was conch, a large mollusk that could be found ten to fifteen feet underwater among the grassy beds of seaweed. It has thick, firm, white meat that is a staple in the Caribbean diet. The difficult part was the unpleasant process of removing, cleaning, and preparing the meat, which had to be pounded paper-thin. Once accomplished, though, the meat could be prepared as ceviche or in salads, soups, and stews. My favorite was to prepare the conch as one would tempura, a messy project on a boat but, when cooked properly, a delightful meal.

Georgetown, at the southern end of the Exuma chain, is a well-populated community with a good airport, a full service marina for those boats seeking docks, and a commercial port to accept supply vessels. On any given year, over four hundred cruising sailboats spend a considerable amount of time there during the winter and early spring. So the different anchorages were beginning to fill up as we arrived. Having shoal draft, we were able to sneak by monohulls and into shallow and more protected waters. As I stood on the bow and handled the anchor, Sally took the helm and maneuvered the boat. With hand signals from me, we quietly anchored.

With many crews, anchoring was a loud and combative process between the captain at the helm and the first mate on the bow. Sally's first experience with this was years earlier during a visit with me at Great Stirrup Cay, in the northern Berry Islands, where we initially had the anchorage to ourselves. One morning, we heard a vessel arriving in the midst of much yelling. We looked out and saw an old wooden sailboat, thirty feet in length, with a long bowsprit. A lady of at least seventy years was out on the sprit struggling with a heavy anchor. The boat had no stanchions or lifelines, and the bowsprit had no safety net. At the helm was the captain, who also appeared to be in his seventies.

"Drop it starboard," he yelled over the noise of his thumping engine.

She shouted back in a weak voice, "I know what the hell I'm doing."

His voice bellowed with a British accent. "Well, if you knew what you were doing, you'd have bloody well done it."

"If you'd bring the damn bow into the blasted wind, I would." She was leaning into the wind and fighting to keep her balance on the sprit as she cradled the anchor.

The captain continued to holler, "Well, you look like you're going to drop it to port."

"I'm about at the end of my tether with you, I am." Her voice was barely audible over the sounds of the engine.

The skipper circled us in an attempt to bring their boat back into the wind.

"That's a bit much, don't you think?" she said.

"Oh, keep your wig on." His voice echoed around the anchorage.

"What?" She was clearly agitated.

"Just drop the bloom'n anchor, or you're going to put me in a sticky wicket."

The anchor hit the water with a splash, and she somehow didn't follow it in. As their boat settled back, she secured the line.

Upon seeing us watching, the skipper's voice growled across the water. "Give us a minute to get squared away and then come over." He emphasized with a wave of his arm.

Sally grimaced. "Do we really want to go over there?"

"That's boating," I said, laughing as I prepared the dinghy.

Sally remained uncertain as we motored over. I could tell she wasn't sure if she wanted to meet this angry couple. With the captain's permission, we boarded their vessel. They bore a resemblance to each other, and I couldn't tell if she were his sister or if their marriage endured so long that their genes had bonded into a common denominator.

As is customary, we signed their guest log. It was leather bound and looked like an old Bible. The first mate directed us to the last couple of pages, where she had Sally sign in a small space. I was allowed to look at the beginning of the log where I saw that their first entry was in 1946 when they sailed over from England. Husband and wife, they had been living aboard in the Bahamas since, even while raising two boys.

We found the crusty couple delightful and enjoyed their story. During the dinghy ride back to our boat, I could see on Sally's face that they had expanded her horizons regarding the cruising lifestyle.

Life in Georgetown was a pressure cooker. Sally was on the beach by 0930 for calisthenics while I puttered around *Harmony*. In the afternoon, the boaters gathered for volleyball. Afterward, I headed out in the dinghy to fish. We spent our evenings reading books or playing Scrabble.

Sally often took long walks along the pristine beach on the windward side of the island, looking for elusive sea-beans along the water's edge. Sea-beans are large, hard, and buoyant seeds from fruits or tropical plants that, after falling into the ocean from places like Africa or South America, are carried by sea currents and often land on beaches thousands of miles away. Early sailors and scientists such as Christopher Columbus and Benjamin Franklin learned about ocean currents from the discovery of these drifting disseminules.

European folklore surrounds the sea-bean. Women would clench them in their hand to provide relief during childbirth. They were given as good luck pieces to those who went to sea because the seeds had been washed ashore in good condition. The most precious was Mary's bean, a distinctive seed that features a cross-shaped indentation on one side and gave religious meaning to those who found them. It thrilled Sally to find a sea-bean on a beach that was thousands of miles from where the plant grew. I would shine a bean to a high gloss and make a necklace for her.

Across the bay from Georgetown in the Exumas.
Harmony *is one of the two boats closest to shore in the cove.*

We were living in an idyllic world, but I was unable to escape that previous adversarial existence. *Harmony* was anchored in a small cove across the bay from Georgetown, and I was reading at the settee in the main salon when I heard a dinghy, its outboard spewing bubbles of gas, oil, and smoke.

"Mista Jones, you home, mon?" someone called out in a heavy Bahamian accent.

I stepped out in the cockpit to find one of the staff from the Peace and Plenty Hotel.

"You have a phone call," he said.

I stepped inside *Harmony* to get a piece of paper and pen.

"No, I do not know who it is. He is waiting, mon."

I wasn't sure I understood. The Peace and Plenty Hotel was a good ten-minute dinghy ride across the channel. "They're on hold?"

"Climb aboard. I'll bring you back. No problem, mon."

As we skimmed across the water, though, I did have visions of a problem. Was it my mom or my son? At the hotel desk, I found a phone with the receiver off the hook. Someone had been waiting twenty or thirty minutes.

"This is Russ."

"Robert Russell Jones?"

"Yes."

"Rivera here. Colonel Smith, Army Counter Drug Division, is expected your way this afternoon for a tour of OPBAT.[32] Mr. Regan from DOD[33] will accompany him. Are you available for a briefing?"

The caller was the last person I expected, and I was confused. "Who is this again, and how did you find me?"

Rivera laughed and ignored the last question. "Daniel Rivera, State Department. It's been suggested that you meet these guys. They're going to be checking into the hotel around 1730. Just ask for a quick rundown on the situation with the army, counter drug division, DEA, and drug running in the Bahamas."

"Are they expecting me?"

"No, just mention my office and your contacts with Pully."[34]

Ah, that's how they know. Through Pully. Rick Moore, a DEA agent who occasionally passed through Georgetown, had put me in phone contact with Pully, who had briefed me on the drug smuggling situation in the Bahamas. Pully

---

32. OPBAT stood for Operation Bahamas, Turks and Caicos. It was a joint US Army and DEA operation based in Georgetown.

33. Department of Defense.

34. John Pully was a DEA agent at the embassy in Nassau.

reported that smuggling had been greatly reduced since the corrupt government under Prime Minister Pindling had been removed and the Bahamians started cooperating with the DEA. I found it interesting that Moore and Pully complained that their bosses weren't interested in hearing of reduced smuggling activity. All headquarters wanted to hear were how many were arrested and the amount of drugs being seized. Or as I would have put it, they were only interested in the "body count."

In the cool of the evening, I was back at the Peace and Plenty, sitting on the patio. I enjoyed a mixed drink while Colonel Smith and Mr. Regan explained OPBAT. The army supplied Blackhawk helicopters, equipment, pilots, and other personnel in a supportive role to DEA. Besides flying patrol missions over the islands and routes across the Gulf Stream to Florida, the army assisted with signal intelligence and radar interpretation, along with language and topography training.

"Just for the record, DOD is not in agreement with this role the army has been given," Mr. Regan said.

"Sounds like the War on Drugs is eroding the law that prevents the military from law enforcement activities," I said.

"Exactly," he replied.

I turned to Colonel Smith. "Do you see progress in this war?"

"The counter drug division isn't involved in arrests, seizures, or the chain of custody with evidence, so our progress isn't quantifiable."

"But Colonel, as chief of the counter drug division, you do have a view of the overall interdiction situation, don't you?"

"Four or five years ago," he said, "we saw conflict on the borders of South and Central American countries over drug smuggling. Tensions have been relieved, and operations are now coordinated. Drug smuggling, though, is like a multiheaded hydra. Cut off one head, another appears."

I wondered aloud, "From Bolivia and Columbia to Panama, El Salvador, and then the Caribbean. Where's the next narco state? Mexico?"

"Only a matter of time," Regan said. "Like a fast-moving grass fire, the drug trade and resultant government corruption is already spreading there."

I thought I'd slightly change the subject. "What's the most popular drug from Mexico shipped to the United States?"

"Marijuana," they said simultaneously.

"No. It's beer and tequila. How much violence, crime, and corruption by cartels are involved with those regulated drugs?"

Regan and Smith looked confused. It was a rhetorical question on my part, though, and not the time to get into that provocative discussion. *Perhaps I planted a seed that would later sprout.* I thanked them for their time and left.

———•••———

Life in Georgetown continued to be a running holiday. The first week in March was the Cruising Regatta, an event for visiting yachts. It involved boat races around the island, softball games with the Bahamians, volleyball tournaments, and fishing contests. Friends from far and wide continued to arrive, such as Garland and Joyce Thacker on *Joyland*, who were working their way down island, and Stan and Donna Tice on *Snowgoose*, who had sailed from California, traversed the Panama Canal, and were now sailing up the island chain. Stan was a retired San Jose police sergeant.

The annual Bahamian National Family Island Regatta was held in April. This event was about competition and excellence. World-class Bahamian crews were pitted against one another in extreme competition that tested skill and endurance. The racing rules dictated that the sailing vessels be designed and built with strict restrictions on the materials to keep the boats as closely related to their traditional origins as possible. After watching the afternoon races, we roamed town, which was alive with parades, police bands, carnival attractions, and booth after booth selling scrumptious local cuisine.

In the evenings, across the channel and under the coconut palms on soft sandy beaches, the boaters gathered around a fire. The men discussed the depth of their boat's keel, the length of their anchor lines, or the size of their holding tanks. Sally sought first mates who were looking to discuss good books, spirituality, or the meaning of life while living aboard in the Caribbean. She was usually disappointed as she learned that, to most first mates, a properly functioning toilet on their vessel was "the meaning of life."

As spring approached, cruising vessels moved on. Some headed back to the States. Others, such as our good friends, Frank and Dee Zachar on *Vagabond Tiger*, headed south for Venezuela. Several weeks after most had departed, we weighed anchor and headed north, meandering toward the eastern chain of islands called San Salvador, Cat Island, and Eleuthera. We looked forward to exotic out of the way ports such as Rock Sound, Governor's Harbor, Spanish Wells, and Hope Town.

We anchored one afternoon off a small island, miles from any hint of civilization. A light breeze held us gently off a sparkling beach lined with palms. The coral rocks offshore beckoned, as lobsters had been rare in the populated area of Georgetown. Sally hovered the dinghy above as I floated down through liquid air, scouted out, and snared two.

Back at *Harmony*, while Sally showered, I shimmied up a palm tree and cut down an immature coconut that yielded plenty of coconut milk. With fresh pineapple and my spiced rum, I then made piña coladas to enjoy before dinner. I garnished Sally's with a fresh flower I had picked from a plant along the beach. As we sat in the cockpit and quietly enjoyed our drinks, I lost myself in the glittering sunlight that danced off the water. Memories bounded around my mind.

"What are you thinking?" Sally startled me back to the present.

"Aw, geeze maneez," I mumbled to myself. I hated that question. "Nothing."

"Yes, you were. I see it in your face. You've slipped into one of those moods."

I smiled. "I have moods?"

"Yes, an hour ago, you were diving for lobsters, climbing trees, and making drinks. Then you slid deep in thought and became distant. It's like I've lost you. I can see pain in your face, and I'd like to know what's going on in that head of yours."

"I'm sorry."

"Don't be sorry. Just talk to me."

I was quiet for a spell and looked out over the sparkling water. The subject wasn't going to change, so I finally spoke. "You wouldn't understand."

Sally silently sat while looking at me. "And who else have you said that to?"

Sally with her fresh Pina Colada.

I looked at her as she cocked her head and then raised her eyebrows in anticipation of my answer. *I'm on a sailboat anchored off an uninhabited island in the middle of the ocean. Where am I going to go to avoid this conversation?*

Sally asked again, "Who else in your life did you decide wouldn't understand?"

"Susan, Lucy, Terri," I said, barely audible.

"How well did that turn out?"

"Look at my life with you these last couple years, the Florida Keys, the East Coast, and the Bahamas. Look at what we have right here." I waved my arm around our little paradise. "This is what dreams are made of, what most people only read about in travel magazines and adventure stories. This is the stuff of movies."

"So you think you don't deserve all this?" Sally asked.

"Deserve is not the word." I hesitated. "There's nothing new here, Sally. It's the same old question. Why me?" I remained still for a spell. "Don't most people ask 'Why me?' when something bad happens to them instead of something good?"

Sally didn't answer. She softly looked and waited for me to continue. I didn't want to continue with the subject, and I struggled. I finally explained about flight school friends such as Ortego, McAllister, and Jantz. I told the story of Lieutenant Phung and the pictures of his wife and children. I continued with the events of the day when Gary George and Joseph Neske, the two young boys with Delta Company, lost their lives. I explained how police officers Richard Huerta and Gordon Silva died.

"How did I escape destruction while involved in this turbulent history? Why am I here enjoying this with you while their lives were cut short? Why me when someone as kind and gentle as Trent continues to be confined to his wheelchair?"

We quietly sat and looked out at the approaching sunset. Sally then looked at me as if it were time for me to continue.

"Intellectually, I know there's no answer to the question. Emotionally though …" My voice trailed off, and I didn't finish the statement.

"Maybe," Sally suggested, "asking 'Why me?' keeps you from feeling the awful sadness about all that death and waste." I wasn't sure what she meant, and Sally sensed I was lost. "What would happen if, whenever you started asking 'Why me?' you instead let yourself grieve?" She let that comment sink in a bit. "The 'Why me?' seems to keep you stuck and unable to have the feelings. It's a deep sadness for all of them and all the wrongs in the world. It's a lot of sadness to feel."

"There's not a day in my life," I said, "that I haven't thought about the loss of those young men's lives and the randomness of it all."

"So why not you? Could it not be destiny or grace?"

"'Tis grace that brought me safe thus far, and grace will lead me home," I softly sang.

Sally smiled, then brought me back to the subject. "Do you feel our young men in Vietnam died in vain?"

I took a moment to gather my thoughts. "Since our politicians involved in that war now admit it was a failed policy, today, loved ones of those who died in Vietnam hold each other and ask why." I started to get angry. "Now we have the same situation with this failed policy in the War on Drugs."

"You see similarities with Vietnam and the War on Drugs?" Sally asked.

"The war in Vietnam and the War on Drugs aren't parallel, but, with Vietnam, we failed to learn the lessons of the French experience. In the War on Drugs, we have failed to learn the lessons of alcohol prohibition. When prohibition was lifted and we again took control of the alcohol trade, ending the violence, the loved ones of police officers and civilians who had been killed wondered how we were led into that fiasco. They held each other and asked why." I looked out over the ripples of water around the boat. "What saddens me now is that our politicians will someday come to their senses and admit the War on Drugs has failed. They'll take control of the drug trade away from the cartels, ending the bloodshed. Then the loved ones of police officers and civilians who have been killed in this violence, wondering how we were led into prohibition again, will hold each other and ask why."

I finished my piña colada and then thought of Sally's earlier question. "As to whether I believe our soldiers died in vain, I don't know how to answer that. I can say that our young men in Vietnam served honorably. They had faith their government was doing the right thing. The same holds true for the men and women serving today on the front lines in the War on Drugs. They have honorable intentions, but a misguided faith that our government is doing the right thing."

"So are you going to talk about this when we eventually settle back ashore? Are you willing to stand up to the cartels? After all, they're the ones you want to put out of business."

"Oh, it's much worse than that. Today we have the drug war industrial complex. It's an unintended consequence, but there's a symbiotic relationship between the drug cartels, politicians, DOJ and law enforcement agencies, the prison system, and the drug treatment industry. A lot of money is involved, and each group has a vested interest in keeping this war, their little empires, and their careers going."

"So you're willing to take them all on?" she asked with concern in her voice.

"Sure, I'll make some waves."

"Perhaps this is your answer to 'Why me?' Maybe you can do your part by fighting this failed policy, for those you grieve."

Epilogue

As of 2011, the War on Drugs is in its fourth decade. It took only thirteen years to recognize and abandon the disastrous policy of alcohol prohibition, yet we continue not to learn from that experience. Drugs are cheaper, stronger, and more plentiful than before the war began.[35] Yet every year, for forty years, our government has stated that we're winning the war but need more money to fight it. The amount of our national, state, and local tax dollars now spent annually for the war, in excess of $70 billion by some estimates, is so obscene that the National Office of Drug Control Policy obscures the true amount by shifting its methodology for calculating and reporting it.[36] Jeffrey Miron, senior lecturer in economics at Harvard University, estimates that the total cost of drug prohibition, when including lost tax revenues, is $88 billion.[37]

The number of personnel assigned to the War on Drugs, including those from DEA, FBI, Customs, Immigration, military, state police, county and municipal narcotics officers, joint task forces, and other agencies, continues to expand on an annual basis. These men and women are serving honorably, some dying in the process, yet their interdiction efforts, as evidenced by low prices, aren't making a dent in the supply of drugs.

As more money and equipment are used in the war, police tactics have become more violent, and the constitution has become collateral damage. Hundreds of botched police raids have resulted in the loss of lives of innocent

35. Peter Hakim. "Rethinking US Drug Policy." *The Beckley Foundation.* Web. 25 Aug. 2011. <www.thedialogue. org/PublicationFiles/Rethinking%20US%20Drug%20Policy.pdf>

36. Matthew B. Robinson and Renee G. Scherlen. *Lies, Damned Lies, and Drug War Statistics: A Critical Analysis of Claims Made by the Office of National Drug Control Policy* (Albany: State University of New York Press, 2007).

37. Jeffrey A. Miron and Katherine Waldock. *The Budgetary Impact of Ending Drug Prohibition.* (Washington, DC: Cato Institute, 2010).

victims, nonviolent offenders, and police officers.[38]

Corruption associated with the War on Drugs has reached its slimy tentacles into the ranks of police officers and narcotics detectives, DEA agents, chiefs of police, prosecutors, and judges. Entire narcotics divisions and drug task forces have been disbanded, arrested, and convicted of crimes related to narcotics prohibition.

Over 1.6 million citizens are arrested each year for drugs.[39] The result is that the "land of the free," with less than 5 percent of the world's population, holds 25 percent of the world's prisoners.[40] Of the arrests for drugs every year, nearly half are for marijuana, and 88 percent of those are for simple possession.[41] Since the beginning of the war in 1970, over 41 million people have been arrested for a nonviolent drug crime and saddled with a criminal record.[42,43]

We can treat addiction, but our young adults will never get over a conviction, for which the penalties can be more damaging to them than the use of the drug itself. A drug conviction may follow them the rest of their lives and prevent them from becoming doctors, lawyers, or professors or obtaining jobs that require licensing, such as realtors or beauticians. Yet those who use illegal drugs without being arrested can admit their prior drug use and still become teachers, police officers, DEA agents, physicians, and politicians.

Across the Americas, the violence between gangs in the battle over territory continues, and thousands die annually. Between 2007 and 2011, thirty-five thousand lives were lost in the violence in Mexico.[44] Today, that battle

38. Radley Balko. "Botched Paramilitary Police Raids." *The Cato Institute.* Web. 25 Aug. 2011. <http://www.cato.org/raidmap/>.

39. Douglas A. McVay. "Crime." *Drug War Facts.* Common Sense for Drug Policy, 2007. Web. 26 Aug. 2011. <http://www.drugwarfacts.org/cms/node/235>.

40. Adam Liptak. "U.S. Prison Population Dwarfs That of Other Nations." *The New York Times,* 23 Apr. 2008. Web. 25 Aug. 2011. <http://www.nytimes.com/2008/04/23/world/americas/23iht-23prison.12253738.html>.

41. Douglas A. McVay. "Crime." *Drug War Facts.* Common Sense for Drug Policy, Nov. 2007. Web. 25 Aug. 2011. <http://www.drugwarfacts.org/cms/node/235>.

42. Brian C. Bennett. "Arrests (1970 - 2004)." *Homepage of Truth.* Web. 25 Aug. 2011. <http://www.briancbennett.com/charts/fed-data/pot-arrests.htm>.

43. Douglas A. McVay. "Crime." *Drug War Facts.* Common Sense for Drug Policy, Nov. 2007. Web. 25 Aug. 2011. <http://www.drugwarfacts.org/cms/Crime>.

44. Daniel Hernandez. "How Many Have Died in Mexico's Drug War?" *Los Angeles Times,* 7 June 2011. Web. 25 Aug. 2011. <http://latimesblogs.latimes.com/laplaza/2011/06/mexico-war-dead-update-figures-40000.html>.

is spilling across our border as cartels are growing marijuana and operating methamphetamine laboratories in the middle of our state and federal forests.

Numerous studies have validated my personal experience and subsequent indictment of this war. The most recent is the June 2011 report from the Global Commission on Drug Policy, which is comprised of former presidents or prime ministers of five countries, a former secretary-general of the United Nations, human rights leaders, and business and government leaders, including Richard Branson, George P. Shultz, and Paul A. Volcker. Their report sent a jolt throughout the world when they concluded that, by all measurable standards, the global war on drugs has failed.[45]

We do have distinguished voices in America willing to speak out. The United States Conference of Mayors passed a resolution in 2011, calling the War on Drugs a failed policy that drives mass incarceration and racial disparities. The group of 135 speakers with Law Enforcement Against Prohibition (LEAP), all current or former members of law enforcement, includes retired California Superior Court Judge James Gray, retired Texas State District Judge John Delaney, former Chicago prosecutor James Gierach, retired San Jose Chief of Police Joseph McNamara, and retired Seattle Chief of Police Norm Stamper. But our nation's leaders will not have or allow the debate. Job descriptions, regulations, and administrative rulings prohibit government employees from discussing or debating anything that questions the current policy of prohibition.[46] Law enforcement officers have been fired for suggesting, even in private conversations, alternatives to our drug laws.[47]

Nonprofit organizations, such as the Drug Policy Alliance (DPA) and the Drug Policy Forum of Texas (DPFT), have sprung up in opposition to the War on Drugs. LEAP and DPFT believe drugs are too dangerous to leave in the control of gangs, and a system of regulation rather than prohibition, coupled with education and treatment, is a less harmful, more ethical, and more effec-

---

45. Global Commission on Drug Policy. *"War on Drugs."* June 2011. Web. 25 Aug. 2011. <http://www.global-commissionondrugs.org/report>.

46. Office of National Drug Control Policy. *Reauthorization Act of 1998, Sec. 704 (12).* Web. 25 Aug. 2011. <http://www.whitehousedrugpolicy.gov/about/98reauthorization.html>

47. Lucia Graves. "Border Patrol Agent Fired For Views On Drug Legalization Files Lawsuit." *Huffington Post.* 26 Jan. 2011. Web. 25 Aug. 2011.
<http://www.huffingtonpost.com/2011/01/26/border-patrol-fired-drug-legalization_n_813999.html>

tive public policy than using the blunt tool of law enforcement.

There is no better example than the results we've had with tobacco, the deadliest, most addicting, and most abused of all drugs, legal or illegal. Over the last twenty years, the number of tobacco users in the US has been reduced from forty-two to twenty percent.[48] This was accomplished without firing shots, kicking in doors, or arresting and jailing anyone.

Despite the evidence that the war has failed and alternatives work,[49] the divide over our country's policy seems to be an unbridgeable abyss. We are suffering from groupthink, a pattern of belief characterized by self-deception, manufacture of consent, and conformity to a set of values and ethics without critically testing, analyzing, and evaluating alternative ideas.[50] Therefore, we stand neck-deep in a popular decision to continue this war.

Insanity has been described as "doing the same thing over and over and expecting different results."[51] Yet for forty years we have been pursuing a policy that is not producing the desired results—to reduce death, disease, crime, and drug use. Our nation must look beyond the moral and ideological argument that drugs are bad and that the government must prohibit them in order to protect society. Yes, drugs are harmful, but the facts show that our current policy is not only failing to achieve its goals, it is making matters worse.

If we are serious about addressing the problem of harmful drugs, then we must find methods that actually work. Politicians occasionally propose legislation to study alternatives, but these proposals are rarely discussed and usually die in committee. For real change, it is going to take a groundswell of support from the public that legislators cannot ignore. After all, it is possible to be anti-drug while, at the same time, being pro-reform of this failed policy.

48. Centers for Disease Control and Prevention. "*Cigarette Smoking Among Adults-United States, 2006.*" US Department of Health and Human Services. Web. 25 Aug. 2011. <http://www.cdc.gov/mmwr/preview/mmwrhtml/mm5644a2.htm>.

49. Global Commission on Drug Policy. "*War on Drugs*". June 2011. Web. 25 Aug. 2011. <http://www.global-commissionondrugs.org/report>.

50. Irving L. Janis. *Groupthink: Psychological Studies of Policy Decisions and Fiascoes.* Second Edition. New York: Houghton Mifflin, 1982.

51. WikiAnswers. "*Answers.com.*" Web. 25 Aug. 2011
<http://wiki.answers.com/Q/Who_first_said_the_definition_of_insanity_is_to_do_the_same_thing_over_and_over_and_expect_different_results>

Appendix

Anders. Troy "Muleshoe" Anders married and raised a family near Muleshoe, Texas. Today, the town of Muleshoe has a bronze statue of a mule modeled after "Ole Pete," Troy's father's finest mule.

Andrews. Tom Andrews flew Chinooks in Vietnam where he suffered an AK-47 wound to a leg. He recovered, married, and raised three children. Divorced from his first wife, Tom lives with his wife Anne in Texas, where he works in commercial property management.

Atkins. Walt Atkins rose through the ranks and, in 1998, served as the first African American chief of police for the city of San Jose.

Anton. Warrant Officer Frank Anton endured five years in brutal prisoner of war camps. After his release, Frank went on to serve twenty-one years in the Army. He then flew ten years for American Airlines. He has two daughters, and today he and his wife reside in Florida.

Bartley. Major Don Bartley, chaplain, died from a roadside bomb in Vietnam in June 1969.

Castiglia. Salvador "Columbo" Castiglia had a prior conviction for robbery in 1971. In 1986, while on parole for the 1974 murder conviction of Turco, he was arrested and returned to prison for another robbery.

Bontempi. After twenty-five years as a Hell's Angel, Dirty Doug grew discontented with the club. He left of his own free choice and found a job driving trucks. He gave up his bad habits—alcohol, cigarettes, and other drugs—and died shortly thereafter.

Brady. For his actions as a medevac pilot during the vicious battle in Death Valley, Major Patrick Brady was awarded the Congressional Medal of Honor. After two tours of duty in Vietnam, he continued his army career, retiring at the rank of major general.

Brandes. James "Jim Jim" Brandes committed suicide while in jail on a homicide case in which he testified.

Class 68-503. It graduated one hundred and sixty-one army helicopter pilots. Ten were killed in Vietnam, for a loss rate of 6 percent, which is consistent with the loss rate from other helicopter flight school classes. This death rate of helicopter pilots, though, is double that for the 1.6 million men who fought in combat, provided close combat support, or were at least fairly regularly exposed to enemy attack in Vietnam.

Common Sense for Drug Policy (CSDP). Common Sense for Drug Policy is a nonprofit organization dedicated to reforming drug policy and expanding harm reduction. CSDP disseminates factual information and comments on existing laws, policies, and practices. They publish *Drug War Facts*, which provides reliable information with applicable citations on important public health and criminal justice issues. It is updated continuously and can be found in its entirety at www.drugwarfacts.org.

Conover. Jerry Conover recovered, although he lost some use of his right arm and hand. He has his own heavy construction equipment business and lives with his wife in New Jersey, where they raised a son and a daughter.

d'Arteney. Jim d'Arteney earned a Purple Heart during two tours in Vietnam. Upon leaving the service, he earned multiple degrees and worked in the field of employee assistance programs, eventually retiring from University of California San Diego. He works with his wife, Ruth, in her real estate business in California.

Drug Policy Alliance (DPA). The Drug Policy Alliance is the nation's leading organization promoting alternatives to the drug war that are grounded in science, compassion, health, and human rights. For more information, see www.dpa.org.

Drug Policy Forum of Texas (DPFT). The Drug Policy Forum of Texas is an educational organization, which believes that, when it comes to the War on Drugs, the information given to the public is one-sided and distorted. They hold the basic belief that a well-informed public will choose rational policies. For more information, see www.dpft.org.

DuPont. In 1988, John DuPont turned his eight hundred-acre estate into a wrestling camp where, in 1996, he shot and killed Olympic wrestling champion David Schultz. DuPont was found guilty of third-degree murder, but was also declared mentally ill. He was sentenced to thirty years, which was to be served either in prison or a mental institution. He died in prison in 2010.

Eliason. While flying a Cobra gunship, Ross Eliason was shot down in his sixth week in Vietnam. The aircraft commander dragged his unconscious body out of the burning aircraft. After Ross regained consciousness, they escaped and evaded for several hours before being rescued. Ross was evacuated home to recover from shrapnel, compressed spine, broken neck, and multiple fractures of the mandible. He married and raised two daughters, and both he and his wife had successful careers in law enforcement. They reside in Texas.

Fair. Trent Fair remains a quadriplegic, confined to a wheelchair.

Hell's Angels. While the Hell's Angels learned valuable lessons from their win in the RICO case, apparently law enforcement did not. In 1997, a San Jose Hell's Angel was arrested for murder. As District Attorney George Kennedy stated, the case against the lone defendant should have been handled as a routine homicide. Instead, law enforcement tried to turn it into a case against the San Jose Hell's Angels. Search warrants were served at clubhouses and personal homes of Hell's Angels, during which dogs were shot and truckloads of Hell's Angels items, unrelated to the murder, were seized. The homicide case against the individual Hell's Angel was lost, and a civil suit against the municipal agencies involved resulted in a court ruling that the law enforcement searches were "unnecessarily intrusive." The San Jose chapter of the Hell's Angels was awarded $1.8 million dollars.

Henderson. Walt "Sugar Bear" Henderson spent over three years in the hospital and several more in physical therapy. He married his physical therapist, Kathy, and they raised a son and daughter. After his successful career as a strategic planner for several corporations, they are now retired in Texas.

Huey 66-16094. The Americal Division's daily report for March 7, 1969, states that, "at 1605 hours, the C&C helicopter for the 196th Brigade Commander landed to dust-off wounded at BT 165180. They received four mortar rounds, automatic and fifty-caliber fire, and possibly a B-40 rocket (rocket propelled grenade), resulting in three onboard wounded."

Hull. In 1989, Costa Rican authorities arrested John Hull and charged him with drug trafficking and using "Costa Rican soil for hostile acts" against Nicaragua. In 1990, Costa Rica added an additional indictment of murder against Hull, and he was added to Interpol's "most wanted" list. Hull, though, had already fled Costa Rica with the assistance of the DEA. The US Department of Justice did not pursue the matter because Costa Rica dropped the drug charges, probable cause did not support the murder charges, and the Costa Rican government did not pursue the "hostile acts" charge. Furthermore, Costa Rican President Roberto Calderon made it clear that his government had no interest in extraditing Hull.

Jones. During a tour of duty with the marines, my son Robert "Joey" Jones was sent to the army jump school at Fort Benning, Georgia. Joey never looked back. Upon his discharge from the military, he entered competition skydiving, eventually earning five world championships and fourteen national championships. He has set several world records and has held the title of all-around champion of combined formation skydiving three times. Today, he contracts for specialized military skydiving training. His clients have included the US Naval Special Warfare Development Group, along with Belgium, British, Canadian and Danish special forces. He also contracts with several national skydiving competition teams, which he has coached to numerous championships. He and his wife Lena, a gold medal winner with the Swedish women's skydiving team, reside in Empuriabrava, Spain.

Joey, second from left in back row, with his gold medal winning team at the World Cup, Portugal, 1998.

Joey and Lena.

Kimmich. Carl Kimmich safely completed his tour in Vietnam. Today, he is a captain on the B-777 with Delta Airlines. He lives in Connecticut.

Kroesen. Colonel Kroesen was treated for his wounds in country and was able to finish his one-year command of the 196th. In 1971, he returned for a second tour as a major general, where he commanded the Americal Division and, later, the First Regional Assistance Command. During the post-Vietnam, Cold War years, he served as commanding general of the 82nd Airborne Division in North Carolina, the VII corps in Germany, and the Army Forces Command in Georgia. Finally, after an assignment as vice chief of staff of the army, he took his last active duty job as commander-in-chief, US Army, Europe, and commander in central group, NATO. He retired as a four-star general. He was wounded during each of the four wars in which he served: World War II, the Korean War, the Vietnam War, and the Cold War. He sustained the last of the wounds in 1981 in an assassination attempt in Heidelberg, Germany. Using an RPG, a "Kommando" of the Red Army faction hit the car he and his wife, Rowena, were riding in. After leaving the army, he became chairman of the board of Military Professional Resources Inc., and a senior fellow at the Institute of Land Warfare of the Association of the United States Army. He also served as the vice president of the American Security Council Foundation.

Krutschewski. In 1981, Peter Krutschewski was convicted of importing $15 million worth of marijuana, a charge he didn't deny. Instead, his attorneys argued that Krutschewski was a highly decorated army helicopter pilot who was temporarily insane as a result of post-traumatic stress syndrome (PTSD) from Vietnam. To win his freedom, Krutschewski offered to donate $1.75 million to convict rehabilitation programs, bringing a storm of criticism from the US attorney who argued, "It would further encourage persons engaged in criminal activity to set aside a nest egg for the rainy day they're caught and brought to justice." The judge agreed and handed down a ten-year sentence in federal prison. Krutschewski died in 1996.

Lafferty. Robert Lafferty's experience and connections as a rogue aircraft broker enabled him to become a highly valuable government asset who provided critical information on the Medellin and Cali Cartels. He either died, as reported, in a 1986 aircraft accident, or disappeared into a witness protection program.

Lambie. Brian Lambie recovered from his physical wounds, but suffered mental anguish for years over the loss of close friends in Vietnam. He raised two daughters. Today, divorced, he lives in Minnesota, where he nears retirement from the state as a Web site administrator.

Law Enforcement Against Prohibition (LEAP). Law Enforcement Against Prohibition is an international nonprofit organization that gives voice to current and former members of law enforcement who believe the War on Drugs is a failure. Their goals are to educate the public, the media, and policy makers about the failure of current policies and to restore the public's respect for police, which law enforcement's involvement in enforcing drug prohibition has greatly diminished. For more information, see www.leap.cc.

My Lai massacre. On March 16, 1968, up to 507 unarmed citizens—women, children and elderly men—we murdered by elements of the 11th Brigade, Americal Division. The incident, which became public knowledge mainly due to the efforts of WO Hugh Thompson, prompted widespread outrage around the world and increased domestic opposition to the US involvement in the Vietnam War.

Passaro. After Passaro had been sent to prison, I heard rumors that the Hell's Angels were unhappy with him over my discovery of his meth lab, which figured heavily in the RICO trial. I visited him and attempted to get him to accept the witness protection program and turn informant. He laughed off any suggestion that the Hell's Angels were unhappy. In 1985, only weeks after his release from prison, Altamont Al Passaro was found floating in one of the Santa Clara County reservoirs. On his body was $10,000, so it wasn't the result of a bad drug deal. He found himself on the wrong side of the Hell's Angels, his murder a message.

Perkey. William "Wild Bill" Perkey remained with the San Jose Hell's Angels after his release from prison. He died in 1996.

Reid. Terry Reid finished his tour of Vietnam unscathed. He had a successful career as a civilian medevac helicopter pilot.

Schneider. Only days after Gary Schneider was wounded, while he was in the hospital recovering, his wife gave birth to their son. Gary went on to work as an electrician for the railroads, and he and his wife also raised a daughter. Their son served six years in the army. Today, Gary and his wife are retired in Michigan.

Solano. In the case where I identified William "Black Bill" Solano delivering heroin, he skipped bail before sentencing. When discovered in a small town in Mexico, a US law enforcement agency paid the local Mexican police chief several thousand dollars. Days later, law enforcement in Phoenix received an anonymous tip from Mexico that a wanted felon was arriving on a flight from Mexico. Solano was found seated on the arriving flight, handcuffed. His lawyer's argument to the court that Solano was illegally extradited was ignored. As a result of his having been involved with heroin, a drug not tolerated by the Hell's Angels, he was stripped of his club membership.

Sumner. Ted Sumner left the police department in 1980. He raised two children, a son who is now a San Jose police officer and a daughter who is a global risk management executive. He and his wife live in San Jose, where he is the owner and head instructor of San Jose Kenpo Karate. He holds a ninth-degree black belt and was an inaugural inductee into the Kenpo International Hall of Fame. Sumner is involved in research using Karate training to treat US soldiers who have recently suffered a traumatic brain injury.

Taft. Kenneth Taft recovered from his wounds and lives in Illinois with his wife. They raised two sons, the youngest having served with the army in Afghanistan. Kenneth is now retired from the Illinois State Department of Transportation.

Thompson. Hugh Thompson's report on the events at My Lai was key to the subsequent investigations and court martials of the soldiers involved. He retired from the army at the rank of major in 1983. In 1998, thirty years after My Lai, Thompson and his crew were recognized for their actions with the award of the Soldier's Medal, the US Army's highest award for bravery not involving the enemy. Thompson passed away in 2006.

Vehige. Kenneth Vehige recovered from his wounds and lives in Missouri.

3rd Battalion, 21st Infantry. Its lineage can be traced back to 1861 where it fought continuously throughout the Civil War. It was the first infantry unit to engage the Japanese in World War II and the first combat unit to arrive in Korea and engage the North Koreans. Known as the "Gimlets," a tool that bores holes in stone for the purpose of placing explosives, its motto is "Duty," and its battle cry is "Bore Brother Bore." In 1972, the 3rd/21st was the last combat unit to leave Vietnam.

INDEX

20491919R00168

Made in the USA
San Bernardino, CA
13 April 2015